The world's largest collection of visual travel guides

DELHI, AGRA & JAIPUR

Edited by Manjulika Dubey
Photography by David Beatty,
Shalini Saran and others

Executive Editor: Bikram Grewal
Editorial Director: Brian Bell

INSIGHT GUIDES
DELHI, AGRA & JAIPUR

CONTACTING THE EDITORS: We would appreciate it if readers would alert us to errors or outdated information by writing to:
Apa Publications, P.O. Box 7910,
London SE1 1WE, England.
Fax: (44) 20 7403 0290.
e-mail: insight@apaguide.demon.co.uk.
www.insightguides.com

First Edition 1991
Second Edition 1995 (Updated 2001)

Distributed in the UK & Ireland by
GeoCenter International Ltd
The Viables Centre, Harrow Way
Basingstoke, Hampshire RG22 4BJ
Fax: (44) 1256 817988

Distributed in the United States by
Langenscheidt Publishers Inc.
46–35 54th Road, Maspeth, NY 11378
Fax: (1) 718 784 0640

Distributed in Canada by
Thomas Allen & Son Ltd
390 Steelcase Road East
Markham, Ontario L34 1G2
Fax: (1) 905 475 6747

Distributed in Australia by
Universal Press
1 Waterloo Road
Macquarie Park, NSW 2113
Fax: (61) 2 9888 9074

Distributed in India by
Om Books Services
4379/4b, Prakash House, Ansari Road,
Darya Ganj, New Delhi-110002, India
Tel: (91 11) 326 3363/326 5303. Fax: (91 11) 327 8091
e-mail: obi@del2.vsnl.net.in

Worldwide distribution enquiries:
APA Publications GmbH & Co. Verlag KG (Singaporebranch)
38 Joo Koon Road, Singapore 628990
Tel: (65) 8651600. Fax: (65) 8616438

Printed in Singapore by
Insight Print Services (Pte) Ltd
38 Joo Koon Road, Singapore 628990
Fax: (65) 8616438

This guidebook combines the interests and enthusiasms of two of the world's best-known information providers: Insight Guides, whose range of titles has set the standard for visual travel guides since 1970, and Discovery Channel, the world's premier source of nonfiction television programming.

The editors of Insight Guides provide both practical advice and general understanding about a destination's history, culture, institutions and people. Discovery Channel and its website, www.discovery.com, help millions of viewers explore their world from the comfort of their own home and also encourage them to explore it first-hand.

Now a teacher on the history faculty at the Jamia Millia Islamia University, **Dr Narayani Gupta** studied history in Delhi and Oxford and is a founder-member of the Conservation Society of Delhi. She is the author of the definitive *Delhi Between Two Empires (1803–1931)*, published by Oxford University Press, and has written extensively on modern Indian urban history. Her substantial contribution to this volume brings to APA readers her rare gift of combining erudition with infectious enthusiasm.

Dr Shobita Punja is a regular contributor to Apa guidebooks. Presently working with the Ministry of Education in the field of culture, Dr Punja has studied art history at Stanford University. She has written two books, on Indian museums and on the fabulous temples at Khajuraho in Madhya Pradesh. For this *Insight Guide*, she provides an introduction to the art and architecture of the Golden Triangle.

A senior journalist with one of India's most influential dailies, **Nandini Mehta** has lived in Delhi since she was a child. Her work enables her to keep in touch with the cultural life of the city, on which she has written.

Reena Nanda's interest lies in the field of history, art and architecture. She has conducted tours around the historic areas of Delhi and has published a series of articles on conservation. As her essay on the Red

Grewal

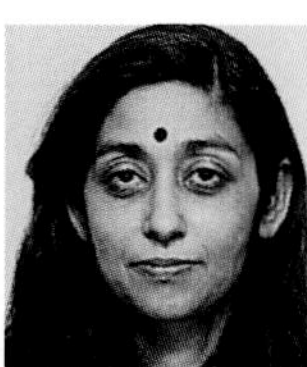
Mehta

Sharma

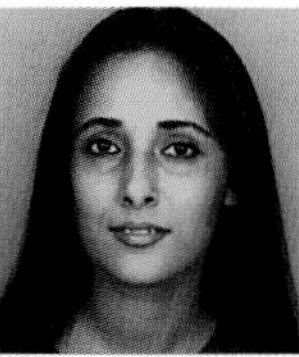
Tayebbhai

Menon

Dubey

Fort demonstrates, her concern is not so much with architectural history as with how people lived and how they used the built structures they have left for posterity.

Nigel Hankin is a member of the small number of British who opted to stay on in India after Independence. He set out to make a living conducting tours and writing on the Delhi of the Raj. His article on some of the significant British sites in northern Delhi judiciously evokes the nostalgia and mystique of a bygone era without losing sight of contemporary political realities.

Gillian Wright's first visit to India in 1977 inspired her to study Indian language, in which she holds a first class honours degree from the School of Oriental and African Studies in London. She has contributed to a number of travel books, and worked with Mark Tully, previously the British Broadcasting Corporation South Asia correspondent, on three books dealing with Indian politics, history and culture. She has also worked on several television documentaries on India and is interested in wildlife and ornithology. Wright lives in Delhi in Nizamuddin and her articles in this book communicate her intimate knowledge of the area.

An artist and nature writer, **Bulbul Sharma** is widely known to Delhi citizens for her syndicated nature column. She also works with children, combining art and nature while holding camps and workshops. She has also produced a short film on birds. For this guide she discusses the large population of birds and animals of Delhi, where she has lived for many years.

Dr Asok Das, a specialist in Mughal painting and decorative arts, has published books, portfolios and papers on Mughal and Rajasthani arts. Having worked for 16 years as Director of the Maharaja Sawai Man Singh Museum in the City Palace of Jaipur, he organised several exhibitions throwing new light on the history and development of the city and its unique position in the cultural life of Rajasthan.

Tripti Pandey is actively involved in the Rajasthan State Government's Department of Tourism, Art and Culture and has published a number of articles and a book on Rajasthani culture. She has always lived in Jaipur and brings her intimate knowledge of the city to her articles on its places of interest, crafts and food.

John Lall is a retired member of the Indian Civil Service who, while he was posted as Commissioner to Agra, resumed his interest in history and studied the monuments of the city. Lall has published, amongst others, books on the *Taj Mahal* and *The Glory of Mughal Agra.*

Yasmeen Tayebbhai is a practising architect in New Delhi, whose graduation dissertation involved research into the principles underlying the town planning of Fatehpur Sikri. Her article on the subject written for this guide brings to the reader her understanding and appreciation of this architectural marvel.

Another contributor who is an architect is **A.G. Krishna Menon**, also based in Delhi. As part of his work on the conservation and renewal of historic towns around the country, he has developed an intimate knowledge of the Mathura region. His article on the allure of the Braj Bhumi region communicates these insights.

Amitabh Dubey put together the article on the wildlife parks and other sites of tourist interest around Jaipur.

Thanks are due to **Toby Sinclair** for editorial help rendered in conceiving and commissioning the book and assisting in the picture research and also for preparing the maps for the first edition of this guide.

Yasmeen Tayebbhai and **Mandakini Dubey** were both gracious and helpful far beyond the call of duty. Thanks are also due to writers who worked on previous versions of this book: **Radhika Tandon**, **Shekhar Aiyar**, **Jug Suraiya** and **Kushwant Singh**.

The book was updated by **Maria Lord**, an Insight Guides editor, who complied the Travel Tips, wrote the article on the political life of Delhi since Independence and rewrote the sections on performing arts, Delhi festivals and Hauz Khas village.

CONTENTS

History

The Golden Triangle
by Narayani Gupta 21

A Tale of Three Cities
by Narayani Gupta 25

A Cultural Synthesis
by Shobita Punja 33

The Forever Capital
by Narayani Gupta 48

Places

The Political Centre
by Maria Lord 59

Performing Arts
by Maria Lord and Nandini Mehta 64

Sunset Splendour – Imperial City
by Nandini Mehta 69

Connaught Place
by Nandini Mehta 82

Museums and Galleries
by Nandini Mehta 84

Delhi Festivals
by Maria Lord and Nandini Mehta 92

Old Delhi
by Narayani Gupta 96

The Red Fort
by Reena Nanda 102

The Northern Ridge
by Nigel Hankin 111

The Old Fort
by Gillian Wright 119

The Living Museum
by Gillian Wright 125

Nizamuddin
by Gillian Wright 126

Eating the Muslim Way
by Gillian Wright 131

The Cities of the South
by Narayani Gupta 135

Hauz Khas Village
by Narayani Gupta and Maria Lord 142

The Nature-Lover in Delhi
by Bulbul Sharma 147

CONTENTS

Jaipur – The Rajput City
by Narayani Gupta 157

The City of Sawai Jai Singh
by Asok Das 161

Jantar Mantar
by Asok Das 167

Eating Out in Jaipur
by Tripti Pandey 168

The Glory of Amber
by Asok Das 173

A Crafts Bonanza
by Tripti Pandey 181

Anokhi
by Ravi Kaimal 185

Jaipur Beyond the Walled City
by Tripti Pandey 186

Rambagh Palace Hotel
by Tripti Pandey 189

Sanganer, Bagru and Samode
by Ravi Kaimal 193

Around Jaipur
by Amitabh Dubey 199

Agra – City of the Mughals
by Narayani Gupta 209

Taj Mahal
by John Lall 213

Mughal Pietra Dura
by John Lall 221

Agra Fort
by John Lall 223

The Left Bank
by John Lall 231

Fatehpur Sikri
by Yasmeen Tayebbhai 237

Sikandara
by John Lall 252

Mathura and Vrindavan
by A.G. Krishna Menon .. 257

Mathura Museum
by A.G. Krishna Menon .. 260

Maps

Delhi/New Delhi 58
Connaught Place 83
Old Delhi 97
South Delhi 136
Jaipur 156
Agra 208
Fatehpur Sikri 236

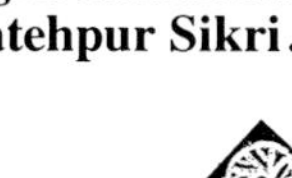

Getting Acquainted

The Place 266
The Land 266
When to Go 266
Etiquette 266
The Economy 267
The Government 267

Planning The Trip

What to Bring 268
Entry Regulations 268
Customs 268
Health 269
Getting There 270
Money Matters 270
Special Facilities 271
Embassies & Consulates 271
Tourist Offices 272
Airline Offices 272
Cyber Cafés 273

Practical Tips

Emergencies 273
Business Hours 273
Tipping 273
Women Travelling Alone 274
Postal Services 274
Telecommunications 274
Media 274
On Arrival 275
On Departure 275
Repairs and Tailors 275
Entrance Fees 275

Getting Around

Travel by Air 276
Travel by Bus 276
Rickshaws 276
Driving in India 276
Car & Taxi Rental 277
Travel by Rail 277
Useful Trains 278

Where To Stay

Agra 279
Delhi 280
Jaipur 282

Where to Eat

Agra 284
Delhi 284
Jaipur 286

Shopping

Shopping in Agra 287
Shopping in Delhi 287
Shopping in Jaipur 288

Wildlife

Wildlife & Bird Parks 289

Language

Traveller's Hindi 289

Further Reading

History 291
Fiction 292
Travel 293

Williamson & Howitt.

Published by Edw.d Orm

No. 1.

J. Clark Etched.

d Street Sept.r 1st 1807 & by B. Crosby & Co. Stationers Court.

VIEW OF DELHI FROM THE RIV

R SHEWING THE KING'S PALACE.

Drawn by W. Purser.

FORTRESS OF SHUHUR

Engraved by Percy Heath.

EYPORE, RAJPOOTANA.

VIEW OF THE PALACE O

This palace was built by the Emperor A

AGRA, FROM THE RIVER.

in the middle of the sixteenth century.

THE GOLDEN TRIANGLE

Delhi, Agra and Jaipur are concertinas: they can fold up into very short tours, or be expanded to fill out a long, leisurely stay. There are not many itineraries which allow so much travel in time within such a small geographical compass. The Golden Triangle between Delhi, Agra and Jaipur has a wealth of sites, both contemporary and historical, from the present-day India of the 21st century, to the medieval era and still further back to the epoch of the Mahabharata.

An ideal itinerary would be for 10–12 days, beginning with 2–3 days in Delhi before moving on to Rajasthan or Agra. A night in Sariska could be followed by two days in Jaipur, with trips to Amber, Sanganer and Samode. A night in Bharatpur could fit in with a midday visit to Deeg, en route to Agra. Two days in the old Mughal capital would allow time for Fatehpur Sikri and Sikandara, and the trip from or back to Delhi could take in the mini-Varanasi pilgrim centre of Mathura and Vrindavan.

For visitors with less time to spare, tour operators in the capital conduct half-day tours of north and south Delhi which take in a dizzying cross-section of the city's rich history. It is well worth spending half a day each in the different cities embedded in Delhi – medieval Delhi, Shahjahan's capital, British New Delhi and the modern metropolis. Jaipur and Amber can also be covered in a one-day tour, affording a splendid glimpse of a planned 18th century city and a typical Rajput fort.

Agra and Fatehpur Sikri can be "done" in a sunrise-to-sunset dash from Delhi, but demand a more leisurely exploration. In Agra, the tomb of Itimad-ud-daula, not always included in standard packages, is essential viewing, while rambling through the old British cemeteries makes an interesting contrast. The Taj is best viewed at early dawn and dusk, and of course the routine recommendation of a full-moon night visit is justified. Fatehpur Sikri, likewise, should be seen as late in the afternoon as possible, when the red sandstone glows and the buildings cast intricate shadows. Mathura and Vrindavan are ancient places of pilgrimage, and the museum in Mathura has an excellent collection well worth the detour in itself.

Jaipur itself, like Delhi, should be explored and not merely viewed. Not far from it are the palaces of Samode and Alwar, where landscape and architecture are wonderfully blended. Sanganer is a traditional crafts village where the manufacturing processes of Rajasthani textiles and the distinctive blue pottery can be observed first-hand. An overnight stay in one of the bird sanctuaries or wildlife reserves (Keoladeo Ghana and Siliserh for birds, Sariska and Ranthambore for tigers) is strongly recommended. The mud fort of Bharatpur, near the bird sanctuary, has the characteristically the rugged architecture of the Jats whose capital it was, while nearby Deeg bears the stamp of the architecture they learned from the Mughals of Agra.

Preceding pages: three 19th century aquatints, showing views of Delhi, Jaipur and Agra. Opposite: three Delhi women carrying water pots.

A Tale Of Three Cities

Travelling in India is now easier but perhaps a little less exciting than it was in earlier centuries. The modern tourist does not have the option of sailing up the Yamuna and seeing the Taj Mahal glowing against an unpolluted sky, or the dreaming domes of the Jama Masjid beyond the walls of Delhi's Red Fort which at one time bordered the river. They can no longer arrive in Jaipur on camel back and see the skyline of the old city or the silhouette of Amber fort. Further back in time, watchmen must have raised the alarm as they saw the distant clouds of dust that warned of an invading army from Afghanistan or Persia. Jaipur had been less vulnerable than Delhi or Agra, for the expanse of desert to the west was a more effective defence than stone ramparts. More recent invasions include the thousands of refugees at the time of Partition, Rajasthani villagers escaping drought in the countryside, and the tourists, who are assailed by crowded, exuberant cityscapes where the architecture and lifestyles of the past jostle with the present.

In present-day Delhi, Agra and Jaipur are embedded many older towns – that of the Tughlaqs (Tughlaqabad), of Sikandar (Sikandara), of Akbar (Akbarabad – the Agra of Jahangir) and of Shahjahan (Shahjahanabad). Jaipur's walled city was laid out by Raja Jai Singh II of Amber, below the existing hill fort, and the city of the plain has now spread far beyond Jai Singh's city walls. For over eight centuries, the northern part of Rajasthan and the Ganga-Yamuna valley have had a shared history, so that these three cities carry within themselves memories of glory and conquest but happily also a thirst for the beautiful.

Historians of modern town-planning study blueprints and multi-coloured maps; it may come as a surprise to them that the Jaipur City Museum has many maps which show how the city was planned – over two and a half centuries ago. The town planning concepts of the Harappan civilisation in the 3rd millennium BC were transmitted through the centuries and written in the *Silpa Sastras* (The Art of Building). Later versions of this were used in planning the layout of Jaipur. The British extravaganza of New Delhi was designed by Lutyens also from Baroque models of an earlier century. Later in the modern capital of Punjab and Haryana commissioned by Jawarharlal Nehru and overseen by Le Courbusier, Chandigarh, we can see elements of Jaipur, and also of New Delhi – all three being interesting examples of the "open" city. In the later extensions built for Delhi and Jaipur, the organic links with the designs of Jai Singh and Lutyens are apparent.

In India it is common practice to have new streets or overbridges "inaugurated" by some suitably senior figure at a time convenient to the great personage. In 1648

Preceding pages: Sultan Mahal, Samode. Faces of the Golden Triangle region: small girl from village near Delhi (left) and young Muslim girl from village near Jaipur (above right).

the emperor Shahjahan presided at the beginnings of his Delhi: "On the night of Friday 25th Zi'l Hijja, in the twelfth year of his auspicious reign...being the time appointed by the astrologers, the foundations were marked out with the usual ceremonies". Jai Singh, likewise, must have bowed to the astrologers, but he is remembered for his fascination with *astronomy. He built observatories in many towns, and saw the Almighty as his suzerain, "the King of Kings...whose power the lofty orbs of Heaven are only a few leaves; and the stars...small pieces of money in the treasury of the empire of the Most High".

five, *ab*, water: thus, "the land of the five rivers"), and the Doab (*do*, two, referring to the tracts watered by the Ganga and the Yamuna). The hills of Rajasthan are very ancient; many millennia ago they were a green and pleasant land. In early historic times the river Saraswati flowed here and joined the Indus, before disappearing underground to become a memory and to provide guessing-games for archaeologists. Brajbhumi, the region associated with Krishna, is the land beside the Yamuna, with its main centres at Mathura and Vrindaran, but it stretches fingers into Rajasthan as far as the shrine of Nathdwara. The temple there

The upward thrust of the Mewar plateau and the Great Indian Desert or the Thar separates the Indus valley from that of the Yamuna-Ganga. "Land divides and water unites" – how true this is of the cultural zones of northern India. Pontoon bridges (formed by upturned boats laid side by side), stone bridges and iron bridges have spanned rivers, but deserts are difficult to cross. On either side of the desert (known as *maru* in the Sanskrit texts of the Vedas and *Mahabharata*) were territories with names which clearly evoked local geography – Sind (from "Sindhu", the Indus), Punjab (*panch*

houses a celebrated image of the cowherd prince who became the King of Dwarka on the west coast, separated from the land of his childhood by the desert.

For centuries the towns on the Yamuna have been crossroads cities, where the road from the west coast to the Himalayas scissored that from Afghanistan to the Bay of Bengal. The lines of pack-animals carrying salt from the sea met those carrying wheat from the Punjab. Jewellery from Rajasthan and ivoryware from Delhi were exchanged for Gujarat silk and Bengal cotton. When these cities were the stable centres of prosperous kingdoms, families of substance – particularly the rulers – indulged a boundless appetite for the beautiful and the unusual, and weavers, carvers and painters busily refined their skills to meet their patrons' demands. Later, a less discriminating but large market developed in countries overseas; after Independence, the handicrafts revival movement helped sustain the crafts.

In the 17th century, European tourists – then called travellers – were exploring North India, marvelling at the forts and towns which made those of Europe seem puny.The armchair travellers back in Europe had read of the Mughal towns of Agra and Delhi; much later, Jaipur became known to them, when Colonel Tod in the 1830s surveyed the desert kingdoms and wrote three volumes of racy prose, combining myth and fact in a spellbinding narrative. The audacious railway construction programme which linked Delhi and Agra to Kolkata (Calcutta) and later to the west coast via Rajasthan brought tourists to the region that was officially called Rajputana. For travellers in the late 19th century, Jaipur was attractive for another reason: Delhi and Agra had been two of the epicentres of the Revolt of 1857, during which the princes of Rajasthan had stood aside, "loyal" to the British. Their loyalty was rewarded: when Queen Victoria was proclaimed Empress in 1877, these princes, along with many others, were designated as feudatories under British paramountcy, and the Maharaja of Jaipur was accorded a satisfactorily large number of gun salutes – the symbol of statehood. The Jaipur ruler was following a tradition of "accommodation". Descended from the Kachchwahas who had established themselves in the desert in the 10th century and who claimed descent through Lord Rama from the sun, the Maharaja's ancestors had in the 16th century accepted Mughal suzerainty, and a Kachchwaha princess had married Emperor Akbar. The kings of Amber served as governors of the Mughals in Bengal and Afghanistan.

Far left, rural patriarch from near Agra. Left, Rajasthani migrant worker. Above, sisters in Id festival finery at the shrine of Nizamuddin.

Jaipur was one of the most important urban centres of North India in the 18th century, much as Delhi had been in the 17th and Agra in the 16th centuries. It was an unusual city for Rajasthan, in that it was not a rugged fort, but one built on the plains – symbolic of Raja Jai Singh's attitude of mind, which eagerly sought knowledge from all quarters. Halls of faceted mirrors sparkled in the palaces of all three cities and stylised floral designs danced through Rajasthani textiles, through jewelled pietra dura in the Taj Mahal and in bas-relief in sandstone in Delhi Fort. Jaipur rulers borrowed Mughal fashions and in periods of crisis in Delhi or Agra, court poets and artists fled to Jaipur or to Amber and were accorded patronage. The durbar of Jai Singh was what Fatehpur Sikri had been under Akbar, a magnificent centre of patronage for the arts.

Jaipur itself did not suffer from Persian and Afghan invasions like Delhi, but the indifference of Jai Singh's successors led to the dispersal of the priceless library he had built. By the late 18th century, the three cities were being buffeted by the incursions of the swift-footed Maratha warriors from the southwest. Had the raiders been able to consolidate what they had gained for a few decades, there would in truth have been a Maharashtra (*maha*, great, *rashtra*, kingdom) over much of Rajasthan and the northern plain. But they were outmanoeuvred by the British armies moving up the Ganga valley from Calcutta. With military and diplomatic skills, the British established a firm line of control. One decisive battle in 1803 won them a swathe of territory which included both Agra and Delhi. From there, their eyes turned to Afghanistan and, therefore, to Sind and Punjab which lay in between. Rajasthan escaped a conquest and after the Revolt of 1857, the British came to an accommodation with the ruling Rajputs which averted this danger permanently, although keeping them well under British influence. Thus the rulers of Rajasthan had again done the impossible; retained their identity and established good relations with the sovereign power.

The game of shifting capitals has been played since the 12th century. Delhi was Sultanate and Mughal capital, alternating with Agra, until 1857. The year after, it was "punished" by being made just another provincial town of Punjab; in 1911, in a surprise move, it was chosen as the capital of British India. Initially, Agra was capital of the Northwestern Provinces, but later had to yield its place to Allahabad which became the capital of the huge United Provinces. Jaipur was a Rajput state till after Independence, when it was selected as the capital of the new state of Rajasthan. Today, Delhi is a huge modern city and the political centre of the country, Jaipur is the gateway city of Rajasthan, and Agra a busy and crowded town with remnants of Mughal splendour nestling in it.

These cities take their pasts for granted, in a modern India of mind-boggling problems and a sense of hurry. All Indian cities have been growing in size and population in the last four decades. This explains the crowds and chaos which, for the first-time visitor, can be a disconcerting encounter. It also explains the land-hunger which leads to all available urban (including public) spaces being occupied or encroached upon. In the contemporary pandemonium of these three cities the legacy of their historic and beautifully crafted buildings, shines out all the more unexpectedly.

Religious mendicants – Sufi seeker (above left), and Hindu holy man (right).

عمل حاجی مدنی

تقسیم نمودند تمام روز در منزل بابا خرم بخرمی و خوشحالی گذشت و اکثر پیشکشهای او پسندیده افتاد

A Cultural Synthesis

It was courageous travellers and early traders who carried the message of India's wealth to the distant shores of Europe and East Asia. Buddhist pilgrims and scholars from both the west and east journeyed into South Asia 2,000 years ago, to study Buddhist philosophy and to visit the sites associated with him. Such diverse interests in religion and commerce created an image of an India rich in resources of timber, minerals and precious stones, of skilled artisans who crafted the finest textiles, jewels and household artefacts, of gurus, teachers, mathematicians and scholars, hermitages, universities and glorious cities.

It was the lure of this wealth that opened up trade routes along the shores of India and through the Himalayan mountains. In the early years of the Christian era, Arab traders had established contact with India and East Asia, bringing them closer through the exchange of ideas and innovations. With the birth of Islam in Arabia in AD 622, power and conquest followed these vital trade routes, encompassing the distant lands of Spain, Africa, Middle and Central Asia, China and Java. Once again, India was linked to other countries by a subtle network of ideas stemming from the theology of Islam, politics, trade and sociology, bringing about a complex synthesis of technological innovations and culture.

Indo-Islamic art, growing and flowering over many centuries, retained in essence its international link while acquiring a flavour that is unique to India. It was nurtured by both highly skilled indigenous artists and artists brought from the Central Asian and Iranian courts.

A place for prayer: Central to Islamic belief is communal worship, and for this the new settlers in India required appropriate sites.

Preceding pages, detail from 17th century miniature – the wedding procession of Prince Dara Shikoh, Shahjahan's heir. Left, ceremonial weighing of Prince Khurram on his 16th birthday by the emperor Jahangir. Above right, Dara Shikoh and Princess enjoying a music recital.

There are three kinds of mosques or *masjids* which serve the need for prayer and prostration before Allah: the Id-gah for mass congregation during Id and religious festivals; the mosque for Friday mass worship, called Jama, Juma or Jami Masjid; and for private prayer five times a day, a small space where on the prayer rug one could kneel facing Mecca and the Ka'ba, the *axis mundi* of Islamic cosmology. Since worship of images is prohibited by Islam,

the little carpet, a portable mosque, was a treasured item of religious ritual. The art of carpet weaving developed in the Middle East, Iran, Afghanistan and in India, and produced a wide range of wool, silk and cotton prayer rugs to serve the needs of all worshippers. They are embellished with decorative borders and, sometimes, calligraphic quotations from the Quran.

A mosque consists of an enclosed courtyard with a central wide open area for prayer. One wall of the courtyard is aligned to point towards Mecca, to indicate the direction of prayer. This wall, called the *qibla*, is given prominence by the construction of a carved niche called the *mihrab*, with borders of Quranic calligraphed verse. In the open courtyard in front of the *qibla* is a tank or fountain for the ritual washing of hands, feet and face before prayer.

The first mosque of this kind to be built in India was the Quwwat-ul-Islam ("Might of Islam") in 1192, attributed to Qutb-ud-din Aibak. The Qutb Minar was constructed by him beside the mosque which, although built as a tower of victory, became the model for all subsequent Indian mosque minarets. The *minar* is an essential feature of all mosques and served as a high tower from which the muezzin or priest traditionally called people to prayer. A mosque could have either a single *minar*, or two, or four, to lend a symmetrical balance to the structure. The evolution of the design for the *minar* in the Middle East, Cairo and Iran can be traced from simple square towers, to elaborate circular, many-sided constructions.

The next problem that confronted craftspeople was the construction of an arched prayer hall for the *qibla* wall. The engineering principle of the arch was a technological innovation brought by Islam to India. For the first time the bridge between two walls or pillars did not have to be limited in span by the use of single stone or wooden beams. With the use of the arch-wide openings, tall broad doorways and windows were possible, which transformed construction. Local artisans were initially hesitant to use the arch, and often supported it with beams and brackets, or even filled up the archway, creating a mixture of Hindu and Islamic building styles. In time, arches and domes lost their tentative form, acquiring lofty heights and spanning wide areas to create airy buildings full of muted light, which became the signature of Indo-Islamic architecture. The increased confidence of the architects is reflected in the later mosques built at Fatehpur Sikri by Akbar, and the private royal mosque for daily prayer, the Moti Masjid, built by Aurangzeb at the Red Fort in the 17th century. The perfection of building technique, the restrained use of decoration, the indigenous lotus design, Islamic inlaid calligraphy and the reposeful symmetry of the domes and arches of the Jama Masjid, in Delhi, represent the high point of mosque architecture in India, the culmination of an artistic endeavour pursued over centuries.

Tombs of saints and rulers: As in Christian belief, Islam speaks of Judgement Day, when the souls of the dead will be divided according to their deeds and sent to hell or to paradise. Throughout the Islamic world the dead were buried in graves aligned to face Mecca, with sometimes a low tombstone raised above the ground and covered only by the "canopy of the sky". Later, for important tombs, the metaphor of the "canopy" was converted into cloth hangings and masonry domes. Tombs of saints and poets were included within the mosque complex to serve as pilgrimage centres; to visit them was to commune with the spirit of goodness and faith. These tombs attracted hundreds and thousands of pilgrims of different faiths, and to this day, these *dargahs* or mausoleums resound with devotional music (*qavvalis*), recitation of prayers and the bustle of people. To celebrate the life of the saint, the annual Urs (anniversary of the saint's death) and religious festivals were arranged at the tomb. The tomb of the 13th century saint Hazrat Nizammuddin in Delhi, of Sheikh Salim Chisti at Fatehpur Sikri, and of Khwaja Moinuddin Chisti in Ajmer are perhaps the most important Islamic pilgrimage centres in this region of India.

Similarly, royal tombs evolved from simple square domed structures into buildings of dramatic proportions. The ruler built his own tomb during his lifetime as a monument to his life and deeds. The raised grave was placed in a bare room, where devotional music and recitations of the Quran were held throughout the year. Often a false grave was placed at ground level and the real grave within a well-guarded chamber underground, so that no one could defile the body of the king. The tomb was surrounded by a garden and often enclosed within a boundary wall, so that entrance could be restricted to family members and friends. Often a mosque was built on the western side for prayer, with a complementary building on the east to provide symmetry to the plan. The poetic metaphor for paradise was the surrounding garden, full of sweet-smelling flowers, evergreen trees like the cypress, with the gentle sound of birds and the continuous gurgling of life-giving water.

Entrance to the Qila-i-Kuhna mosque in the Old Fort, New Delhi (far left) and in the Agra Fort (left). Above, congregational prayers at Jama Masjid, Delhi.

The theme of gardens, with floral motifs, is repeated in the architectural decorations, textiles and carpets of that period in the Islamic world. The plan for the tomb building was first square and later octagonal. These features are combined in an irregular octagonal plan in the Taj Mahal and in Humayun's tomb. The roof over the tomb was usually a dome, with the exception of Akbar's tomb at Sikandara and Itmad-ud-Daulah's tomb in Agra. Akbar used the Hindu architectural design of carved pillars supporting flat roofs, stone beams, overhanging eaves, and brackets, similar to his Panch Mahal in Fatehpur Sikri. The structure is light and airy, with open halls supported by pillars on several storeys. The tombs, like the palaces, were built of rubble covered with smooth plaster work, and stucco designs that were either painted or inlaid with ceramic tile patterns.

In Islamic structures in Delhi from the 13th to the 15th century, artists used coloured tiles to create borders and panels on gateways and arches in accordance with the artistic heritage from the Middle East. Local pink sandstone and white marble created colour variations in the decorated facades of buildings. Ornamentation in geometric forms, squares, circles and interlocking shapes, existed side by side with arabesques of creepers, flowers and trees that seem to have been inspired by paintings. The juxtaposition of red sandstone and white marble created a pleasing visual effect and, since a variety of stone was available in plenty in India, it gradually replaced tile work and became a distinctive feature of Indo-Islamic architecture. In the tombs of Ghias-ud-din Tughlaq and Humayun, the main body of the structure is faced with pink sandstone, with the dome in white marble. Itmad-ud-Daulah's tomb in Agra and later the Taj Mahal were faced completely in white marble, giving to these buildings a new quality of weightlessness and brightness.

Geometric designs cut out from coloured marble and sandstone were joined together and set into the stone wall in elaborate patterns. Akbar's grandson Shahjahan used pietra dura work in the Taj Mahal, but reduced the scale of the areas to be covered and introduced semi-precious and precious stones into the marble inlay. A single flower on Shahjahan's tomb comprises more than 60 cut stones of subtle hue that capture, as in a painting, the turn of the petal, the fall of the leaf, and the stain of pollen-laden stamens.

The Hindu royalty of Rajasthan were perhaps most influenced by Mughal culture, for historical and political reasons. The Hindu belief in reincarnation negates the need for tombs, but there was an ancient practice of marking the place where a warrior died or was cremated. The Rajputs therefore constructed *chatris* or raised open pavilions with pillars and domes to mark the place of their heroic dead.

It is in the forts and palaces of Delhi, Agra and Jaipur that one gets a glimpse of the lifestyle of the rulers. The concept of the fortified palace or living quarters for the rulers embodied the fundamentals of Islamic domestic architecture: public and private areas were clearly defined, whether within a house, a palace complex or a fort. The private areas, shielded from the public eye, were placed at a distance from the entrance; like the protective veil worn by Muslim women, stone walls and screens further segregated the living areas for the family and the harem. Rooms had little furniture and hence could be used for multiple purposes. Depending on the wealth of the owner, they were adorned with cloth hangings, carpets, bolsters, cushions, low book stands with illustrated Qurans and manuscripts, and household objects that could be moved around at will. The palaces of Delhi, Agra and Jaipur are empty now, but a close look at contemporary miniature paintings helps to recreate the beauty that once furnished these buildings.

Great care was taken by the architects of these palaces to build in a manner that was suitable to the climate, and to ensure comfort in all seasons for the occupants. Delhi, Agra and Jaipur share a common climate – torrid and dusty during the summer months – and rooms were built with thick walls for insulation and large windows and doors for cross ventilation. The intense summer sunlight was diffused and scattered by the use of stone lattice screens or *jalis*. Perfumed water was sprayed on cloth and grass mats hung across openings to cool the interiors. In the Red Fort in Delhi, there were fountains within the building and the gardens around it to cool the air.

There are not many buildings within these forts as the Mughals, perhaps because they

Left, the great mosque beside Mumtaz Mahal's tomb. Above left, the fortified palace of Agra. Above right, Qutb-ud-din's *minar*, for centuries the tallest tower in the world.

were accustomed to an outdoor nomadic life, built relatively few permanent structures within the forts, preferring colourful tents and pavilions in the gardens where they could enjoy the cool perfumed evenings of summer, and the warmth of an Indian winter's day.

As well as the colour and sparkle on their buildings, they embellished their clothes with gold, silver and gem sequins. Their rooms glittered like the star-studded night sky, with the use of glass and mirrors that caught the multiple reflections of candles and lamps, as in the Shish Mahals in the Red Forts in Delhi and Agra, and Amber Fort.

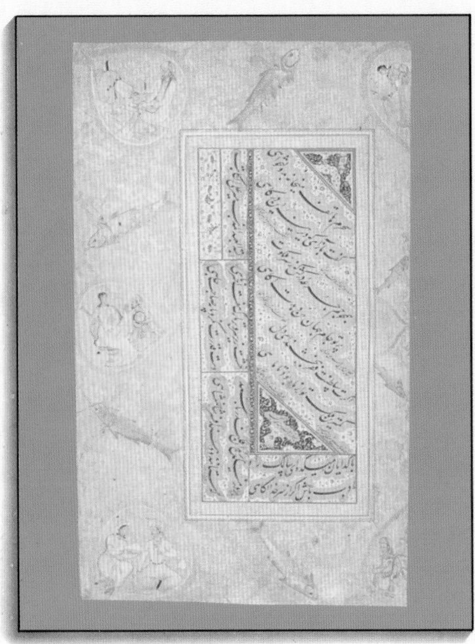

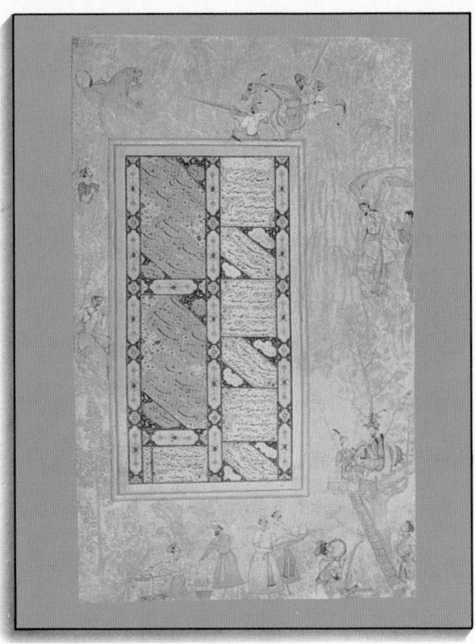

Landscaped gardens were laid out with water channels to catch and reflect the changing moods of the sky, and filled with flowers identified in Mughal paintings as irises, roses and narcissi. The whole plan of the palace was oriented towards the creation of a tranquil, luxuriant mood.

Beyond the fort walls, the moat and the protective gateways lay the houses of the noblemen and other people, and the markets. It was trade and conquest, and the protection of important trade routes by land and sea, that brought wealth into the cities of Agra, Delhi and Jaipur. These cities still retain some flavour of the old caravanserais and market places. Like the *souks* of Damascus, each area was marked out for the sale of a particular commodity, which enabled travelling caravans of specialised traders to locate their market, find appropriate resting places and transact business. These specialised market streets still bustle with trade.

Painting and Calligraphy: To these great cities of Delhi, Agra and Jaipur came artists and scholars seeking the patronage of emperors and courtiers. Amongst the most cherished objects was the handwritten book, and of all books the most honoured was the Holy Quran, God's message transmitted by the Prophet Muhammad. In cities and *madarsas* (theological colleges) throughout the Islamic world, books were copied by hand by generations of scribes. The art of calligraphy flourished as many styles evolved, and borders of arabesque and geometric designs were added to make each book a work of art. Earlier in India, manuscripts and holy texts had been recorded on dried palm leaves bound together by cord, also illustrated with minute drawings of figures, animals and trees. The Indian artist was thus quite accustomed to working on a small or "miniature" scale when paper, an invention brought from China, was introduced during the medieval period. The pre-Islamic and Islamic styles differed in the content of the illustrations and the nature of the painting. The older tradition illustrated Hindu, Jain and Buddhist texts in bright primary colours – red, blue, yellow, gold, white and black. The drawings were bold and stylised, abstract and densely symbolic. From Iran, the tradition of painting was a synthesised art form and tended to be more naturalistic and lyrical with intricate details of landscape, "Chinese" clouds, birds and animals. details of textiles, wall decorations, jewellery, animals, birds and trees.

In the Hindu tradition, landscape and architectural details were used as a backdrop for human beings. Artists knew, but rarely employed, the rules of perspective; their focus was on the "action" of the story. A range of brushes with camel, squirrel or even human hair was used and colours obtained from plant and mineral sources were mixed with a binding material to be applied on absorbent paper. The treatment of the paper before painting, and its polishing with a smooth stone after, were also important components of the process.

Colours were mixed to produce shades of pink, lilac, soft greens, browns and blues. When the two traditions met in India, a wide range of styles emerged, from the Persian-influenced paintings of the time of Babur and Humayun to the powerful dramatic style of the early Akbar period. Manuscripts like the *Akbarnama* have pictures crowded with people engaged in a myriad of activities, colours are vibrant and every inch contains

Left, pages of calligraphy from the illuminated album of Jahangir. Above, detail of script on Akbar's cenotaph at Sikandara.

Mughal emperors maintained large ateliers where several artists collaborated on works of painting and manuscripts. The *Nama* or royal diary was produced by each successive ruler and re-copied by his heirs. The *Baburnama*, *Akbarnama* and others were royal treasures that took years to create. The subject matter of Mughal paintings varied from illustrations of events in the life of the emperor to scenes of everyday life. Babur is said to have taken great interest in recording animals and plants that he saw for the first time in India – banana trees, the elephant and the rhinoceros, and several birds. Some of the best collections of such manuscripts can be found in the National Museum in Delhi, and the British Library and V&A in London.

In Rajasthan (where artists from the court of Aurangzeb found employment), and in the hill states of Punjab and Himachal, painting was indebted to the Mughal school. They incorporated the use of Hindu symbolism and bold, primary colours, and each school evolved its own style of portrayal of human figures and landscapes. Under the influence of European painting, Indian artists attempted new themes, portraits and studies of nature – the so-called "Company style".

In the workshops of these rulers of Delhi, Agra and Jaipur, many other crafts were patronised and precious jewellery handcrafted. Jaipur is even today an important centre for gem cutting and for gold and silver enamel work. Jade brought from China and Central Asia was fashioned into handles for daggers, wine cups, *huqqa* stands and other treasured items. From various corners of the Mughal empire, textiles were brought to furnish houses and to attire the nobility: fine muslin and cotton from Bengal, woven brocade silk from Banaras, carpets and shawls from Kashmir, printed and painted fabrics from Rajasthan, gold, silver and silk embroidery from Delhi, Uttar Pradesh and the western states.

Endings and Beginnings: By mid-18th century, the Mughal empire had lost much of its power, following the devastating raids of Nadir Shah from Iran. Fabulous jewels, enormous quantities of gold and treasures, including the exquisite Peacock Throne, were lost, and palaces and homes were destroyed.

Delhi and Agra lost their status while the French, Portuguese and British came to colonise Mumbai, Goa, Chennai (Madras), Pondicherry and Kolkata (Calcutta). Years after the extinction of the Mughal Empire, Delhi returned to prominence when she was chosen once again in 1911 to be the capital city of the British empire in India.

British architecture in Delhi is distinct from the styles in Mumbai, Kolkata or Chennai. The empire was seemingly secure, and there was an attempt to develop what was called the Imperial Anglo-Indian style of architecture. Rashtrapati Bhavan (the Viceregal residence) makes extensive use of classical Greek and Roman motifs, doric columns, archways and colonnades along with Indian elements of design – the lotus and the elephant – and extensive use of coloured sandstone. Several buildings were constructed for administrative purposes in Delhi, Agra and Jaipur – railway stations, town halls, courts, post offices, barracks and prisons. Residential buildings for British officials exhibited a mixture of Indian and European features to suit the climate of this region, with high ceilings, large windows and doors, verandahs along the sides to shade the building from the strong sunlight, and gardens and lawns with their favourite English trees and flowers.

Today, the cities of Delhi, Agra and Jaipur form a gigantic collage, in which the old monuments co-exist with the new, and conservationists are anxious to preserve the the past in the planning and design of the contemporary city.

Above left, traditional textiles – tie-dye process. Right, block printed hanging in Sanganer palace.

Delhi has many gates of entry, but none for departure: this local saying has been borne out by the city's history. It has served as a frontier post for empires located to the east, and as a centre for those which spread over the Ganga plain and Afghanistan. Situated at a point where the Yamuna is easy to ford, it has been a strategic border between the regions of Haryana and modern Uttar Pradesh. Before South Asia was partitioned, young school children located Delhi on the map by first drawing straight lines across the widest and down the longest stretch of the country, then marking the point of intersection of the two lines.

To stumble upon traces of earlier habitations is commonplace in Delhi. If it were not so continuously occupied and built upon, large sections of the present city could have been cordoned off into archaeological parks. Medieval arches and columns and old coins surface in the soil disturbed by pickaxe or plough. During the 19th century, census officials were surprised to notice a group of people in Delhi who earned their living by searching for coins among the ruins of the Tughlaqabad fort.

Over the centuries, sections of the built area have reverted to rural use, and back again to urban. Names get forgotten, distorted, deliberately changed (for example, Mongolpuri, the Mongol township, becomes Mangalpuri, "town of good fortune"; Youngpura, named after a local British official, becomes Jangpura, "town of the great battle"). Even so, many have survived for centuries. One of the fourteen villages which emperor Ferozeshah Tughlaq bought in the 14th century to build his citadel was Hastinapur, which had a history going back to the *Mahabharata*. Likewise, Indraprastha, again of epic vintage, survived as a village in revenue records until the present century. Tools of the paleolithic period have been found on the hills that cross the city, and late Harappan pottery was excavated on the plains further north, giving the city an even older ancestry. The emperor Asoka in the 3rd century BC left his signature in the form of an edict on a rocky outcrop in

south Delhi. A remarkable non-rusting pillar of the 4th century stands in an architectural complex of the 12th century, its origin a mystery. Names of different localities remind us that in another age they were independent settlements or suburbs (*pur* signifies a town, *kot* a fort, *abad* a town, *serai* a market town). In the popular mind, Delhi is the forever capital, just as Varanasi is the sacred city. Both power and glory, as well as wanton assault and the scars of adversity, are woven into its fabric.

The mental image of the eternal city becomes three-dimensional for the period after the 12th century, with strong visual elements. The political regimes that dominated North India (and sometimes sections of the South) each stamped their seal on the Delhi landscape. Ancient and medieval empires in South Asia did not stop at natural frontiers, and Afghanistan was part of many North Indian empires. The Buddhist and Hindu diaspora was matched by the Islamic one when Muhammad of Ghur (in Central Afghanistan) expanded his kingdom westward to Khurasan and eastward to India. From the 10th to the 13th centuries, South India and parts of Southeast Asia were controlled by the powerful Cholas. In the north, the Chauhan dynasty of Rajasthan ruled Delhi until in 1192 the army of Muhammad Ghuri wrested it from Raja Prithviraj at the second battle of Tarain. The conqueror returned to his base, leaving in charge his deputy Qutb-ud-din Aibak. Qutb-ud-din's tower is the most distinctive image of Delhi in the popular mind.

<u>Preceding pages</u>: the lion capital of the emperor Ashoka, adopted as India's emblem, on the gates of Rashtrapati Bhavan; contingent of the Border Security Force of the Bikaner Camel Corps at the Republic Day parade, held every year on 26 January; the courtyard of the 17th-century Jama Masjid. <u>Above</u>, ceremonial unveiling of Baker's four Dominion columns in front of the Secretariat on 10 February 1931.

Qutb-ud-din's reign was the beginning of the Sultanate of Delhi, with a succession of dynasties: the Il-baris, earlier known as the Slave Kings, the Khiljis, Tughlaqs, Sayyids and Lodis, ending in 1526 with the victory of the Mughal (a Persianised form of "Mongol") Babur. The cultural links with West Asia remained close. The boundaries of the Sultanate were fluid, as were those of other Indian states. At their maximum extent, these reached Bengal and present-day Tamil Nadu; the rise of the powerful kingdom of

Vijayanagara in South India in the mid-14th century was a barrier to expansion there.

Delhi has not had a tranquil life. Its history is as sharply varied as its climate, which swings sharply from frosty winter through a colour-laden spring, followed by long months of simmering heat broken by the fury of howling dust-storms, stilled in torrents of rain. There have been springlike periods of animation, of laughter, poetry and shimmering colour, which have been shattered by the plundering armies of Mongols, Persians, Marathas and the British; years of desolation have been followed by revival, when the caravans of camels, or the clattering railway trains, moved again, when the shutters of shops were lifted, when the people ventured out again into the lanes and streets. Much has been lost – many lives, many precious collections of books, many nuances of a gracious life-style, many elegant buildings. The Delhi we see today is what has survived, more by accident than by design. Of its present inhabitants, relatively few families have an association with the city that is of more than three generations.

The surface has been turbulent, but many things have settled at the base which have an enduring quality. Delhi has been a capital, but this has meant more than domination and aggrandisement. Because people from so many parts of India, Central Asia and West Asia have coexisted here, a cosmopolitan culture has developed; poets and writers have been proud to be known by the sobriquet "Dehlavi" ("of Delhi"). The short reigns of many rulers suggest an ephemeral glory; perhaps this was why many of them built so compulsively, so that their works might endure. In design and material, the architecture of the Sultanate period blended the best of local craftsmanship with Persian designs and building techniques. Whether it was the design of walls and bastions to protect the city, or an awesome network of great canals to irrigate its gardens, or mosques and mausolea, elegance and durability were combined in a manner that is the envy of modern architects.

The successive rulers marked out their distinct spaces – the Il-baris in Rai Pithora on the southern Ridge, the Khiljis in Siri on the plains further north, the Tughlaqs in a bewildering range of construction, from

St James's Church, built near Kashmiri Gate in 1824 by Col. James Skinner.

Jahanpanah, near Siri, to Ferozabad on the river further north, and in a massive outpost, the fort of Tughlaqabad on the east. The Sayyids and Lodis left no forts but many beautiful mausolea and mosques. Early in the 14th century, many artists and craftsman from West Asia sought refuge in Delhi after the Mongols defeated the Turkish Seljuks. A few decades later, the Mongol marauder Timur (Tamerlane) plundered Delhi of its wealth and its craftsmen: "I had determined to build a Masjid in Samarkand which should be without a rival, so I ordered that all builders and stone-masons should be set apart for my own special service".

If the rulers led charmed lives, the men of religion who chose to settle near the capital lived more securely, and built up followings that have endured till today. Roshan Chiragh-e-Delhi and Hazrat Nizamuddin were men of piety who lived in the 14th century and who have given their names to localities in Delhi. The shrine of Bakhtiyar Kaki in Mehrauli also attracts many worshippers. The shrines of many saints in Delhi are equally sacred to Hindus and Muslims, since their mysticism, whether Bhakti or Sufi, tended to be richly eclectic. Another great gift to India as a result of the West Asian connection was language: Arabic, Turkish and Persian met and mingled with Indian languages. One of Delhi's earliest Persian poets, Amir Khusrau (1253-1325) wrote with equal facility in Hindawi (early Hindi).

Timur, who had devastated Delhi, had been struck by the grandeur of the city. His descendant Babur, who was to become the first emperor of the Mughal dynasty, did not share his enthusiasm. "The country and towns of Hindustan are extremely ugly," he wrote, and observed that "the populousness and decay of cities is almost instantaneous". During his brief reign, and the much longer ones of his successors, Delhi and Agra alternated as the capital.

By the 16th century, however, the fortunes of Delhi were no longer bound up with the ruling dynasties. Two great Mughals, Akbar and Jahangir, had little to do with Delhi. Together with Lahore, Agra and Patna, it had become one of the major commercial entrepôts of North India. This was underlined by Sher Shah Suri, the rival of Emperor Humayan and an outstanding ruler in his own right, who built the great highway (the Grand Trunk Road immortalised by Kipling in *Kim*) from Lahore to Sonargaon in Bengal, via Delhi and Agra.

Delhi became a busy city with many wholesale and retail markets, and many local crafts, for which the Mughal court was a major patron. The city was ringed with small market towns (surviving today in the names of localities like Yusuf Sarai, Sheikh Sarai and Badli Sarai).

As the population of the city and its suburbs grew, a population was required to service the court, the nobles, the gardens and canals, mosques and schools. Almost unconsciously, there developed a hybrid language called Urdu ("the language of the soldiers", since it began as a soldiers' Esperanto – hence etymologically linked with "horde"). This rapidly became a highly stylised language, which borrowed equally from West Asian languages and from Hindi and Sanskrit. It lent itself to poetry, and the poets of Delhi in the 17th, 18th and 19th centuries (Mir, Sauda, Zauq, Ghalib) became famous individually and as a "school" which engaged in friendly rivalry with the poets of Lucknow.

Those Mughal emperors who lived in Delhi built on an even grander scale than the Sultanate rulers had done. Babur's son Humayun, an amiable and dreamy young man who led a precarious life, found time to construct the massive fort of Din-Panah (now called the Purana Qila, the Old Fort) on the river. Sher Shah Suri expressed in stone his rivalry with Humayun, when he built a massive fort-city across from Din-Panah and separated from it by a waterway. Humayun himself has been commemorated in one of the most beautiful mausolea in India. Akbar, the builder of Fatehpur Sikri, contributed nothing to Delhi, but one of his ministers built a temple at Kalka, now in Himalchal Pradesh, which has become a major shrine; another, Abdur Rahim, is remembered as a gifted poet and translator, and as the commander-in-chief whose mausoleum is a major monument.

Delhi might well have remained a prosperous commercial town surrounded by rich fields interspersed with monumental ruins, if it had not been for Shahjahan. Not satisfied with adding to Akbar's buildings in Agra, he decided to build a vast citadel and a splendid mosque at Delhi. Shahjahanabad still pulsates with life, and many of its buildings and much of its morphology is over three centuries old. In the 18th century Delhi thus became once again synonymous with sovereignty and with wealth. After 300 years of relative peace, therefore, the plundering raids began again. The Persian ruler Nadir Shah left behind in 1739 a desolation like that of the swarms of locusts that periodically devastated Delhi. His removal of Shahjahan's exquisite Peacock Throne was symptomatic of the political decline of the Mughals. Later, the warrior chieftains from Maharashtra, the Jat clans from neighbouring villages and the British from their base in Bengal, all sought to capture the city. In the event it was the British who won, in 1803.

Delhi served as a frontier-post for the East India Company for nearly half a century, until the Punjab kingdom was conquered. The Mughal emperors in their palace coexisted amicably with the Company's representative. The last emperor, Bahadur Shah, took delight in composing gently bantering verse about the British. He and other poets recited verse and the local artists painted miniatures by the score for British clients. This co-existence was broken on 11 May 1857 when a group of Indian soldiers from Meerut dashed across the bridge of boats on the Yamuna, to urge the startled emperor to lead them in a revolt against the British. For more than four months the fate of Delhi hung in the balance, with the soldiers controlling the walled city and the British forces poised on the northern Ridge. In September 1857 they stormed the city and expelled the inhabitants. The people were dazed by the violence of the retribution, and then by the Emperor's banishment to Rangoon; the British troops moved into the citadel, henceforward called the Red Fort.

Nothing could quite take the place of the Mughal court. There were the cardboard substitutes, the Durbars of 1877, 1903 and 1911, elaborate ceremonies where the Indian princes paid homage to the Viceroy or the King-Emperor. These were held on a plain north of the city, cleared of fields and vegetation. At the last of these gatherings,

King George V announced that the winter capital would be shifted from Calcutta to Delhi (for the summer months all the paraphenalia of central government used to migrate to the cool hill-station of Simla).

The Viceroy and the government offices could not be adequately accommodated in Shahjahanabad. After weighing the relative advantages of different sites, and surveying the land from elephant-back, it was decided to site New Delhi south of the imperial city, linking the ruins of the older towns into its landscape design. The new city would rise above the rest by the device of situating the Viceroy's Palace at a higher level, atop Raisina Hill. The team of architects for New Delhi was led by Lutyens, well known for his English countryhouses, and Baker, who had designed the government offices at Pretoria.

In the twenty years that the capital was being built, on a design strongly evocative of Versailles and Washington, the tempo of the Indian nationalist movement increased. The speeches at public meetings near the Red Fort could not be heard in the spacious and somewhat barren expanses around the Viceroy's Palace. When in 1931 Mahatma Gandhi strode up the steps of this beautiful building and shook hands with Lord Irwin, few people would have imagined that 20 years later the President of an independent India would be occupying Lutyens' grandest countryhouse.

For North India, Independence also meant Partition. In the fear and uncertainty of 1947, many Muslim families of Delhi migrated to Pakistan, and a reverse stream of Hindus and Sikhs from west Punjab flooded into the city. They were given land west of the Ridge and south of New Delhi, and many built houses for themselves across the river and to the north. Since then, the infill and extension of Delhi has never ceased, and migrants continue to pour in – poor migrants patching together mud-and-tarpaulin shacks, rich migrants building palatial homes, industrialists seeking a toehold in the capital, young people looking for challenging jobs. The fields of mustard have been covered with asphalt roads, and highrise buildings of concrete and glass dwarf older structures. But the Qatb Minar still dominates the skyline of south Delhi, a magnificent reminder that this is a very old city indeed.

The seat of government: North and South Block, seen from the Boat Club lawns where protest rallies are often held.

THE BANK THAT CARES
Grindlays Bank
फार्मेसी
PHARMACY

HongkongBank
HongkongBank
SHOWROOM
hmt
WATCHES
Carona
Carona
39th WORLD
TABLE TENNIS CHAMPIONSHIPS
Bata Bata बाटा
Bata Bata Bata बाटा
hmt
RAMA
ALLWYN
SUITINGS SHIRTINGS
THE BANK THAT CARES
Grindlays Bank plc

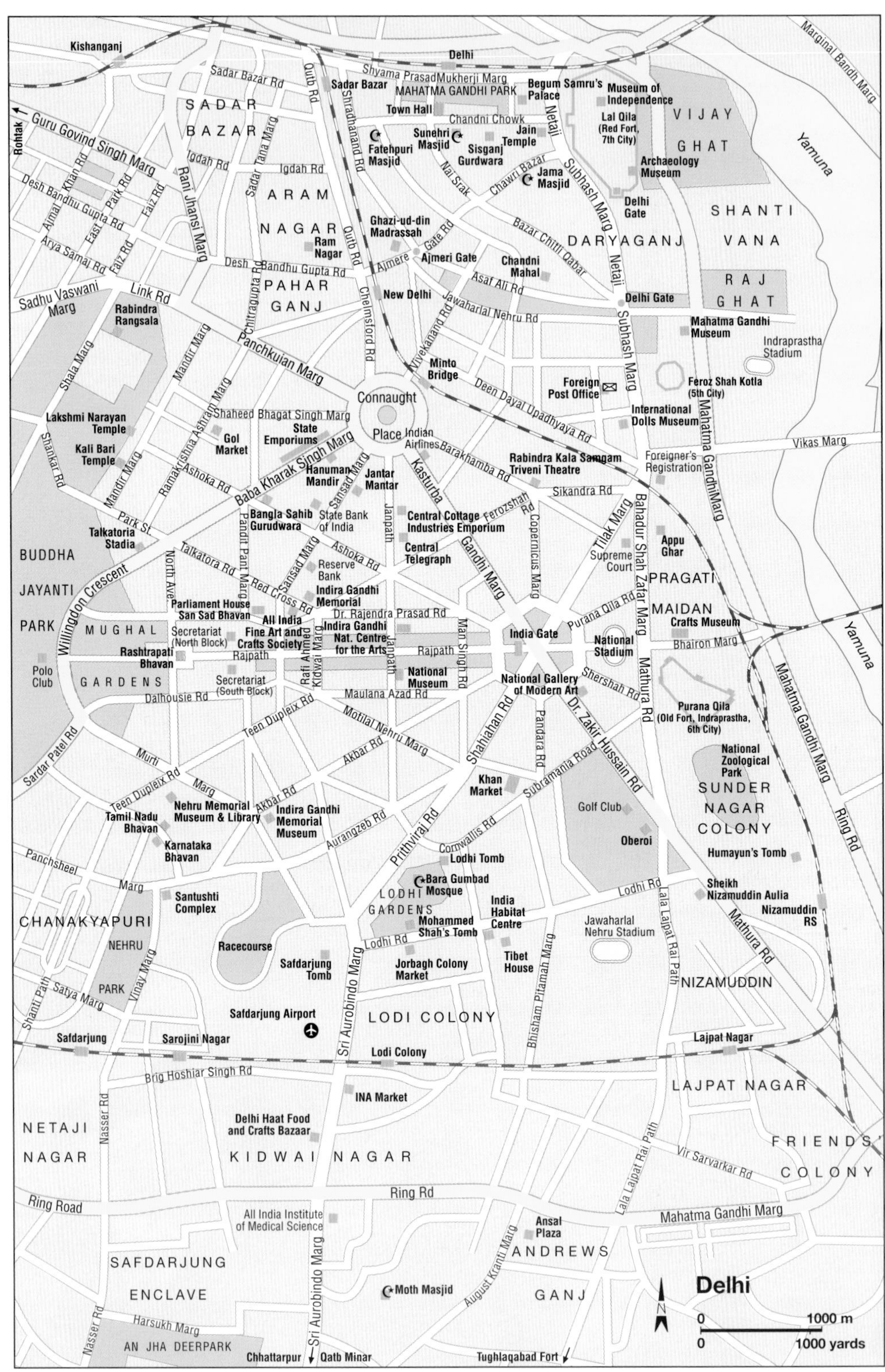
Delhi
0 1000 m
0 1000 yards
Kishanganj
Delhi
Sadar Bazar
MAHATMA GANDHI PARK
Town Hall
Begum Samru's Palace
Museum of Independence
Lal Qila (Red Fort, 7th City)
VIJAY GHAT
Yamuna
Fatehpuri Masjid
Sunehri Masjid
Sisganj Gurdwara
Jain Temple
Jama Masjid
Archaeology Museum
Delhi Gate
SHANTI VANA
SADAR BAZAR
ARAM NAGAR
Ram Nagar
Ghazi-ud-din Madrassah
Ajmeri Gate
Chandni Mahal
DARYAGANJ
RAJ GHAT
PAHAR GANJ
New Delhi
Mahatma Gandhi Museum
Indraprastha Stadium
Rabindra Rangsala
Minto Bridge
Foreign Post Office
Feroz Shah Kotla (5th City)
Connaught Place
International Dolls Museum
Lakshmi Narayan Temple
Gol Market
State Emporiums
Indian Airlines
Kali Bari Temple
Hanuman Mandir
Jantar Mantar
Rabindra Kala Samgam Triveni Theatre
Foreigner's Registration
Talkatoria Stadia
Bangla Sahib Gurudwara
State Bank of India
Central Cottage Industries Emporium
Central Telegraph
Appu Ghar
Supreme Court
Reserve Bank
Indira Gandhi Memorial
BUDDHA JAYANTI PARK
PRAGATI MAIDAN
Parliament House San Sad Bhavan
All India Fine Art and Crafts Society
Indira Gandhi Nat. Centre for the Arts
Crafts Museum
MUGHAL GARDENS
Secretariat (North Block)
Rashtrapati Bhavan
India Gate
National Stadium
Polo Club
Secretariat (South Block)
National Museum
National Gallery of Modern Art
Purana Qila (Old Fort, Indraprastha, 6th City)
National Zoological Park
SUNDER NAGAR COLONY
Khan Market
Golf Club
Oberoi
Nehru Memorial Museum & Library
Tamil Nadu Bhavan
Indira Gandhi Memorial Museum
Karnataka Bhavan
Lodhi Tomb
Humayun's Tomb
Bara Gumbad Mosque
LODHI GARDENS
Sheikh Nizamuddin Aulia
Santushti Complex
India Habitat Centre
Nizamuddin RS
CHANAKYAPURI
NEHRU PARK
Mohammed Shah's Tomb
Jawaharlal Nehru Stadium
Racecourse
Safdarjung Tomb
Jorbagh Colony Market
Tibet House
NIZAMUDDIN
Safdarjung Airport
LODI COLONY
Safdarjung
Sarojini Nagar
Lodi Colony
Lajpat Nagar
LAJPAT NAGAR
INA Market
NETAJI NAGAR
Delhi Haat Food and Crafts Bazaar
KIDWAI NAGAR
FRIENDS' COLONY
All India Institute of Medical Science
Ansal Plaza
SAFDARJUNG ENCLAVE
ANDREWS GANJ
Moth Masjid
AN JHA DEERPARK
Chhattarpur
Qatb Minar
Tughlaqabad Fort
Rohtak
Guru Govind Singh Marg
Sadar Bazar Rd
Qutb Rd
Shyama Prasad Mukherji Marg
Shradhanand Rd
Chandni Chowk
Netaji
Subhash Marg
Marginal Bandh Marg
Idgah Rd
Rani Jhansi Marg
Sadar Tana Marg
Nai Srak
Chawri Bazar
Bazar Chitli Qabar
Desh Bandhu Gupta Rd
Arya Samaj Rd
Ajmal Khan Rd
Park Rd
Faiz Rd
East Park Rd
Link Rd
Sadhu Vaswani Marg
Chitragupta Rd
Chelmsford Rd
Ajmere Gate Rd
Asaf Ali Rd
Jawaharlal Nehru Rd
Vivekanand Rd
Panchkuian Marg
Mandir Marg
Shala Marg
Ramakrishna Ashram Marg
Shaheed Bhagat Singh Marg
Deen Dayal Upadhyaya Rd
Baba Kharak Singh Marg
Barakhamba Rd
Vikas Marg
Mahatma Gandhi Marg
Shankar Rd
Ashoka Rd
Sansad Marg
Janpath
Kasturba Gandhi Marg
Ferozshah Rd
Sikandra Rd
Tilak Marg
Bahadur Shah Zafar Marg
Copernicus Marg
Park St
Pandit Pant Marg
North Ave
Talkatora Rd
Red Cross Rd
Willingdon Crescent
Dr. Rajendra Prasad Rd
Purana Qila Rd
Rafi Ahmed Kidwai Marg
Man Singh Rd
Rajpath
Bhairon Marg
Mathura Rd
Dalhousie Rd
Maulana Azad Rd
Shershah Rd
Teen Duplex Rd
Motilal Nehru Marg
Shahjahan Rd
Pandara Rd
Dr. Zakir Hussain Rd
Akbar Rd
Subramania Road
Sardar Patel Rd
Murti Marg
Prithviraj Rd
Cornwallis Rd
Aurangzeb Rd
Ring Rd
Panchsheel Marg
Lodhi Rd
Lala Lajpat Rai Path
Sri Aurobindo Marg
Bhisham Pitamah Marg
Vinay Marg
Satya Marg
Shanti Path
Brig Hoshiar Singh Rd
Nasser Rd
Vir Sarvarkar Rd
Ring Road
August Kranti Marg
Harsukh Marg

THE POLITICAL CENTRE

With the coming of Independence, Delhi retained its status as the capital city, and – for all India's federal structure – as the centre of politics, playing a part in most of the major political dramas of the last 50 or so years.

At midnight on 15 August 1947 (Independence Day itself) the new Prime Minister, Jawaharlal Nehru rose in the central chamber of Sansad Bhavan to formally take power of independent India. His stirring speech is one of the most famous made by any Indian politician:

> "Long years ago we made a tryst with destiny, and now the time comes when we shall redeem our pledge, not wholly or in full measure, but very substantially. At the stroke of the midnight hour, when the world sleeps, India will awake to life and freedom".

Later that day he addressed a huge crowd (estimated at one million people) from the ramparts of the Red Fort, a tradition continued by all prime ministers since, along with the raising of the Indian tricolour on the Lahore Gate.

However, amid the celebrations at the end of British rule, the tragedy of Partition was being played out on the Indo-Pakistan border. This huge exchange of populations – up to 13 million people – was to change the face of Delhi radically. What had been a predominantly Muslim city became the destination of a large number of refugees from the Punjab, many of them Sikhs, fleeing the communal slaughter of up to one million people as they tried to cross from one new country to the other. If there were Punjabi refugees arriving, then Muslim families from Delhi were leaving for Pakistan. While Delhi retains strongholds of Muslim culture, in Old Delhi and around Nizamuddin's tomb, their former wealth and strength is greatly diminished. Delhi's Punjabi population, on the other hand, is both very visible and, on the whole, prosperous. Many of the city's taxi, bus and auto drivers are members of the Punjabi comunity, as are the emerging wealthy middle class businesspeople.

The early years of India's freedom were marked by intense political activity. The most pressing task facing the new rulers was how to bring the princely states, particularly those of Rajasthan, Hyderabad and Kashmir, within the Union. This task was handed over to Nehru's Home Minister, Sardar Vallabhi Patel. His sympathies as a right-wing Hindu – he had infamously called for the sacking of Muslim civil servants and the removal of protection to Muslims during the Partition riots – and his not inconsiderable abilities as a diplomat, endeared him to the feudal Hindu rulers of Rajasthan. By the early 1950s, all the Rajasthani princely states had been abolished. This assimilation was not so easily acheived in the

Preceding pages: the modern concrete pyramid of the Hall of Nations in the Trade Fair grounds, from the medieval Old Fort; Chandni Chowk, with the Red Fort at the summit of the street. **Right**, election results being posted in New Delhi.

southern state of Hyderabad, ruled by the Muslim Nizam. He was determined either to retain his independence or to join with Pakistan. It was not until 13 September 1948 that riots in the city gave Nehru the excuse to send troops in to take control. Further problems were posed by the ruler of Kashmir. This Muslim majority state was ruled by a Hindu maharaja, who showed a preference for accession to India. This prompted the Pakistani army to invade in October 1948. Immediately, Nehru sent in the Indian army and pushed the Pakistanis back to what is roughly the present line-of-control. India and Pakistan have been to war twice more; in 1965 over Kashmir and 1971 over the newly independent Bangladesh.

The beginning of 1948 had been marked by another shocking event. On 30 January, Mahatma Gandhi was assassinated by a Hindu nationalist in the grounds of the Birla House on what is now Tees January Marg (literally, 30 January Road) in New Delhi. His assassin, Vinayak Nathuram Godse, had been incensed by his tolerance towards people of all religions, expecially India's Muslims, throughout the communal riots that had followed Partition. Ghodse's links with the RSS (a Hindu nationalist organisation), who had bitterly opposed Gandhi's insistence that the money owed to Pakistan under the terms of Partition be paid, discredited the Hindu right-wing for many years.

Gandhi's death not only shocked many people, but united the nation in grief. His cremation procession attracted crowds of millions as the flower-covered hearse drove to Raj Ghat on the banks of the Jamuna where there are memorials to Gandhi and all of India's former Prime Ministers.

On Nehru's death in 1964 rule passed, briefly, to Lal Bahadur Shastri, before Nehru's daughter, Indira Gandhi, took the reigns of power in 1966. Her rise to the top of the Congress Party had been rapid and she was, initially, highly popular, particularly after the 1971

Prime Minister Indira Gandhi.

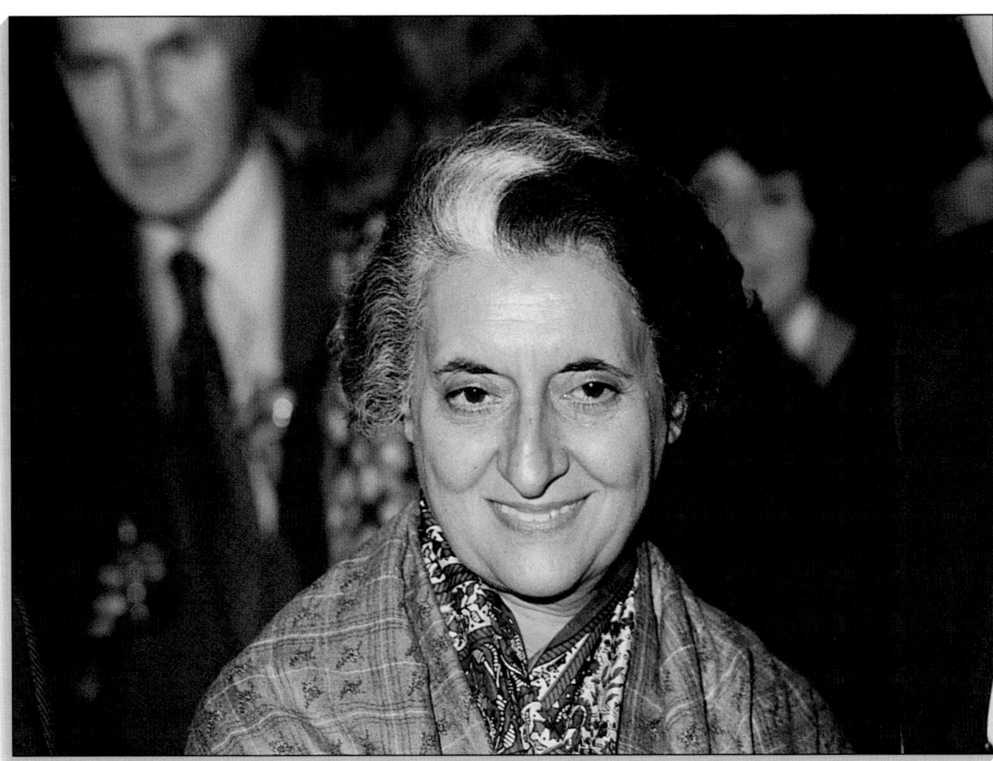

Bangladesh war. However, by 1974 corruption scandals within Congress and the poor state of the Indian economy had severely reduced her support. The calls for her resignation grew stronger, until on 26 June 1975 she declared a State of Emergency, suspending all elections and civil liberties, and imposing strict censorship.

During the Emergency, she imposed stringent economic measures – which did have the effect of cutting inflation – but she also imprisoned her political opponents and handed over considerable power to her greatly disliked son, Sanjay. He was responsible for the infamous compulsory sterilisation campaign, in which men, officially with more than two children, were picked up from the streets and operated on in mobile clinics. This was disproportionately directed at the poor, especially Muslims, as was his widespread demolition of housing in Old Delhi, which was often acompanied by violence against the inhabitants.

Indira called elections in March 1977 in which she was comprehensively beaten by the coalition Janta Party under Moraji Desai. This government was riven by ideological faultlines and, when elections were held again in January 1980, Indira Gandhi and the Congress Party were returned to power.

However, Indira's jubilation was cut short. Her son Sanjay was killed in a flying accident over Delhi's Safdarjang Aerodrome on 23 June. Though very few tears were shed by those who remembered Sanjay's activities during the Emergency, Indira was distraught.

With Sanjay – whom she had been grooming as her successor – gone, she turned her attention to her younger son, Rajiv. He had been happily working as an airline pilot, and had shown no inclination to enter politics. Initially, he resisted the calls for him to stand for parliament, but by June 1981 he had been elected to Sanjay's old seat. By 1984 he found himself leading the country after his mother's death.

Crowds at a political rally in New Delhi.

There had been calls by militant Sikhs for an independent Punjab, Khalistan, since 1947. By the early 1980s, these had coalesced around a charismatic leader, Sant Jaranil Singh Bhindranwale. He had been used by Indira to split the power of the Sikh party, the Akali Dal, who had opposed Indira throughout the Emergency. When she was re-elected in 1980, it had been assumed that support for the Sant (Sikh religious leader) would decline.

This was a severe miscalculation. Increasing violence against Hindus – and non-Khalistani Sikhs – led to severe communal rioting in early 1982, and in June, Bhindranwale and his supporters occupied the holiest Sikh shrine, the Golden Temple in Amritsar. The situation in the Punjab deteriorated rapidly, and the unrest spread to the large Punjabi population of Delhi. By May 1984, Indira determined to act. She sent in the army, and between 30 May and 6 June around 1,000 of Bhindranwale's supporters and 300 Indian soldiers were killed, and the shrine heavily damaged.

This desecration of their holiest shrine deeply shocked the Sikhs. On the 31 October, Indira Gandhi was assassinated by her two Sikh bodyguards as she was walking in the grounds of her bungalow at 1 Safdarjang Road in Delhi. The brutal anti-Sikh riots that subsequently swept the capital killed over 2,000 people. The Delhi police stood by and watched as the killing continued and the new Prime Minister, Rajiv Gandhi, ordered in the army. It was later discovered that much of the violence in Delhi had been orchestrated by Congress-led gangs.

Rajiv Gandhi's fate was to be the same as his mother's. In 1991 he was blown up by a Tamil suicide bomber opposed to India's intervention in the civil war in Sri Lanka.

With the death of Rajiv, the rule of the Nehru dynasty appeared to be over. The next Prime Minister was Narasimha Rao, a veteran Congressman from Andhra Pradesh. It was during the

Atal Behari Vajpayee being congratulated by L.K. Advani on becoming Prime Minister.

period of Rao's rule that the economic liberalisation policies that had been started by Indira and Sanjay really took hold. Rao's government was marked by a series of corruption scandals (he has recently been sentenced to three years in prison on corruption charges) and an already disillusioned Indian public began to look for alternatives to Congress.

The main beneficiary was the BJP (Bharatiya Janata Party), a right-wing Hindu nationalist party with links to other Hindu organisations, including the RSS. The BJP had grown out of the Janata Party that had won the 1977 elections. Its next taste of power came in 1989 as part of the minority government of V.P. Singh. This goverment fell when the leader of the BJP, L.K. Advani, embarked on a countrywide *yatra* (pilgimage) to raise support for the destruction of the Babri Masjid (mosque) in Ayodhya, said to have been built on the site of the birthplace of Rama.

Advani was arrested before he could approach the shrine, but in 1992 hundreds of members of militant Hindu organisations descended on Ayodhya and tore down the mosque. This led to some of the worst communal rioting (this time largely targeted at Muslims) the country has known. These shocking scenes dented the electorate's enthusiasm for the BJP, and it was only in Delhi that they held on to power – although Delhi's current Chief Minister, Sheila Dikshit, is from the Congress Party.

However, they soon regained ground, and when a general election was held in May 1996, the BJP emerged as the largest party. They were kept out of government by a coalition of regional parties known as the United Front. The tables were turned at the next election in March 1998 when, under Atal Behari Vajpayee, the BJP again received the most seats and formed its own coalition government – which included some parties who hd previously supported the United Front, notably the TDP (Telugu Desam Party) from Andhra Pradesh.

Vajpayee soon courted controversy by conducting nuclear tests at Pokhran in the Thar desert, bringing worldwide condemnation, retaliatory tests from Pakistan and sanctions from the United States. There has also been a worrying rise in attacks on minority religious communities, especially Christians. This first BJP-led government was brought down in 1999 when Jayalitha Jayaram – the ex-Chief Minister of Tamil Nadu and another politician sentenced to 3 years in prison for corruption – walked out of the coalition.

The BJP strengthened its position at the 1999 polls and forged a new coalition, the National Democratic Alliance (NDA). Continuing economic liberalisation, they have discarded their support for *svadeshi* (Indian-made goods), and face escalating unrest in the troubled state of Kashmir.

The recent reappearance of the Nehru dynasty in the form of Sonia Gandhi, Rajiv's widow, as the leader of the Congress Party has attracted some support, and, at present, Congress appear to be the most credible challenger to the BJP.

Sonia Gandhi waving the flag at a Congress rally.

As the seat of power of successive dynasties that ruled India, Delhi has always attracted great painters, musicians, dancers and craftsmen from all over the country, but perhaps never more so than today. When the princely states and great landed estates were abolished after Independence, Indian artists lost their traditional patrons, and ever since then have found their new patrons – politicians, government cultural institutes, broadcast media, industrialists and diplomats – concentrated in Delhi. As a result Delhi offers the most varied cultural life of all Indian cities, with the best of court and local traditional styles in dance, music and theatre.

The best way to find out what's on in a particular week is to look at the cultural pages of the newspapers – the *Indian Express* on Saturday and the *Times of India* on Friday carry comprehensive listings, as do the listings magazines the *Delhi Diary* and *The Delhi City*.

Delhi's cultural hub is in the centre of town, between Barakhamba Road and Ferozeshah Road, concentrated around Mandi House Chowk. Here are located the **Kamani** and **FICCI auditoriums** and the **Shriram Kendra**, venues of major cultural performances. Nearby is the **Triveni Kala Sangam** with its art galleries and theatre; and **Rabindra Bhavan**, the government-funded cultural academy, which holds art exhibitions and festivals of dance, theatre and music.

Among the big annual events that Delhi stages are four "classical" music and dance festivals – the Shankarlal and Dhrupad festivals in February and March, the Vishnu Digamber festival in August, and the SPIC-MACAY festival in September. The greatest musicians in India, representing the different *gharanas* (schools) of Hindustani (North Indian) music, participate. The concerts often beginning late and continue into the night, way beyond the schedule, as the musician warms up and the audience responds. The music most often heard is that derived from the music performed at the North Indian courts.

The *gharana* (male lineages of musical instruction, usually hereditary) of the court musicians generally traced their ancestry back to Tansen, a musician at the court of Akbar (1556–1605). He is said to have been one of the greatest performers of *dhrupad*, a vocal genre held by many musicians to be the "purest" form of *raga* music. Although initially very popular at the courts, during the time of Muhammad Shah (1719–48) *dhrupad* was supplanted by *khayal*. Muhammad Shah's court musician, Niyamat Khan, is usually credited with popularising the form (which legend says was invented by Sultan Husain Sharqi in the 15th century).

Khayal is now the vocal genre most commonly heard in the concert hall. A *khayal* composition (*bandis* or *ciz*) comprises two short sections, known as *sthayi* and *antara*, which are in contrasting registers. Usually two compositions are presented, the first in a slow tempo, known as a "big" (*bara*) *khayal*, the second, a "small" (*chota*) *khayal* in a faster tempo, which speeds up towards the end of the performance. A *khayal* concert starts with a short unmetred section introducing the *raga* (mode or pitch collection), followed by the *ciz*, which is in *tala* (rhythmic cycle), the most common of which is the 16-beat *tintal.* It is accompanied by the *tabla* (paired kettledrums) and, traditionally, the bowed lute, *sarangi* (this is now usually replaced by the harmonium, a small hand-pumped organ introduced to South Asia by French missionaries). The drone-lute *tambura* provides a constant background, sometimes played by a supporting singer and usually tuned to *sa* and *pa* (roughly corresponding to the Western doh and soh). The compositions are explored in a series of elaborations and improvisations.

Another popular genre often performed on the concert stage, particularly by female vocalists – is *thumri*. This is a "light-classical" form which

Floor seating at an evening recital in New Delhi.

developed at the courts of Avadh (present-day Lucknow), consisting of a sung poem performed in a slow tempo with a highly melismatic melodic line. The Hindu texts are highly charged and devotional – even though the singers were usually Muslim – and often mildly erotic and written in a dialect of Hindi called Braj Bhasa. The accompaniment is the same as for a *khayal* performance.

Instrumental music, particularly of the *sitar* and *sarod* (both plucked lutes), follows a slightly different pattern, and draws on both *khayal* and *dhrupad* traditions. Compositions are known as *gat* (analogous to those of *khayal*); they are preceded by a long *alap* section, an unmetred presentation of the *raga* introducing each note in turn, in a similar fashion to that of *dhrupad* singers. The soloist then uses a variety of improvisational techniques to explore the material presented in the *gat*, and will usually present two different compositions, the second of which is faster. Instrumentalists usually consider themselves part of the Seniya *gharana*, which is traced back to Tansen.

Diligent student at the National School of Drama.

Leading dancers of all the main "classical" styles – *bharata-natyam*, *kathak*, *kathakali*, *kuchipudi*, *manipuri*, *mohiniattam* and *odissi* – give regular concerts in Delhi. Delhi society turns out in force at these events, to see and be seen, and afterwards to catch up on all the gossip and intrigue of the cultural world.

The dance-style you are most likely to see advertised is *bharata-natyam*. Although it originated in Tamil Nadu, it is now taught and performed across India as well as overseas. It is derived from Tamil temple dance and has been a concert form since the early 20th century.

The female hereditary temple dancers *(devadasis)* took part in rituals in praise of the temple deity and were considered "married" to the god. This made them auspicious women as they could never become widowed. They would also be the sexual partners of the temple priests and local king (sponsor of the temple). It was this aspect of their duties that outraged Victorian sensibilities and an "anti-nautch" (from the Sanskrit naca, "dance") was started, culminating in the banning of temple dancing. At the same time, growing Indian nationalism was seeking to legitimise claims for independence by presenting elements of South Asian culture as evidence of a strong national identity. Led by the Brahman dancer and teacher Rukmini Devi, moves were made to establish a "pure" form of the dance on the stage, the result was present-day *bharata-natyam*.

It is a solo dance, still performed largely by women, with an accompaniment of Karnatak (South Indian) music played by an ensemble known as the *cinna melam* and led by the *nattuvanar*, who keeps time with a pair of cymbals and calls out the dance patterns, or *jati*. The dancers wear pellet bells *(ghungru)* around their ankles which add to rhythmic texture of the music. A *bharata-natyam* performance ideally consists of seven pieces: the introductory *alarippu* which is a prayer to the presiding deity; a *jatisvaram*, a technical piece using *nrtta* (abstract movement); the *sabda*, which introduces *nrtya* (movement expressing emotion); a complex dance known as *varnam*, that uses both *nrtya* and *nrtta*; a *padam*, a piece expressing love through *nrtya*; a technical and fast *tillana*; and a concluding *sloka* (rhythmic recitation of a religious verse).

The other "classical" dance-style widely performed in Delhi is *kathak*. The origins of *kathak* are closely linked to the rise of Hindustani music at the North Indian courts, particularly *khayal*, *thumri* and *dadra*. Traditionally danced by courtesans, it is characterised by its fast pirouettes and rhythmic patterns created by pellet bells *(ghungru)* worn on the ankles. Regular concerts are held by the Kathak Kendra in Bahawalpur House on Bhagwan Das Road.

Theatre in Delhi offers a variety that ranges from Molière and Brecht translated into Hindi, to the best of contemporary regional theatre selected and brought to the capital – experimental plays as well as traditional forms, like puppet theatre from Karnataka and Rajasthan.

The **Pragati Maidan** exhibition ground is another hub of cultural activity, from art cinema to regional plays and performance by the most promising young dancers.

MCMI XIV
INDIA
MCMI XIX
TO THE DEAD OF THE INDIAN ARMIES WHO FELL AND ARE HONOURED
IN FRANCE AND FLANDERS MESOPOTAMIA AND PERSIA EAST AFRICA GALLIPOLI AND ELSEWHERE
IN THE NEAR AND THE FAR EAST AND IN SACRED MEMORY ALSO OF THOSE WHOSE NAMES ARE HERE
RECORDED AND WHO FELL IN INDIA ON THE NORTH WEST FRONTIER AND DURING THE THIRD AFGHAN WAR

SUNSET SPLENDOUR – IMPERIAL CITY

When the British decided in 1911 to move the capital of India from Kolkata (Calcutta) to Delhi, they were following in the footsteps of other conquerors of India before them. The ruins of at least seven (some say fifteen) other capital cities already dotted Delhi, from ancient Indraprastha to Mughal Shahjahanabad. Now, at the beginning of the 20th century, it was the turn of the British. Their hold over the country had never seemed more secure; and what better way to proclaim the power and permanence of the British Raj than to build a new capital, in a city with such historic imperial associations?

The decision was announced on 12 December 1911 with suitable fanfare, at a Royal Durbar held by King George V and Queen Mary at a vast arena in the north of Delhi. The Durbar was perhaps the most glittering display of imperial pomp and splendour Delhi had ever seen, attended by 300,000 people, among them 562 bejewelled and turbanned Maharajas, accompanied by their retinue of wives (average of 5.8 per prince), children, courtiers, elephants, Rolls-Royces and personal railway carriages. With great solemnity, the king and queen laid the foundation stones of the eighth city of Delhi, wielding a pair of ivory mallets and silver trowels set with amethysts. The new capital of British India, King George declared, was to be built "with the greatest care and deliberation, so that the new creation may be in every way worthy of this ancient and beautiful city".

Two decades were to pass before the new capital was complete – the last and largest imperial city to be built in the 20th century. Unmatched in its monumental scale and extravagance, it included a palace larger than Versailles, the most visible symbol of the might and majesty of the British Empire. But the progress of this grand imperial project was by no means smooth. From the very beginning it was dogged by controversies, quarrels between the two main architects, delays, shortage of funds and, indeed, by an extraordinary number of ill omens.

The first controversy arose soon after the departure of King George and Queen Mary when a commission of planners arrived and, after much debate, deemed the site for the new city unsuitable: it was damp, malarial and simply not big enough. Travelling around on elephant back, they began looking for another site – about 64 sq km (25 sq miles) in area, close to the existing city of Shahjahanabad, and with scope for expansion without disturbing any of the existing shrines, tombs and ruins in which Delhi abounded.

Eventually they settled on a desolate plain called Raisina, dotted with a few small villages and camel thorn shrubs, the haunt of jackals and black buck. One day the Viceroy, Lord Hardinge, out

Preceding pages, Lutyens' Central Vista, Rajpath, illuminated for Republic Day's festivities. **Left**, India Gate at the eastern end of Rajpath, with the King George V canopy beyond. **Right**, bust of the architect of New Delhi, from Rashtrapati Bhavan.

riding on the site, galloped up a small hill and came upon a magnificent view – on one side the dark, imposing silhouette of the Old Fort, on the other side the domes and minarets of Shahjahanabad's Jama Masjid, and in the distance the winding silver streak of the river Yamuna. Here on the hill was where the Viceroy's House must be, he declared. So the foundation stones laid by the King and Queen were stealthily dug up in the dead of night, wrapped in gunny sacks and taken in a bullock cart to be reinterred at the new site.

Now the planning of the new city could begin in earnest – and begin it did, with a great big bang. For when Lord Hardinge arrived in Delhi from Kolkata, formally to inaugurate the start of the grand project, a bomb was thrown at him as he rode in ceremonial procession through Chandni Chowk, gravely injuring him and killing his umbrella bearer. This was not the only ill omen. At the Royal Durbar the previous year, the splendid silver-poled marquee in which the Indian Princes were to receive the King Emperor had mysteriously burnt to the ground. And bazaar gossip in Delhi had it that the foundation stones were actually tombstones, procured in a hurry from a local stone merchant. Wasn't Delhi also known as "the graveyard of dynasties", said the prophets of doom, with every new city built there presaging the end of the dynasty that built it?

Such dark auguries, however, were firmly pushed aside as the gigantic task began of levelling the land and laying out water and sewage pipes and electricity lines. In 1913, Edwin Lutyens, the most original and creative English architect of the day, was chosen to design New Delhi. A builder on a grand scale, especially renowned for his beautiful country houses, Lutyens also had a reputation for extravagance.

New Delhi, Lutyens decided, would be a garden city, with wide, straight vistas – so essential for the ceremonial parades and processions that an

Waiting at New Delhi Station.

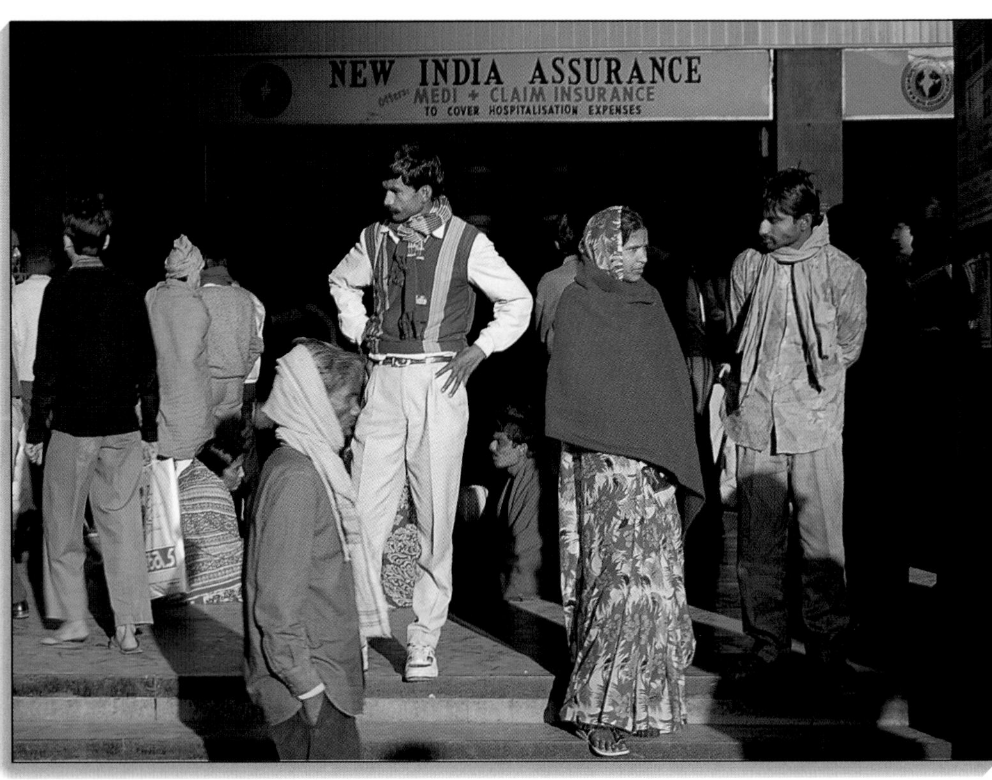

imperial capital must stage from time to time – low buildings, spacious avenues, and plenty of trees and parks to combat the harsh climate. His master plan was a vast hexagonal grid encompassing the Viceroy's House, the Old Fort and a commercial area. Dominating the hexagon was the Viceroy's House on Raisina Hill, from where a straight processional route, Kingsway (now Rajpath) led to a great plaza (now Vijay Chowk) and continued down all the way to the Old Fort. On either side of Rajpath would be the residential area, divided into triangles by avenues and roundabouts. Here would be the bungalows of senior Raj officials: the closer they were to the Viceroy's House, the bigger the bungalows. At the very edges of the hexagon, and spilling out of it, were smaller houses for legislators, junior officials and clerks. Midway down, the processional route would be cut across at right angles by another straight road, Queensway (now Janpath), leading to the commercial area of the city. The plan thus reflected not only Lutyens' aesthetic vision, but also the hierarchy and social structure of the Raj. If you stand on Raisina Hill just outside the iron grille of Rashtrapati Bhavan and look down, the perfect symmetry of Lutyens' plan is immediately evident.

Lutyens chose as his associate Herbert Baker, whose credentials for the job were impeccable: he had built the new administrative capital at Pretoria in South Africa, displaying his skilful use of architecture as a tool for expressing the imperial ideal. The two had worked together earlier when Baker had invited Lutyens to collaborate with him briefly in South Africa. They decided that while Lutyens would be responsible for the overall concept of the new city, the Viceroy's House and the War Memorial, Baker would design the administrative buildings and the legislative assembly.

Now began the great debate on the architectural style of the new capital. Both King George and Lord Hardinge were insistent that it should be chiefly inspired by Indian architecture. Lutyens, however, was adamantly against this: "Fancy Shakespeare being asked by Queen Elizabeth to write an ode in Chaucerian metre", he wrote indignantly to his wife. Lutyens made clear, too, his disdain for the kind of Raj architecture he had seen in Kolkata and Mumbai (Bombay), which grafted Mughal domes and arches and canopied balconies onto pseudo-Baroque and Victorian-Gothic structures. Nevertheless, at the Viceroy's urging, Lutyens and Baker set off on a tour of the monuments of India, visiting Agra, Jaipur, Bikaner, Mandu, the great Buddhist stupa at Sanchi and the palace forts of Datia and Dhar. Both came back more determined than ever that they were not going to build in an Indian style. In his characteristically arrogant fashion Lutyens wrote: "Personally, I do not believe there is any real Indian architecture or any great tradition". He sent Baker two "recipes" for Indian architecture:

"Hindu: Set square stones and build child-wise, but before you erect, carve every stone with lace patterns and horrifying shapes. On top – set an onion.

Mughal: Build a vast mass of rough concrete, elephant-wise, on a very simple rectangular cum octagonal plan, dome in anyhow. Overlay with a veneer of stone patterns. Inlay jewels and cornelians if you can afford it...Then on top of the mass, put three turnips..."

Baker, too, dismissed Hindu architecture as largely "grotesque meaningless carving" and Mughal as "masses of brick covered with decoration".

Both agreed that the new city must be "neither Indian nor English nor Roman, but Imperial"; that it must be spacious and symmetrical, in sharp contrast to the crowded and organic feel of Old Delhi, and must, above all, symbolise the system and order that the British administration felt it had imposed on this sprawling, crowded, disorderly country.

But the grand tour of Indian monuments had had more of an impact on Lutyens and Baker than they perhaps realised or cared to admit. In their final drawings, both architects incorporated several elements of Indian architecture that were both decorative and practical – such as *chajjas* (stone cornices), *jalis* (carved stone screens), *chatris* (canopies), and Indian decorative symbols like lotuses and bells. Lutyens justified this synthesis succinctly: he was "not building in fancy dress", but "as an Englishman dressed for the climate".

It was with supreme confidence in the permanence of British rule in India that the building of Imperial Delhi began. The new city was being built to last a thousand years and, after that, to make the most splendid ruins of all those that littered the landscape of Delhi. As the new city rose, some 29,000 labourers and 3,500 stone cutters worked round the clock. Cream and red sandstone was brought in from quarries in Dholpur and Bharatpur; green, yellow, pink and white marble from Makrana, Vadodara (Baroda) and other places in central India and Rajasthan; and no less than 700 million bricks were baked. To bring all this material to the construction sites, as well as tons of sand and rubble, earth and manure (for the parks and lawns), a 24-km (15-mile) railway track was laid, with 8 km (5 miles) of siding. Day and night the little train chugged along, and by the time the city was built it had carried 500 million tons of material.

The pace of work slowed down suddenly in 1914 when World War I began, and to pare expenses down during the war years a number of Lutyens' grandiose schemes were abandoned. These included an amphitheatre on the Ridge, a cultural complex along Queensway and an ornamental lake at the end of Rajpath in whose waters would be reflected the ramparts of the Old Fort.

To add to Lutyens' chagrin, Baker now wanted his Secretariat buildings to share the elevation on top of Raisina Hill with the Viceroy's House.

Below left, melange of motifs on Rashtrapati Bhavan gates. Below right, graceful colonnades of Connaught Circus.

Viceroys came and went, he reasoned, but it was from these buildings that the real power and authority of the British Raj would be exercised. This meant pushing the site for the Viceroy's House 1,200 m (400 ft) back from the brow of the hill. Lutyens gave in, without realising how this would affect the view of the house. In fact, it turned out to be, literally, a monumental blunder. As one approaches the Viceroy's House along the ceremonial route up Raisina Hill, the dome begins to disappear from view, and then reappears again as one comes closer. By the time this architectural gaffe became evident, it was too late and too expensive to set things right. Lutyens never forgave Baker – he had finally met his "Bakerloo", he said bitterly – and the two barely spoke to each other again. Today, however, few visitors notice the mistake, and among those who do, many find a charming mystery in the way the dome recedes and then reappears in its full splendour.

The Viceroy's House, now known as Rashtrapati Bhavan, the residence of the President of India, is Lutyens' magnum opus, with its subtle and graceful fusion of Western classicism with Indian architectural features – an example of Lutyens' remarkable gift for combining grandeur of scale with the small, perfect, often whimsical detail. It was a typical touch of Lutyensesque genius, for example, to use red and cream sandstone here as well as in the other major buildings of the new capital – colours which so imaginatively echo the hues of the grand Mughal capital, Shahjahanabad.

Rashtrapati Bhavan, as architectural historian Robert Irving describes it, is "at once a giant Indian bungalow, embattled Rajput fortress and Mughal tomb" – with English country house comforts. Over 180 m (600 ft) from end to end, with its 340 rooms and its vast internal courtyards covering 18,580 sq m (200,000 sq ft), it is indeed larger than Versailles. Unlike the tall Raj buildings of Kolkata and Mumbai (previously

Lutyens' city centre is now dwarfed by new high-rise construction.

Bombay), this one is emphatically horizontal, its austerity enlivened by touches of Lutyens' wit and originality. Sculpted stone Indian elephants and bulls coexist happily with British lions; juxtaposed against the austere facade of the South Court is a marvellously sinuous cobra fountain; the severely classical columns of the palace's porticos and corridors are hung unexpectedly with bells typical of traditional Indian architecture; and the floor of an upstairs family room is a giant red and white chessboard, with charming screens in the shape of a parrot cage.

Girdling the building at two different levels is a wide *chajja*, which not only creates dramatic shadows, but effectively keeps out the heat, drains water clear of the building during the monsoon, and protects the rooms from what Lutyens called "the tremendous violence of Indian light".

The vast copper-clad dome is circled by a stone railing, clearly inspired by the Buddhist stupa at Sanchi, and surrounding it are four saucer-shaped rooftop fountains, meant not only to keep the building cool but to provide a shimmering reflection against the metallic surface of the dome. Some years ago, alas, the rooftop fountains were turned off – they seemed too conspicuous an extravagance in water-starved Delhi.

At the centre of the great court in front of Rashtrapati Bhavan, Lutyens designed another imperial symbol, the Jaipur Column (from money donated by the Maharaja of Jaipur). Commemorative pillars had long been a tradition in India, from those built by emperor Asoka in the 3rd century BC to the 11th century Qatb Minar in Delhi. Lutyens also envisaged the 43.5-metre (145-ft) tall Jaipur column as a symbol of victory, like a giant stake or flag driven into conquered ground. Carved with very English oak leaves, it culminates brilliantly in a bronze Indian lotus from which bursts forth a crystal star. At its base is a rather pompous inscription that

Sansad Bhavan.

was composed by Lutyens himself:

In thought, faith
In word, wisdom
In deed, courage
In life, service
So may India be great.

The 4.3-metre (14-ft) high iron grille at the entrance to Rashtrapati Bhavan is another manifestation of Lutyens' exuberant creativity. As decorative and airy as antique lace, it conveys at the same time an impression of solidity with its red stone piers and sentry posts, and elephants carrying lamps and urns.

It may be possible to visit the interior of Rashtrapati Bhavan by writing to the President's Deputy Military Secretary. The rooms the public are allowed to see are: the Durbar Hall, Ashok Hall and the dining room.

Mughal Gardens: In the 100-hectare (250-acre) grounds of Rashtrapati Bhavan, Lutyens created another masterpiece – a terraced Mughal water garden, cascading over three levels, intersected by channels of water that reflect the colours of the flowers and the sky. Ornamental fountains in the shape of 16-tier lotus leaves throw jets of water in the air, and in the centre is a 18-sq. metre (200-sq. ft) island of green.

At the end of the garden is a round pool around which Lutyens created his famous "butterfly garden" – planted with flowers specially chosen because they attract butterflies. In Lutyens' days, 418 men were employed to look after the Mughal gardens, of whom 50 spent their entire day scaring off birds. The great viceregal palace required a staff of 2,000. The gardens are open to the public during February.

Lutyens also built the palaces in New Delhi of two of the most powerful Indian princes – the Nizam of Hyderabad and the Gaekwar of Baroda. Both houses have a butterfly-shaped plan, with a central dome and two symmetrical wings. Like Rashtrapati Bhavan, they are an elegant synthesis of styles – classical columns and round Roman arches with *jalis*, *chatris* and

Present-day Connaught Place.

chajjas. Hyderabad House, which also has a Mughal garden, is now the venue for official banquets and receptions and has been restored to its former elegance, Baroda House is today the Railway Booking Office. The domes in these two palaces as well as at Rashtrapati Bhavan were built according to an ancient Indian method, without the use of any temporary support – one of the many skills of Indian craftsmen and masons that Lutyens learnt to admire. As Irving describes it, a ring of labourers, brick in hand stood around the void which had fresh mortar laid on its rim. Music played in the background, and then, at a pre-arranged signal, usually a drum beat, each labourer simultaneously laid a brick, creating an instant circle.

Vijay Chowk and India Gate: At the foot of Raisina Hill is Lutyens' great plaza, bare of any ornamentation except six red sandstone obelisk fountains, to serve as a stage for the elaborate ceremonies that the Raj revelled in. From Vijay Chowk, Rajpath continues for over 2 km (1.2 miles), with waterways, green lawns and trees on either side, intersected by Janpath. Here Lutyens had planned a National Library, an Ethnological Museum, an Oriental Institute and Archives Office, but in the end only the latter was built, a dignified, colonnaded structure.

Further down the central vista is India Gate, the War Memorial Arch which Lutyens built in honour of 60,000 soldiers who died overseas in World War I. In cream sandstone, 42 metres (139 ft) high, it is inscribed with the names of over 13,000 Indian and British soldiers, missing presumed dead. Now an eternal flame burns beneath the arch in memory of those who died in the 1971 war with Pakistan.

The Canopy: In 1936, after New Delhi had been inaugurated, King George V died, and just beyond India Gate, at the terminus where all the vistas meet, Lutyens built his last imperial monument – a stone canopy, framed

Peanut seller on Janpath.

within the 9.2 metre (30 ft) arch of India Gate. Here he placed a marble statue of King George in imperial robes, crown and orb. The canopy is empty now – it would be inappropriate, it was felt, to have any Indian leader's statue in so imperial a setting.

Beyond the canopy is the National Stadium, built in 1931 despite Lutyens' angry protests that it ruined the view of the Old Fort he had planned at this end of the vista. The stadium was the idea of the then Vicereine, Lady Willingdon, who with her execrable taste had also wrought havoc in the Viceroy's House, changing the colour schemes to her favourite colour mauve (Lutyens called her a *mauvais sujet*) and ruining his landscaping by planting sad cypresses in the garden.

The Secretariat Buildings: Lutyens and Baker, though they barely spoke to each other, continued to work side by side, and by 1930 Baker's massive Secretariat blocks had risen on either side of Raisina Hill, flanking the Viceroy's House. Three stories high and nearly a half a kilometre long, each block contained a warren of high-ceilinged rooms built around open, arcaded courtyards, grand staircases and halls connected by over 9 km (6 miles) of corridors. Like Lutyens, Baker too had borrowed ideas from traditional Indian architecture – decorative canopied *chatris* (an ancient royal symbol in India), Mughal recessed porches (known as *nashimans*) and jutting stone *chajjas*. The domes of the Secretariats made lavish use of Indian ornamentation – carved *jalis*, sculpted elephants and lotuses. For seven of the Secretariat rooms Baker commissioned Indian artists to paint murals, and rather to his dismay they chose traditional allegorical and mythological Hindu and Islamic themes. For the entrance to the buildings, Baker chose what he thought was a properly inspiring inscription: "Liberty will not descend to a people; a people must raise themselves to liberty; it is a blessing which must be earned

Sari shop in Connaught Place.

before it can be enjoyed". At a time when the jails of British India were bursting with freedom fighters, even the Viceroy found Baker's little homily provocative.

In the courtyards in front of the buildings Baker placed the Dominion Columns representing Australia, Canada, South Africa and New Zealand, each surmounted by a globe and a ship, symbolising the oceans that linked this vast empire on which the sun never set.

The two wings of the secretariat are known as North Block and South Block; North Block houses the finance and home ministries, South Block the foreign ministry.

Parliament House: Baker's other major project was the Legislative Assembly building. Lutyens had decreed that it should be in a circular colosseum design and then left Baker to get on with it. Sited north of the Secretariat buildings, the Parliament has a red stone foundation, a cream stone middle storey with 144 pillars, and a top storey in plaster (money had begun to run out). It had a diameter of 174 metres (570 ft) and a low central dome which is not visible from ground level.

Inside are three semicircular halls – two richly wood-panelled legislative chambers, now the Lok Sabha (Lower House) and Rajya Sabha (Upper House), and an opulent Chamber of Princes, now the library and reading room – with carved benches, coloured marble pillars and *jalis*, and the gilded enamel shields of the princely states set into the wall.

The large circular central hall with its 28-metre (90-ft) dome was designed for special occasions, as when the Viceroy addressed the Assembly. It was in this hall, in 1947, that a bugler dressed in white *khadi* (hand-spun cotton) blew on a conch shell to herald the birth of a new nation, and here, too, that the Constitution of independent India was drafted.

Connaught Place: The plan for New Delhi included another giant circle – Connaught Place, named after the King

Peak hour traffic in busy "CP".

Emperor's uncle, the Duke of Connaught. This was the imperial capital's commercial hub, and with its three concentric circles of shops opening onto wide colonnaded arcades, a sharp (and deliberate) contrast to the crowded bazaars of Chandni Chowk in the Old City. No longer would the Memsahibs need to pick their way through its narrow alleys, jostled by hawkers and assailed by pungent smells. The shops in Connaught Place would be airy and spacious, with polished wooden counters and comfortable chairs, the most elegant of them displaying the sign "By Appointment to His Excellency the Viceroy". Here they could buy fashionable chintzes and Scottish marmalade, promenade along the arcades with friends and stop for tea and cakes at Wengers or Standard, where a live band played dance music in the afternoons.

Connaught Place was the work of another architect, Robert Tor Russell who, though now forgotten, was in fact responsible for the largest number of buildings in Delhi, among them Eastern Court, now the Central Post Office, and Western Court on Janpath, which were designed as hostels for legislators. Russell also built the Commander-in-Chief's house (now called Teen Murti Bhavan), later the residence of India's first Prime Minister Jawaharlal Nehru and which houses the Nehru Memorial Library and Museum, and the National Stadium. As chief architect to the Government of India, Russell and his team were responsible for most of the bungalows, post offices, hospitals and police stations in the new city.

Baker, however, built the bungalows on King George's Avenue, now Rajaji Marg. (Lutyens dubbed them *bungle-ohs* and a rather warm house on Akbar Road "Baker's oven".)

The bungalow at 1 Safdarjang Road was the residence of Prime Minister Indira Gandhi, Nehru's daughter. This has also been opened as a memorial museum. In the grounds, the place

Sikh women at Bangla Sahib Gurudwara.

where she was assassinated has been marked by a glass walkway.

Lutyens' own characteristically extravagant plans for an Anglican cathedral were turned down and, instead, he was asked to judge a competition for the cathedral building which was won by one of his disciples, Henry Medd. Medd eventually designed both the rather Italianate Roman Catholic Church on Alexandra Palace (near Gole Post Office) and the sober brick and stone Anglican Church, the Cathedral Church of the Redemption, near Rashtrapati Bhavan.

With great foresight, even before the building of New Delhi began, the main avenues were marked out and tree planting began. The man responsible for the greening of New Delhi was a former Kew Gardens expert, W.R. Mustoe, who together with Walter Sykes George landscaped the city. Mustoe chose the trees with great care and imagination – mostly indigenous species that were sturdy, shade-giving and long-living, with a variety of flowers and foliage. He gave each of the major avenues a separate botanical identity by planting each with a different species. Akbar Road has the feathery-leaved tamarinds, for example, whose sour pods are much used in Indian cooking; Aurangzeb Road has neems whose twigs are used as toothbrushes, and whose leaves make an excellent insecticide. The Central Vista lawns have the jamun, which has delicious purple berries. And the junction of Janpath and Aurangzeb Road is lined with majestic arjun trees. In all, some 10,000 trees and 112 km (70 miles) of hedges were planted.

In February 1931, New Delhi was officially inaugurated, setting off a round of festivities – banquets and garden parties at the Viceroy's House, and balls at the favourite watering hole of the sahibs and memsahibs, the Gymkhana Club (described by one French visitor as "a cross between St Pancras Station and a Turkish *hamam*").

Oddments along Janpath.

The most spectacular celebration was the People's Fête at the Red Fort, organised by the contractors who had built the city. There were fireworks and tent-pegging displays, bagpipers, jugglers, acrobats and dancing bears, and a splendid pageant depicting life on the historic Grand Trunk Road, with processions of camels, elephants, palanquins, horse-drawn tongas, rickshaws and bullock carts. Among the crowd of 50,000 who watched were the labourers who had toiled for nearly two decades to built New Delhi. Many of them were born on the site and had grown up there, joining the work force as soon as they were big enough to carry a headload of bricks.

But casting a shadow over the festivities was an ominous portent: the previous year, when the Viceroy Lord Irwin had arrived in Delhi to take up residence in his newly-completed palace, a bomb was thrown at his train, evoking memories of the attack on Lord Hardinge at the start of the imperial project.

The new city had cost nearly £15 million to build – a staggering figure in those days – provoking Indian leaders like Gandhi and Nehru to deplore such "wasteful extravagance" and "vulgar ostentation". Against this barrage of criticism from Indians, Lutyens countered plaintively that the entire city had cost "no more than two battleships", and anyway, "it was all Indian work and much better to do than spin *khaddar*".

Amidst all the euphoria of the inaugural celebrations the British Raj may have seemed, as the Prince of Wales said, "solid, secure and timeless", but the more perceptive among the revellers knew better. Only 16 years later, the Union Jack would be lowered for the last time from the bastions of the Raj, bringing the imperial adventure to an end.

The line between Old and New Delhi has begun to blur. The city that Lutyens built for 70,000 people now has a population of 7 million. Connaught Place has acquired some of the colour and bustle of a bazaar, its arcades spilling over with pavement vendors. When Parliament is in session, Lutyens' grand processional route is often thronged with banner-waving, slogan-shouting protest marchers and demonstrators, while on balmy evenings and sunny winter days India Gate and the surrounding lawns is where the crowds head for, to buy balloons and squeaky toys, littering the lawns with ice cream cups, peanut shells and paper cones of spicy *chana chor garam*.

Several new office buildings have been built on the on the main vistas by the Central Public Works Department, which emulate Lutyens' and Baker's architecture. These include the Supreme Court on Tilak Marg (built 1958), the National Museum on Janpath (built 1956), and the government "bhavans" (offices) dating from the 1950s and 60s. High-rise towers, like those of the Taj Mahal and Meridien Hotels, have also appeared, looming over the tidy gardens and white-painted bungalows.

Migrant entertainer – snake charmer with mongoose.

Connaught Place

Despite the mushrooming of many new shopping centres in Delhi, Connaught Place with its three concentric circles of shops and its immediate environs remains a good place for a shopping expedition. A good place to start is at the **Imperial Hotel** on Janpath, a mixture of Raj and Riviera architecture, and you might consider fortifying yourself beforehand at the Imperial's coffee shop, the Garden Party, from where you can gaze out at its lush green lawns and avenue of palm trees. Once outside the hotel gates, the bustle of Janpath hits you with its overflowing stalls and throngs of shoppers.

On the opposite side of the road in the distinctive Jawahar Vyapar Bhawan is the best one-stop shop in Delhi for Indian handicrafts and handlooms – the **Central Cottage Industries Emporium**. It is government-run, the prices are fixed and reasonable, and the selection is good. Its six floors have a huge range of goods. On the ground floor you can find carpets, metal work, bronze statues and wood carvings. The second floor has furniture, leather goods, home furnishings and curtain fabrics. Moving up to the next couple of floors there is an excellent selection of fabrics sold by the metre (silks and cottons) and woollen shawls (including ones from Kashmir), there is also a good selection of saris and ready-mades, including *shalwar kamiz*. At the top of the store you can find jewellery in gold and silver, gem stones and costume jewellery, handmade paper and greetings cards, a few musical instruments and items made from basket work and coir. When you have selected what you want on each floor, take your goods to a desk where you are issued with a receipt which you present to the payment desk on the ground floor. Your purchases will have been packaged up and will be waiting for you there. It is also possible to have items posted back.

Further on, towards Connaught Place, is the **Tibetan Market**, a good place to find distinctive Tibetan jewellery, often set with turquoise and coral, prayer scrolls *(thankas)*, beads and other bric à brac – much of it fake curios, but sometimes you can stumble across a genuine piece. Further on, Adivasi women from western India spread out their wares on the pavement – cushion covers of old brocade, exquisite pieces of embroidery and mirror work, painted cloth *pichwai* wall hangings. Be prepared for some energetic bargaining.

From here, turn left on Indira Chowk, past **Jeevan Bharati Bhawan**, the modernist glass-and-stone landmark designed by the Indian architect Charles Correa. It is the headquarters of the Life Insurance Corporation of India. Just by Jeevan Bharati Bhavan are a series of **pavement stalls** for cotton clothes; these are mostly export surplus or rejects, in the latest fashion, and it's worth rummaging here for blouses, skirts, T-shirts and nighties at giveaway prices. Continue on from here to Regal Building on Sansad Marg. This is location of the **Gaylord** and **Kwality Restaurants** which can be relied on for honest standard North Indian fare – tandoori chicken and kebabs, and the Kwality's house specialty, *chole bhature* (spiced chickpeas with fried bread).

A few doors down is the **Khadi Gramodyog Bhavan**. Don't be put off by its dreary air, it is the best place for handspun cotton *khadi* (ideal for summer), made by Gandhi into a symbol of India's national aspirations and worn by Indian politicians and others who aspire to political power. Other good buys here are raw silk, Kashmir woollen fabrics and shawls, leather Kolhapuri sandals, and *papads* and spices – all the produce of Indian villages.

The market below Jeevan Bharati Bhavan.

Keep going round Regal Building, past Rivoli Cinema, and cross the street to Baba Kharak Singh Marg: here are the **State Government Emporia** in a long row, with handlooms and crafts from the different states. Among the best are Gurjari (Gujarat) for ethnic clothes in earthy colours, Utkalika and Lepakshi (Orissa and Andhra) for weaves and *kalam-kari* textiles, Zoon (Kashmir) for papier mâché, embroidered rugs, crewel work fabric, carpets and shawls, Himachal for woollen shawls in traditional weaves, Ambapali (Bihar) for silk and Madhubani traditional painting, Kairali and Cauvery (Kerala and Karnataka) for sandalwood, and the Assam, Manipur and Tripura emporia for basket work and fine reed and bamboo mats and blinds.

If it's a Tuesday or Saturday, drop in at the Mangal (Tuesday) Bazaar across the street near the Hanuman Temple. It has all the colour and bustle of a village fair, with stalls selling glass and lacquer bangles, toys and small objects of daily use. There are women at the bazaar who will decorate your palm in intricate designs with henna paste *(mehndi)*.

There is also the nearby underground market at **Palika Bazaar**. This is mostly full of touts and over-priced goods aimed at tourists; probably best avoided.

Among the good bookshops are **The Bookworm**, specialising in paperbacks, and **Galgotia** both, in B Block, and the **People Tree** in Regal House. For records and cassettes of Indian music try **Berco's** (E Block).

Perhaps the most popular eating place in Connaught Place is **Nirula's** (L Block), pioneers in McDonalds-style fast food. Their hamburgers, pizzas and ice creams sell faster than hot *samosas*. Above the fast food counter is a restaurant called the Potpourri, with a salad bar and wholesome American salads and steaks. The Potpourri is also an excellent place for breakfast.

Other good places to eat include the **Rodeo** on A Block – a Tex-Mex with a good bar, **Zen** on B block for good Chinese and a few Japanese specialities, and down Kasturba Gandhi Marg, the **Parikrama** revolving restaurant which serves good North Indian dishes.

A pleasant place to round off your shopping expedition is the **Coconut Grove** in the Hotel Indraprastha at the bottom end of Janpath, on Ashok Road – one of the few restaurants in Delhi that specialises in Keralan and Andhran cuisine. Among the good dishes is the mild coconut flavoured stew, *avial*, eaten with *appams*, a type of rice-flour pancake.

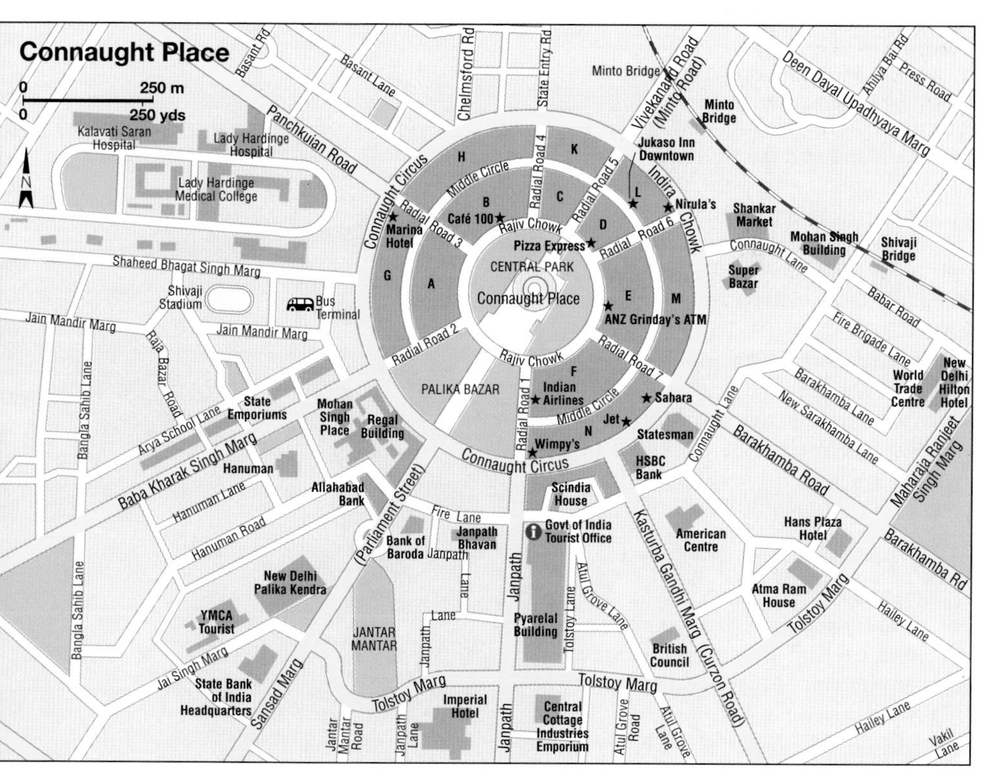

MUSEUMS AND GALLERIES

When the British built their grandiose new capital, they didn't think it necessary to build a single museum or gallery in New Delhi. Today, Delhi has over 20 museums and dozens of art galleries. Together, they provide a visitor to the city with an excellent idea of the wealth and variety of traditional and contemporary Indian art. What follows is a detailed description of the major museums and galleries, and a listing of those which have a more specialised appeal.

The National Museum: For a museum that was built only in 1960, the National Museum has an extraordinarily rich collection, continually being added to (open 10am–5pm, closed Mondays). Its nucleus was an exhibition that was put up in Burlington House in London in 1947–48, of some of the finest paintings, sculptures and decorative objects from museums all over the country.

The collections begin, appropriately enough, with prehistory, going on to the "classical" period of Indian art from the 3rd century BC to the 17th century (when sculpture using stone and bronze flourished), then on through galleries of miniature painting, textiles, decorative art, arms, Adivasi art, Central Asian and pre-Columbian antiquities, costumes and musical instruments. There are also special galleries with rotating exhibits from the museum's own collections, or on loan from foreign museums.

Start at the first gallery on the left which concentrates on prehistory and protohistory, tracing the evolution of humans in India from half a million years ago to around 2000 BC, the later period covering the Harappan Culture which appeared around 2500 BC in Mohenjodaro and Harappa, now in Pakistan. The finds at Mohenjodaro, exhibited here reveal a remarkable degree of urban planning, a high level of material comfort and links with other Middle Eastern cultures. Of particular interest are the finely sculpted toys, ceramics, jewellery and small figures, and seals inscribed with a script that is still to be deciphered.

The next gallery is an introduction to first historic periods of Indian art, notably during the reigns of the Maurya (3rd century BC), and Sunga (2nd century BC) dynasties. The Mauryan period, during which the great emperor Ashoka reigned, is famous for its monumental pillars topped by animal capitals. Ashoka also inscribed edicts on rocks, addressed to his people and laying out his moral code; a bronze replica of one of them is in the front garden of the museum.

Three major Indian schools of sculpture of the 1st to 3rd century AD, from North, South and Central India, are represented in the next gallery. Outstanding here are a standing Bodhisattva in speckled red sandstone, the Buddha heads in the distinct Greco-Roman style of Gandhara in North India (an area conquered by the Greeks during the

National Gallery of Modern Art, formerly Jaipur House.

time of Alexander), and some superb carved slabs and friezes depicting scenes from everyday life, from the ruins of Nagarjunakonda in South India, an important centre of Buddhism at the time.

To the left of the previous gallery are the **Gupta galleries.** These contain magnificent sculptures from a period (4th to 6th century AD) renowned for its monumental yet delicate style.

The **early medieval galleries** (6th to 12th century AD) which follow after the Gupta gallery, are notable for the stone images of the Pala and Sena dynasties of eastern India, the carved lintels from the great South Indian kingdom based at Hampi, and the Pallava sculptures from Mamallapuram.

Following these are two dedicated galleries on the ground floor – the **Bronze gallery** and the **Buddhist gallery**. The bronze Chola sculptures (10th century), especially the dancing four-armed Nataraj figures (replicas of varying quality of these are sold in souvenir shops all over India) are full of rhythm and grace and an almost mesmeric power.

The Buddhist gallery, opened in 1990, has as its prized exhibit Buddha's relics unearthed in Piprahwa in Uttar Pradesh in 1972. But perhaps more compelling are the Buddha sculptures in different styles – the Apollo-like Gandhara head, the classically graceful sculpted scenes from Buddha's life from Sarnath, and two most unusual stucco heads from Central Asia.

The new jewellery gallery has a sumptuous display of gold and gems, dating back to around 2500 BC. The plain gold Harappan pieces make an interesting contrast with the more ornate Mughal designs incorporating pearls and emeralds.

The first floor galleries have permanent exhibitions of miniature paintings, manuscripts and Central Asian antiquities, as well as special exhibition rooms.

The **Central Asian antiquities** in two galleries on this floor have attracted scholars and art historians from all over

Triennale exhibit at the Trade Fair evokes interest.

the world. They are the fruits of three expeditions made by Sir Aurel Stein between 1900-16, along the ancient Silk Route to China – an area that was an extraordinary meeting place of peoples, cultures, arts and religions, as is borne out by the sculptures, coins, silks, murals and ceramics dating from the 3rd to the 12th century that he found in the region.

The **History of Indian Painting gallery** to the left is the pride of the National Museum – the largest and richest collection of Indian miniatures anywhere in the world. Originally introduced into India by Persian artists at the courts of the Mughal emperors, there came into existence several distinct schools of miniature painting. Richly detailed, incredibly fine and with jewel-like colours, they depict a variety of themes: animals and plants, episodes from myths and legends, scenes from court life, portraits.

These galleries also have the quaint Company School paintings (18th and 19th centuries), the work of Indian artists who painted subjects appealing to European tastes, and the richly decorative Thanjavur paintings from South India, many of them on glass, which gives them a marvellous translucence.

Terracotta deity from Crafts Museum.

The Manuscripts section with its large collection of manuscripts on parchment and palm leaf, many of them beautifully illuminated, presents an impressive review of the art of the book in India. Of particular note is a fine collection of exquisitely calligraphed, illuminated Qurans, and a beautiful edition of the *Baburnama*.

The **second floor galleries** are devoted to anthropology, Pre-Columbian art, decorative and applied arts, especially in textiles, metal and jade, arms, and wood carving.

The **Anthropological galleries**: Centre stage here is given to the remarkable Verrier Elwin collection of Adivasi art – from the northeastern states of Nagaland and Arunachal Pradesh and from eastern and central India. The collection of costumes, jewellery, wood carving, textiles, and objects of daily use, as well as photographs and charts, gives an idea of a great variety of peoples who inhabit India.

The Arms Gallery: Dating from the 17th century, the arms collection includes battlefield as well as ceremonial arms. Many are exquisitely worked, set with jewels or ivory, and chased in gold.

Wood-carvings gallery: The collection includes intricately carved fragments of wooden temples from Gujarat, shrines, door and lintels with figures in bold relief, and carved panels from temple chariots in South India.

Decorative Arts gallery: Textiles have pride of place here – embroidered Kashmir shawls in the finest wool, fine muslin, heavily brocaded saris and court costumes. There are also fine examples of Mughal jade, ritual lamps in metal, old coins, and samples of ornamental calligraphy.

Pre-Columbian gallery: The gift of an Indian art dealer who had settled in New

York, Nasli Heeramaneck, this is an exceptional collection beginning from 900 BC and covering successive cultures on the American continent before the arrival of Columbus. It includes Mayan terracottas, Inca metalware and wooden objects, as well as examples of the art of North American Indian tribes.

Gallery of Musical Instruments: This collection of over 300 items was donated by the *sarod* player Sharad Rani. It has a large range, with instruments coming from Tamil Nadu to Kashmir.

The Railway Museum: A must for rail buffs and those with children in tow. This delightful museum's star exhibits include the Fairy Queen, the oldest locomotive in the world still in working order, and over 20 other vintage locomotives and carriages, most of them parked in the 4-hectare (10-acre) railway yard in the museum, laid out with tracks of different gauges. They include the Prince of Wales saloon coach (1876), the gleaming white Viceregal Dining Car (1889) and the Maharaja of Mysore's saloon, all with their splendid original fittings intact.

There are a number of oddities on display. One is an early 20th-century locomotive from the Nizam of Hyderabad's railway, sliced in half so that its engine can be examined; another is a two-tier van, complete with sunshades, built to accommodate some 200 sheep; and there's also a monorail steam engine which ran on a single track with an adjacent wheel running on the road outside.

There is also a toy train on which children can ride around the yard; and in the display galleries inside are models of different types of trains used by the Indian Railways, teak furniture and fittings from old coaches, station clocks, and signalling equipment (open 9.30am–7pm, April to September; 9.30am–5pm, October to March; closed Mondays).

Nehru Memorial Museum and Library: This is dedicated to India's first Prime Minister, Jawaharlal Nehru, who lived

Fragment of Buddhist relief in National Museum.

in this house for 16 years until he died in 1964. Known as Teen Murti Bhavan, it was originally built for the British Commander-in-chief and is a fine example of the Lutyenesque imperial architecture. The 16-bedroom house, with 11 hectares (28 acres) of impeccably tended lawns, shrubbery and rose gardens, has been preserved in all its colonial splendour – Burma teak panelling, solid brass fittings and a copper banister. The rooms too are as Nehru left them – and this private ambience is what makes the museum particularly attractive, giving an insight into the kind of man Nehru was – austere yet elegant. The rooms overflow with well-thumbed books, and bowls of roses – he wore one every day in his buttonhole.

The galleries of photographs are a record of the world figures who were Nehru's contemporaries, as well as a visual introduction to the history of the freedom movement in India. Next to the museum is the library, which has an excellent collection of private papers, books and microfilms relating to modern Indian history. The house is open 10am–4.45pm, closed Mondays, and a *son et lumière* show is held in the gardens every evening (except during the monsoon).

Indira Gandhi Memorial Museum: Prime Minister Indira Gandhi's bungalow at 1 Safdarjang Road has been, like her father's residence, preserved as a memorial. There are well-laid-out exhibitions and a number of rooms kept as she left them. In the garden, the spot where she was assassinated is marked by a glass walkway (open 9.30am–5pm, closed Mondays).

Tibet House Museum: A small but fascinating museum, representing the best of the Tibetan arts and crafts tradition, which draws on Chinese, Indian and Nepalese traditions and indigenous styles (open 9.30am–5pm, Monday–Friday). The museum, presided over by a scholarly lama, has an especially fine collection of old *thangkas* – painted prayer banners which used to line the

Art exhibition at AIFACS gallery.

walls of monasteries in Tibet. They are from all parts of Tibet, and date from the 15th to the 18th centuries.

The jewellery exhibits include earrings, belts, purses, lockets, and hair ornaments in silver studded with giant corals and turquoise. On the floor above is a library with rare manuscripts, and on the ground floor a shop with a small number of antiques for sale, as well as good replicas of some of the jewellery and ritual objects displayed upstairs, woven textiles and herbal medicines.

Sanskriti Museum of Indian Terracotta and Museum of Everyday Art: Two museums next door to each other. The first has a large collection of figures, tiles, pots and reliefs. The second is a small but enchanting collection of objects ranging from the icons and statues found in family altars, to decorative combs, mirrors and toiletry objects, and traditional kitchen utensils. The owner, O.P. Jain, has scoured the villages and towns of India to create these collections and some of his prize exhibits have been rescued from junkyards where they had been sold as scrap. Both museums are open 10am–5pm, closed Mondays.

A Chola bronze from the National Museum.

Gandhi Memorial Museum: This has remarkably few memorabilia, because Gandhi kept his possessions to the barest minimum – a battered pair of spectacles, wooden sandals, a staff and a loin-cloth, and of course his spinning wheel. Together, they present a poignant sight – the sum total of his earthly possessions. The museum also has a large collection of historic photographs associated with Gandhi's life and times, a library of books by and about him, and also some paintings based on episodes from his life.

Air Force Museum: A collection of old aircraft, among them an Ohka Japanese plane of the type that the kamikaze flyers used; a historic Wapiti, which was the first plane to fly through the Khyber Pass in 1929; and World War II aircraft, many of which were abandoned in India by the Americans after the war. The museum is open 10am–5pm, closed on Mondays and Tuesdays.

National Museum of Natural History: A favourite with children, with its wildlife exhibits and its imaginative "Discovery Room" where they can examine and handle rare specimens, observe live animals and do modelling and painting. The museum has in recent years developed into a major centre for environmental education, with daily film shows on ecology and regular illustrated lectures on wildlife and conservation (open 10am–5pm, closed Mondays).

The museum's audio visual presentation on the evolution of life serves as a good introduction to the exhibits that follow – fossils, an aquarium, a birds' egg and stuffed birds collection, and near it an incubator where you can watch a chick being born.

The Musical Instruments Gallery: This collection is displyed at the Sangeet Natak Akademi (Academy of Music and Dance) on Feroze Shah Road (open 9.30am–6pm, Monday–Friday). As well as the Indian instruments on show, the Akademi also has an excellent library on the performing arts.

Sulabh International Museum of Toilets: One of Delhi's more unusual museums is found right on the western edge of the city in Mahavir Enclave. Set up by a NGO specialising in sanitation, it has a wonderfully eclectic collection of chamber pots, replicas of famous toilets and modern toilet technology (open 10am–5pm, closed Sundays).

Art Galleries: Art galleries have proliferated in Delhi as the art market has expanded enormously in recent years, and contemporary Indian artists are getting the kind of exposure and recognition they never had before. Delhi is now the centre of the visual arts in India, taking over from Kolkata, and its art galleries display work in a variety of media, from fibreglass and acrylics to terracotta and wood, and in a wide range of styles, from the most avant garde to those inspired by traditional Indian iconography, and local and Adivasi forms.

National Gallery of Modern Art: Located at Jaipur House, the magnificent town house built for the former Maharaja of Jaipur under Sir Edwin Lutyens' supervision, this art gallery has lent itself happily to its conversion (open 10am–5pm, closed Mondays).

The gallery represents the changes in Indian art over the past 150 years, from the middle of the 19th century to the present day. This museum is renowned for its collection of 19th century "Company paintings", and the work of some remarkable Indian artists of the early 20th century. Among the former are British painters like Thomas Daniells and Tilly Kettle, whose oils, watercolours and etchings of Indian landscapes and monuments are typical of the period.

Interesting, too, are the works of the most fashionable Indian painter at the end of the 19th century, Raja Ravi Varma. He travelled around the princely states, painting stiff Victorian style portraits and scenes from Hindu

Grand old locos pasture in Railway Museum.

myths and legends, full of ethereal looking women. These were copied by the thousands and hung in every middle class Indian home; even today, Raja Ravi Varma's impact on Indian iconography remains, as is evident from the religious calendars and posters in shops and kiosks all over the country.

The National Gallery is rich in its collection of three outstanding Indian painters – Rabindranath Tagore, whose Nobel Prize winning literary work for long overshadowed his powerful original talent as a painter; Jamini Roy, who drew inspiration from the folk art tradition of Bengal; and Amrita Sher Gil whose vivid, passionate canvases capture scenes of everyday life in India.

Garhi: A good place to start an exploration of the contemporary art scene in Delhi is at Garhi, a complex of artists' studios set up by the Lalit Kala Akademi (the National Fine Arts Academy). Located in East of Kailash in South Delhi, Garhi is set in a spacious late-Mughal walled garden with old trees, a well, arcaded stone pavilions and stables which have now been converted into studios.

Lunch break at the graphics studio in Garhi.

Garhi has four large community studios for painting, printmaking, sculpture and ceramics shared by several artists and ten individual studios for senior artists. You can buy directly from the artists at Garhi, at prices much lower than at the galleries.

Another excellent place to start is the government-run **Lalit Kala Gallery** on Firoz Shah Road. Its three floors often hold different exhibitions, and work from a wide range of Indian artists is displayed. This is a good place to buy from as the non-profit-making gallery does not charge commission.

Close by is perhaps the leading commercial art gallery in Delhi today, **Art Heritage** at Triveni Kala Sangam (a complex of four galleries on Tansen Marg), right in the cultural hub of Delhi. Each year, it presents the work of 15 or more artists from all over India – retrospectives of leading painters as well as their latest work.

Within walking distance is the **LTG Gallery** which has held important displays of contemporary ceramics.

One of Delhi's oldest galleries is the **Dhoomi Mal Art Centre** in Connaught Place; it represents a large number of established painters and sculptors, and the owners are friendly and helpful.

In Hauz Khas Village is the **Village Gallery**. The Village Gallery has made a special effort to exhibit leading painters from Kolkata and Mumbai whose works are otherwise rarely seen in Delhi.

Other established art galleries in Delhi are **Gallerie Ganesha** and **Aurobindo Gallery**. The India International Centre, although not an art gallery, often holds high quality small exhibitions.

A number of foreign cultural centres have art galleries, though the exhibits are not always for sale. Among the most active are Gallerie Romain Rolland, Max Muller Bhavan and the Brtish Council.

DELHI FESTIVALS

In common with all of India, Delhi has numerous religious and secular festivals throughout the year. Many of the religious festivals depend on traditional calendars and so have moveable dates corresponding to the lunar cycle. A selection of the best-known festivals follows below, but there are many more local ones.

The biggest crowd-puller of all is the annual **Republic Day** parade on 26 January, when hundreds of thousands of people line Raj Path to watch a procession of soldiers and tanks, camel corps and the cavalry regiments, brass bands and traditional dancers, school children and freedom fighters. On the 29 January, the Republic Day festivities are brought to an end with the **Beating the Retreat**, a parade of India's armed forces and military bands.

Following this is the **Surajkund Crafts Mela**, held for a month in February at Surajkund, the 10th-century ruin of a sun temple, on the outskirts of Delhi. Artisans from all over India camp here for a month, making and selling their goods.

The spring festival of **Holi** occurs at the full moon between February and March. This is a time when social restraint breaks down, people cover each other with coloured powder and there is widespread consumption of *bhang* (cannabis). This is also a time for visitors, especially women, to be wary of going outside as the revelry often gets out of hand.

Shivaratri, the night when Shiva is said to have performed his comic dance *(tandava)*, falls at the end of February/ beginning of March.

New Year in North India falls in the Hindu month of Vaisakha (April–May), and is celebrated by the festival of **Vaisakhi**. This is an important day for Sikhs and it is traditionally celebrated in the Punjab by the dancing of *bhangra*, accompanied by large drums known as *dhol*.

At around this time the Muslim festival of **Id-ul-Fitr** often falls (although Id can occur much earlier or later in the year). This marks the end of the month-long fast of **Ramadan**. This is also the time of the Urs of the Chisti saint, Nizamuddin *(see pages 126–9)*.

Another Muslim festival that depends on the lunar calendar, and is therefore movable, is **Muharram**. This is the period when Shi'a Muslims commemorate the martyrdom of the Prophet's grandson, Hussain. Processions of devotees carrying large, decorated *tazias* (representations of Hussain's tomb at Karbala) move through the streets and many followers beat themselves with chains in grief.

The third great Muslim festival of the year is **Bakr Id**, which usually falls later in the year. This commemorates Ibrahim's sacrifice of his son, and traditionally a goat is sacrificed and eaten on this day.

Young Sikhs at the Guru Nanak Jayanti procession.

Independence Day (15 August) is a national holiday. In Delhi, the Prime Minister speaks from the ramparts of the Red Fort and the Indian flag is hoisted on the Lahore Gate.

The Hindu festival of **Raksha-bandhan** also occurs around this time. Sisters pray for their brothers before tying silk threads around their brothers' wrists. In return a brother will give his sister a small gift and promise to look after and protect her.

Later in August the festival of **Janamashtami** which celebrates the birth of Lord Krishna is the occasion for dance-dramas known as *ras-lilas*, which enact scenes from Krishna's life.

A festival unique to Delhi occurs in early October, the **Phul-walon-ki-Sair** (the flower-sellers' procession), celebrated in Mehrauli in South Delhi *(see page 138)*.

A few weeks later comes **Dussehra**, in October, celebrated with particular gusto in Delhi. This is traditionally the time when the *ram-lila* dance-drama is performed, throughout the month, with episodes from the great epic, the *Ramayana*, telling the dramatic story of the god Rama and his battle with the king of Lanka, Ravana.

Dussehra is followed in November by **Divali**, the festival of lights, when an enchanting Divali Mela (fair) is held in the Mughal Talkatora gardens. The festival celebrates Rama's return to Ayodhya after his 14 year exile, lamps are lit and fireworks set off. This is also when doors are left open to invite the goddess of wealth, Lakshmi, into people's homes.

The most important festival of the year for Delhi's Sikh community is **Guru Nanak Jayanti**, the commemoration of the birth of the first Sikh Guru. It is marked by processions and the reading of the Sikhs' holy book, the Guru Granth Sahib.

Christmas Day is celebrated by India's Christians, and both it and **New Year's Day** are marked by a public holiday in India.

Id prayers at the Jama Masjid.

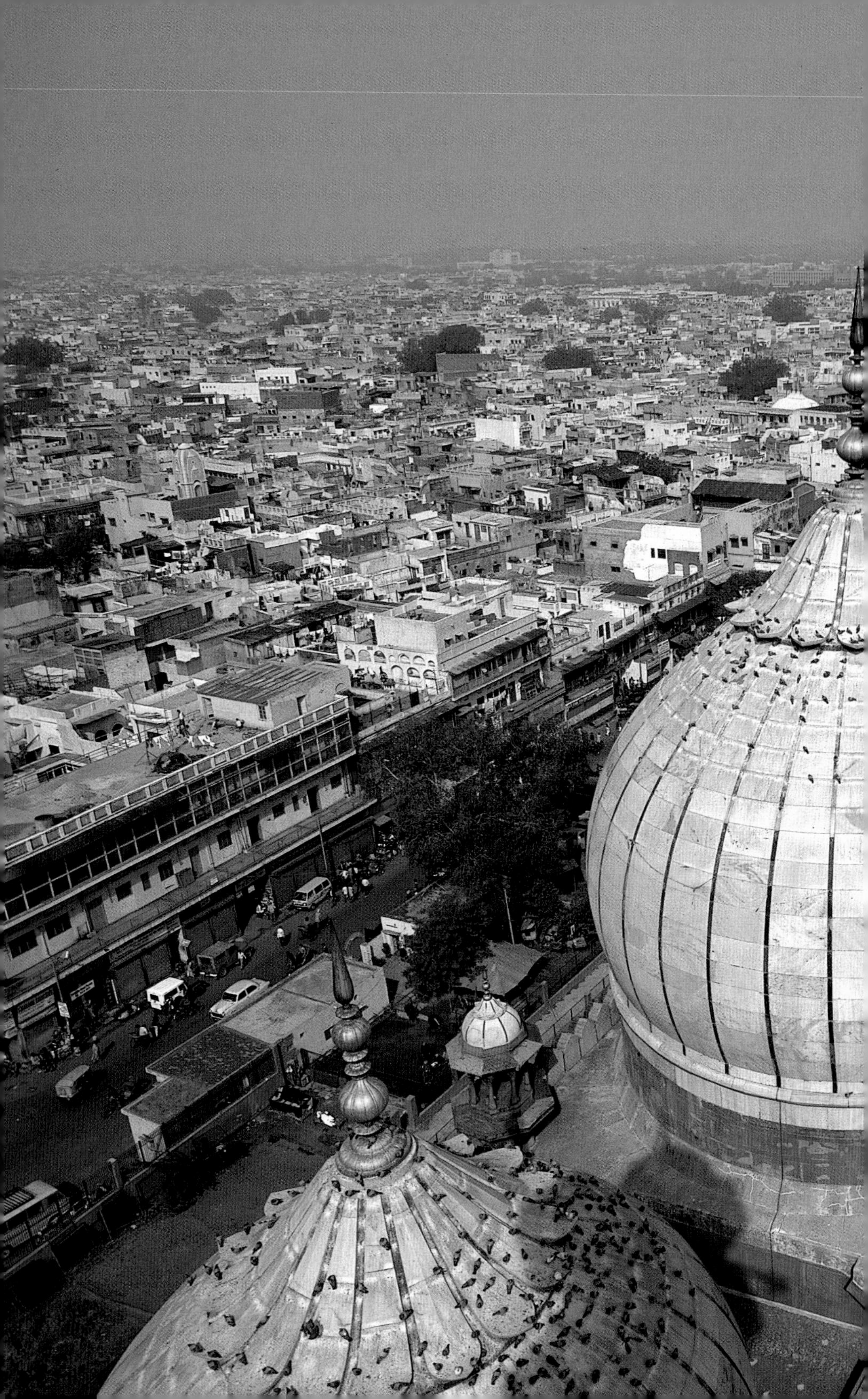

DELHI MUSICAL STORES

OLD DELHI

Known as Old Delhi to most people living in Delhi, and as the Walled City to officials, even though there are many older Delhis, and the town wall survives only in fragments, this area is perhaps more accurately called Shahjahanabad; as both terms above include the Sadar Bazaar, which is in fact outside the wall.

It was the oppressive heat of Agra that decided the Emperor Shahjahan to move the capital back to Delhi. In 1638 he built the Fort Palace (today called the Red Fort), which was the focal point of a new city named after him. Later, the great Jama Masjid was erected on a low hill southwest of the palace. The two axes of Chandni Chowk (running east-west) and Faiz Bazaar (today Netaji Subhash Marg, running due south) were laid out. The rest of the city was built by infill, and building work in Old Delhi has never quite ceased.

Since the 1970s more and more people have been concerned at the deterioration of the urban fabric of this Mughal city, and have pleaded for the need to conserve its distinctive features. What follows is an attempt to convey the quality of life here, rather than a building-by-building description. Like all old settlements, Shahjahanabad should not be seen in a hurry, and a part of the day should be set aside for it. Only by walking through it will you understand its human scale.

Shahjahanabad lies on the Grand Trunk Road which crosses the country from Lahore to Bengal; travellers and caravans from the west entered the city by the gate appropriately named the Lahori Gate (today, only the name survives). Those coming from the east crossed the Yamuna by a pontoon bridge or sailed past the fort and entered the city through the northern gate, the Kashmiri. Some of the other gates – Kabuli, Ajmeri, Delhi – pointed in the direction of those towns.

This little city, focal point of a large empire, was an island in a green sea of fields and woodland, with a skyline punctuated by minarets. In the 1860s the British Government crassly drove the new railway line through the city, with a defiantly neo-Gothic railway station. Today's traveller disembarks in the most crowded part of the city, which they will hardly see for the traffic and the pollution. The best way to get a sense of where the city began and ended is to go north of Bahadur Shah Marg and to turn right at the Delhi Gate crossing.

Delhi Gate is today an island, its height shortened by the repeated layering of asphalt on the roads around it. Northwards, left of Delhi Gate, is the commercial avenue of **Asaf Ali Road**. This follows the alignment of the city wall, which has been demolished. On the right a portion of the wall still stands, set off by a stretch of lawn. A right turn will bring you to Mahatma Gandhi Marg (Ring Road) and the **Gandhi Memorial** at Rajghat.

Preceding pages, the dense urban fabric of the old city around the Jama Masjid. Left, the steps of the great mosque are always alive with activity.

Turn left and go along the Ring Road; on your left you can clearly see the line of the city. In your mind's eye, cover the stretch from the city wall with water, and imagine yourself not in a rickshaw but in a gently-moving boat. Previously the river ran along the walls of the fort, where Mahatma Gandhi Marg now runs. The Ring Road continues northwards; after you've gone under the Mughal and British bridges you reach a huge overbridge: a left turn here brings you to the **Interstate Bus Terminal**. Today's long-distance travellers disembark where earlier the boats used to off-load their passengers. This area used to be Qudsia Bagh, one of the big orchards which ringed the Walled City. The **Kashmiri Gate** on the left marks the northern end of Shahjahanabad. The city can be entered most conveniently from either Delhi Gate in the south or Kashmiri Gate in the north. In neither case will you go through the gate, since both of them have made into islands and are protected monuments. Delhi and Kashmiri Gates are linked as part of a major north-south road which did not exist in the city as originally planned.

If crowded streets worry you, you might not enjoy Shahjahanabad. On the other hand, if not you will find it a refreshing contrast to the open spaces and impersonal character of New Delhi.

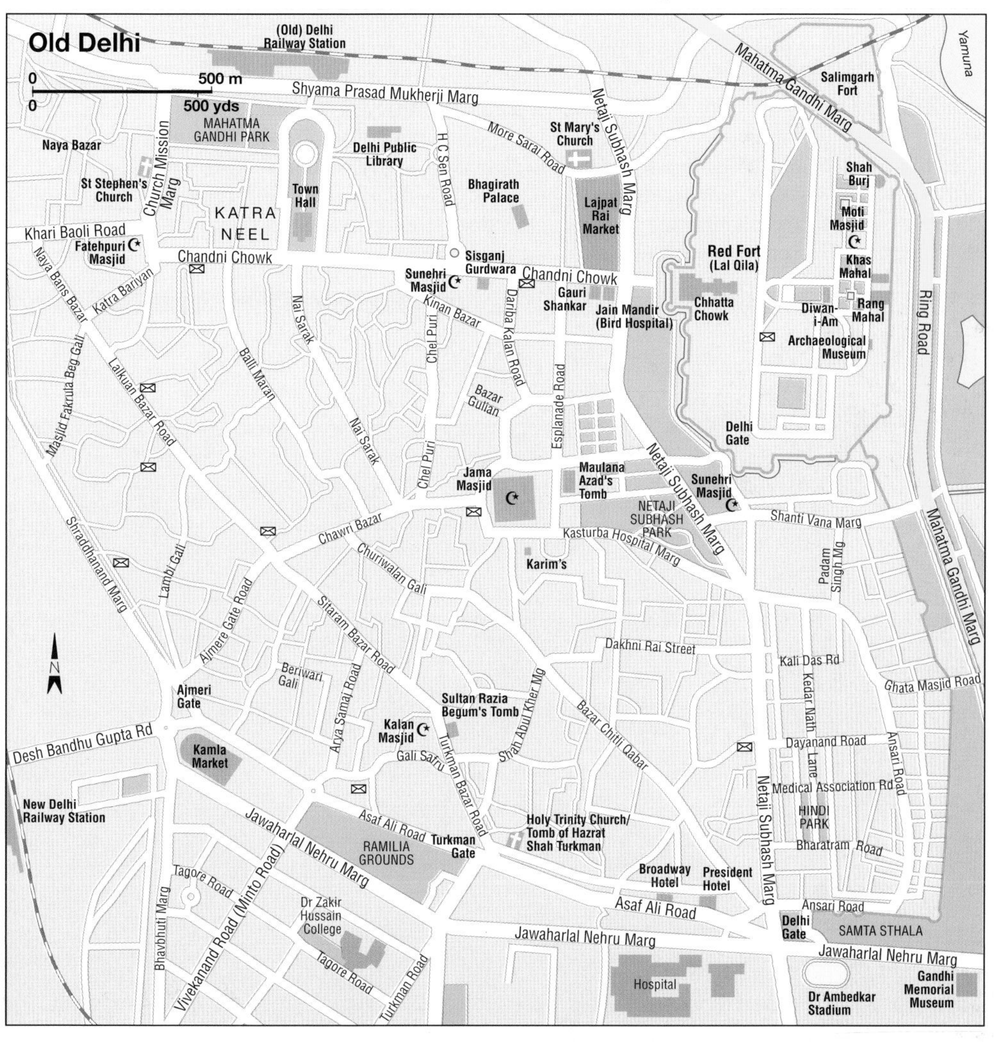

Shahjahanabad has not only monuments but a city fabric which, although inevitably changed, approximates to the original. It is a medieval town: in it you will recognise, not just Cairo or Istanbul, but also Chester and Heidelberg. It will not daunt a pedestrian, though there are times when a cycle rickshaw would be welcome. Cars, buses and scooters have now invaded its roads, have added considerably to the pollution and made the streets even more crowded. Asphalt, cinema advertisements and telegraph poles also now crowd in with the old *havelis*. Although it might now be hard to imagine there were once spreading trees and water channels along the main streets.

The town was earlier divided into wards, separated by roads, each with a sense of neighbourhood based on shared ties of kinship or occupation. The charm of the place – still evident – is that dwellings, shops, restaurants and places of worship are all intermingled in its streetscape. The street was convivial, a place for celebration, for generating political excitement. The city was built right up to the moat of the Fort and spilled out beyond the gates. A great change occurred after the Uprising of 1857: the Mughal fort became British army encampment, the houses around it were swept away to create "Parade Ground", and tourists became poor substitutes for the aristocracy who had patronised the artists and artisans. A vast wholesale market, the **Sadar Bazaar**, was developed near the new railway station, to make Shahjahanabad the bustling commercial entrepôt it still is. An amazing volume of merchandise is stored in very small premises and is carried away by retailers every week. Thus the Mughal capital became a thriving commercial town.

The city suffered another trauma in 1947 when many Muslims left to settle in Pakistan. Many of their houses were occupied by Hindu and Sikh refugees coming in the reverse direction; many *katras* (covered shopping arcades) were

Men in Old Delhi spice market.

also divided up between various families, several of which created occupations for themselves. Today, a startlingly large number of people, as well as shops and workshops, are to be found here. This density does not necessarily indicate poverty: many families live here by choice.

If Shahjahanabad appeals to you, and you have a day or two to spare, it is well worth investing in Gayner Barton and Lorraine Malone's book, *Old Delhi: Ten Easy Walks*, an exceptionally well written guide which helps you explore various parts of Shahjahanabad without getting lost in its winding lanes.

If your time is limited, it is a good idea to hire a cycle rickshaw outside the Red Fort and drive down **Chandni Chowk**. On the left is a microcosm of Indian religions and tolerance – a Hindu temple, a Jain temple with its famous bird hospital, a Sikh gurdwara and a Muslim mosque. After you pass the historic sweet shop, **Ghantewala**, turn left and double back through the narrow lane of **Kinari Bazaar**, ablaze with tinsel and gold braid (these touches of gold or silver are used to decorate everything from saris to the windscreens of trucks). This leads to **Dariba Kalan**, the jeweller's street. The shopfronts conceal houses with cool tree-shaded courtyards behind thick walls which shut off the sounds of the street. If you continue on the Chandni Chowk streets beyond Ghantewala, you will see the classical facade of the British-built **Town Hall** on the right. After which is the fabric bazaar of **Katra Neel.** The **Fatehpuri Masjid** (17th century) is at the end, and just beyond it is **Khari Baoli** (literally, the "Stepwell of Brackish Water" – but there is no sign of the well), an aromatic spice market.

Opposite the Town Hall is the street of **Nai Sarak**, lined with booksellers, mostly catering to college students, and small printing shops. At the southern end of Nai Sarak is **Chawri Bazaar**, that leads to the Jama Masjid. Just off Chawri Bazaar is the amazing spare-car-parts bazaar.

The northern section of Shahjahanabad beyond the railway line is a more open area, and the landscape is more "Indo-British". Indeed this marks the beginning of the British "Civil Lines", concentrated a little further north below the Northern Ridge. **St James' Church** was built by Col. Skinner in the early 19th century and bears the scars of the bullets of 1857. South of it, looking towards Delhi Gate on the right, is the old St. Stephen's College building, in pseudo-Mughal style; on the left after a few shops is the office of the State Department of Archaeology, with a colonnaded facade going back to the early 19th century, when it was the British Residency. It conceals the original building which was the library of Prince Dara Shikoh, the emperor Aurangzeb's erudite brother.

Beyond Kashmiri Gate the road opens out to the Interstate Bus Terminus on the right and Tilak Park and **Nicholson's cemetery**, replete with the graves of 1857, on the left.

Gandhi Memorial at Rajghat.

THE RED FORT

The two approaches to the Red Fort in Delhi give the visitor completely divergent views: from the Ring Road, where the river Yamuna flowed until the beginning of the 20th century, you see beautiful marble buildings with balconies and marble *jali* (perforated screen) windows; from the city side, massive red sandstone walls, ramparts and defensive barbicans in front of the two principal gateways, the Lahore and Delhi Gates. The two views reflect the Red Fort's dual function as residential palace and military fortress – the administrative centre from where the emperor governed North India.

Shahjahan, the fifth of the Great Mughals, who transferred the capital from Agra back to Delhi, devised a plan to divide the Fort into two sections by the avenue that connected the southern Delhi Gate to the northern Salimgarh Gate (no longer in existence). To the north of the avenue lay the private palaces, while the southern part housed the offices and quarters of the officials – the military, *maulvis* (clergy), clerks and household staff – the Kharkhanya or imperial workshops for manufacturing muslins and brocades, and the stables. This palace citadel, twice the size of Agra Fort, completed in 1648 at a cost of 60 lakhs of rupees, was a veritable "city within a city".

Shahjahan intended to build "delightful edifices through which streams of water should flow and the terraces of which should overlook the river". He erected a wide terrace of marble along the river front wall of the Fort, on which were built all the private palaces, of pure white marble, with glistening gold cupolas. At the northern extremity was the three-storey octagonal **Shah Burj** or King's Tower used by Shahjahan for late night conclaves to which only his sons and trusted advisers were admitted. Though it is now in ruins, you can

Preceding pages, the Lahori Gate of the Red Fort, where the national flag is hoisted on 15 August, Independence Day. Below, Shahjahan's marble Diwan-i-Khas.

pick your way through the debris to see the water tank from where the **Nahr-i-Bihisht** or Stream of Paradise originated, the Hammam or Royal Baths (closed to the public), the Diwan-i-Khas, Khas Mahal, and the harem palaces, of which only the Rang or Imtiaz and Mumtaz Mahal survive.

The Emperor used to awake before dawn in his Khwabgah (sleeping chamber) in the Khas Mahal, and after reciting his early morning *namaz* in the adjoining **Tasbih Khana** (both rooms are closed) he would cross the Stream of Paradise to his *baithak* or private sitting room. Above the water channel is a delicate screen filigreed with the scales of justice, the sun and the moon, to remind the Emperor of the symbols of Mughal kingship and its duties. The first of these was the early morning appearance at sunrise in the **Jharoka-i-Darsha**, an octagonal tower jutting out from the *baithak*, both rooms decorated with painted and gilded floral designs. Below the balcony ran the river on whose sandy banks the Emperor's subjects assembled for his *darshan* – literally, viewing – and to submit petitions for justice. Sentences were dispensed on Wednesdays and carried out immediately. Fridays, the Muslim holy day, were a day of rest.

The most elegant of the buildings on the Royal Terrace, north of the Khas Mahal, is the **Diwan-i-Khas**, an open marble pavilion of foliated arches that intersect it into bays. The interior is a bower of roses, lilies and irises made of inlay of precious stones like lapis lazuli, agate and cornelian, and of gilded decoration. Shahjahan, lover of nature, created here a jewelled garden, and on the marble platform in its centre stood the famous Peacock Throne, adorned with his "acquisition of such rare jewels" that it was a blaze of diamonds, emeralds, rubies and pearls. In this Hall of Private Audience, "a secret place where the second audience is given and the council sits", Shahjahan discussed confidential affairs of state and received

Interior of the Diwan-i-Am with marble throne.

important nobles and foreign envoys. On its arches is inscribed the famous couplet:

"If on earth be paradise,
It is this, it is this, it is this."

No longer – its silver and gold ceiling was pillaged by the Marathas (it fetched them 28 lakhs of rupees at the mint in 1760) and the precious stones gouged out. But the traces of its former brilliance still linger.

North of the Diwan-i-khas, steps descend from the marble terrace to a triple-domed mosque which faces the Royal Baths. The **Moti Masjid** or Pearl Mosque was added by the emperor Aurangzeb who, unlike his father Shahjahan, prayed at the Jama Masjid only on special occasions, preferring his own private mosque for daily prayers. In keeping with its poetic name, it is a pure white pearl made of marble, carved with delicate tendrils of leaves. In front of the Diwan-i-Khas was a large courtyard surrounded by arcaded galleries in whose western corner was a doorway hung with a Lal Purdah or red curtain. The privileged few who could enter beyond this curtain were known as "Lal Purdaris" and, as for the harem, no man except the Emperor and his sons was allowed inside. The guards and the Superintendent of the Harem were of course eunuchs.

The **Rang** or **Imtiaz Mahal**, similar in design to the Diwan-i-Khas, is of pure white marble with a beautiful basin in the centre shaped like the petals of a lotus, which used to have a silver fountain. At the four corners are small chambers whose walls and ceilings are encrusted with tiny mirrors from which they derive the name of **Shish Mahal**. Shahjahan would arrive in the Rang Mahal around noon, discuss the affairs of the harem with his daughter Princess Jahanara (the First Lady of the empire after the death of his beloved Mumtaz Mahal), and partake of his midday meal, followed by a siesta. In the hot summer months they could retire to the **Tehkhana** or basement whose red

Palace details: Pearl Mosque (below left) and *hammam* or royal baths (below right).

sandstone ventilation screens as well as the gate that led underground can be seen on the plinth below.

The other palace of the harem further south, the **Mumtaz Mahal**, has been converted into a museum exhibiting artefacts dating from the Mughal period.

In front of the Rang Mahal was a garden which would have had a strong enclosure wall isolating the harem from the rest of the palace. At the end of the garden you see the rear of a building, with a staircase which the emperor took to ascend to his throne in the **Diwan-i-Am**, or Hall of Public Audience. Skirting it, you arrive in front of this red sandstone pavilion with a marble balcony in its back wall decorated with the famous Florentine pietra dura inlay of birds, flowers and Orpheus. Its pillars were covered with a lustrous white plaster painted with floral designs, but are now sandstone denuded of all decoration. (A sample of painted plaster can be seen preserved above the sales counter inside the Naqqar Khana gateway.)

Lower half of "Scales of Justice" screen in the Khas Mahal, imperial private apartments.

As you proceed from the private section, where marble abounds, to the more formal and official buildings, luxury gives way to a subdued grandeur.

In the Diwan-i-Am, the emperor gave "audience indiscriminately to all his subjects, high and low", and the general public could hope to get the emperor's ear – if they could get past the bureaucracy. Once or twice a day, Shahjahan sat here on one of his nine thrones and discussed routine administrative, financial and military matters for the governance of his vast empire. The audience ended with a review of the cavalry and elephants, to check whether they were well cared for and fit for battle. The marble platform below the throne balcony was where officials stood and handed up petitions and letters to the emperor.

The Diwan-i-Am had an immense courtyard of arcaded galleries connecting it to the red sandstone ceremonial gateway opposite, called the **Naqqar khana** because of the ceremonial

naqqars or kettledrums that were played from its open balconies (now enclosed), to mark the hours of the day and the arrivals and departures of the emperor. Beyond this gate, everyone but the emperor and his sons had to dismount and proceed on foot.

After the Revolt of 1857, the British forces occupied the fort and razed to the ground all the buildings south of the Naqqar Khana, erecting in their place military barracks still used by the Indian Army. They left untouched the **Chatta Chowk** or covered bazaar, a narrow alley with vaulted arches and an octagonal court in the centre that terminates in the principal gateway, the Lahore Gate. The shops used to cater to the needs of the imperial household and are still in use, but they sell souvenirs – some of which, like *zardozi* (gold-embroidered) bags and enamelled boxes, are crafts dating to Mughal times.

During the decline of the Mughal power from the time of Muhammad Shah, the Fort was pillaged and looted by Marathas, Jats and Rohillas. When Bishop Heber saw it in 1823 it was "desolate, dull and forlorn", but the gardens and buildings were still there. After the British depredations, all that remains of the two vast gardens at the north eastern end, the **Hayat Baksh** and **Mahatab Bagh**, are two marble pavilions with small arched niches in which lighted lamps were placed, over which water cascaded down. Shahjahan's plan was based on a formal symmetry of interconnecting courts and arcaded galleries that enclosed the royal apartments, the Diwan-i-Khas and the harem. They were not isolated and exposed as they are now. We see them without the rich silk and brocade awnings and blinds (which were let down over the arched openings when required) and the magnificent painted, embroidered and brocaded canopies and carpets that covered the courtyards. For the emperors, like most of the people of North India, lived outdoors more than indoors. Their buildings, with their

Below left, laying bets on quail fight. Below right, private devotions at the Jama Masjid.

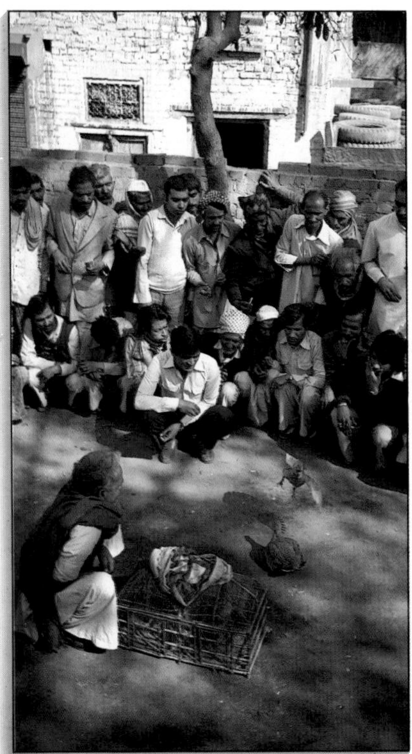

screens and airy spaces, have been aptly described as "tents frozen in stone".

After completing the Red Fort, Shahjahan began the Jama Masjid, the Friday mosque without which no Islamic city is complete. It was finished in 1656 at a cost of one million rupees. Built on a hill in front of the Delhi Gate, the Jama Masjid was connected to the fort by a street of shops called the Khas Bazaar. Shahjahan, seated on a gold throne-like howdah on an elephant or carried on his *takht-rawan* (travelling throne), would leave by the Delhi Gate for his afternoon prayers, never returning by the same gate as that "was considered unlucky in Hindustan"; he would have had a clear view of the eastern gateway of the mosque facing the Palace, and the majestic flights of steps leading to it, a perspective denied to the modern visitor.

The royal entrance is now closed, and visitors have to take either of the gateways on each side of it, also approached by similar steps in red sandstone. In the interior is a vast courtyard, empty except for a tank in its centre, where the obligatory ritual ablutions must be performed before prayers. It is bordered by cloisters whose pattern is broken by the gateways; one of them has a delicate balcony projecting on the inner court, where the royal ladies sat. As customary, the sanctuary is on the western side, facing Mecca, and consists of a wide central arch flanked on each side by five smaller ones terminating in slender, elegant minarets. The interior of the prayer hall is divided into aisles by arches, and its walls and floors are of marble inlay panels with rich motifs of cusped arches. The introduction of black marble strips in the inlay decoration and on the domes introduces a striking effect.

Shahjahan would have knelt on silken carpets facing the central *mihrab* in the prayer hall. To the right are the marble steps of the *mimbar* or pulpit from where the Imam conducts the prayers – never from the top step,

Below left, cricket game through Red Fort window. Below right, chess game behind the Jama Masjid.

deemed sacred to the Prophet. Relics of the Prophet, including his footprint in marble, are kept in the Jama Masjid and can be seen on demand.

From the southern gateway the *muezzin* would climb to the top of the minaret and call the faithful congregation of Shahjahanabad to prayer:

"La Alla illa alla Muhammad resul-alla."

("There is but one God and Muhammad is His Messenger.")

The cry would echo back from the numerous smaller mosques of the city, as it still does today. The mosque is not just a place of prayer, it is a social meeting point for the inhabitants where they shop in the Mina Bazaar, chat and gossip with friends and eat kebabs and sweetmeats from the several vendors crowding the steps.

This impressive mosque, said to be the largest in India, where upwards of 20,000 people can kneel in prayer, has the most perfect proportions. In spite of its size, it is graceful rather than ponderous. Rising loftily from the pinnacle of its hill, it is a visual counterpoint to the high battlements of the Fort, symbolising the supremacy of the One God to whom even sovereigns must bow. The Red Fort and the Jama Masjid are not only linked to each other spatially and conceptually, but are an integral part of the city that Shahjahan laid out around them. If you climb the minarets of the mosque you get a view of the complex urban design that is the walled city of Shahjahanabad.

As we have seen, Red Fort today is a skeleton of what was built. The original plan was a regular and formal composition of quadrangles and arcaded galleries, and the same concept extended to the city. In front of the Delhi Gate was a *chowk* or square, the Sadullah Chowk where dancing girls, astrologers and story-tellers dwelt, while the Lahore Gate gave onto the large "Royal Square" where the nobles took the air, carried in palanquins, with servants fanning them with peacock tails and others

Lizards and snakes for medicinal oils.

running alongside with their silver spitoons. From each *chowk* a main bazaar avenue led to the Delhi Gate and the Lahore Gate of the city, and flowing down the centre was a branch of the Stream of Paradise of the Palace which is said to have "lent happiness to the streets and bazaars".

The principal avenue was the one in front of the Lahori Gate, which had an octagonal pool into which the Stream of Paradise flowed. The striking effect of moonlight shining on the flowing waters gave it the name of **Chandni Chowk**, Moonlight Square. Opposite the pool was the garden and serai of Princess Jahanara, daughter of Shahjahan; its refined beauty caused François Bernier to compare it to the Palais Royal of Paris. On both sides of the two main bazaar streets were arcaded shophouses, and between them a criss-cross of narrow alleys and lanes dividing the city into *mohallas*. Each of these *mohallas* or wards was devoted to workers and trades of different kinds – for the washermen, the leather workers, the silversmiths and the cooks, and interspersed amongst them were the neighbourhood mosques, *madrasas* (schools) and *havelis* (mansions).

The plan of the city had the same symmetry as the fortress palace: the two focal points were the Fort and the Jama Masjid, with an arrangement of spacious public squares from which led wide avenues. After their victory in the 1857 war, the British destroyed these squares and the buildings alongside them, and the subsequent urban sprawl has further obliterated Shahjahan's design. When Aurangzeb added the barbicans to the gateways he had already interfered with Shahjahan's plan, for the Chandni Chowk was also a royal processional avenue that led in a straight axis from the heart of the city to the King's Palace – from where he surveyed his subjects. Shahjahan's design of the Red Fort and Shahjahanabad is a triumphant blend of aesthetics, function and symbolism.

Roadside dentist.

THE NORTHERN RIDGE

The Delhi Ridge as it arises from the Yamuna river is the northern end of one of the world's most ancient mountain ranges, the Aravalli Hills, said by geologists to belong to the pre-Cambrian period of perhaps 1,500 million years ago. They run from Delhi to near Ahmadabad in Gujarat, with peaks in the south rising to about 6,000 feet near Mount Abu in Rajasthan.

Except for the trees and the greatly extended Hindu Rao Hospital, the Ridge is still generally in its natural state – one reason being that to the British, the fighting of 1857 (during the Indian Revolt) made the hilly area sacred ground. It became for them, as it largely remains, a cool resort for gentle recreation, with its woodland rides and walks, its dells and small ponds and glimpses of monkeys, peafowl, mongooses and all the birds of Delhi.

Few visitors know of the Ridge, but for those with an interest in the history of the British connection with India, the tract is important. There are also Muslim relics, mostly buildings of an early sultan. From north to south the monuments are:

The Mutiny Memorial (locally known as the Ajit Garh or victory tower), built by the British army in 1862 to commemorate those on their side who fell in the fighting of 1857. A small force of the governing East India Company were caught on the then exposed and treeless Ridge in 1857 from June to September, following the outbreak in May of what the British called the Indian Mutiny and what post-colonial Indians know as the First War of Independence. The Indian soldiers of the British Bengal army in Meerut, a big garrison town 77 km (44 miles) from Delhi, broke into open revolt against their officers. The immediate cause was a local dispute, but the whole Bengal army was totally dissatisfied with British rule, due as much as to racial arrogance and gross insensitivity towards Indian feelings as to anything else. However, although the Indians as a whole felt that their own ways were adequate and disliked the British passion for change, many either took no part in the uprising, or actively assisted the British government.

Left, the Mutiny Memorial, built by the British in 1863 to commemorate the siege of Delhi.

With both sides emotionally involved, the fighting was marked by appalling brutality. The bloodshed started on 10 May, moved to Delhi the next day and within days and weeks British rule had ceased between there and Allahabad, about 640 km (400 miles) from Kolkata (Calcutta). The claw-back began in June from Delhi with the arrival of a British force from the Punjab of little more than 3,000 men, of whom nearly half were Indian.

Through the remainder of the very hot weather and the monsoon rains until September (by which time its strength was almost 10,000 men), the force stayed on the Ridge attacked by those in the city and by cholera, heatstroke and malaria. The British Commander-in-Chief and his acting successor were carried off by cholera within weeks of each other. The city was assaulted in mid-September at Kashmiri Gate – a good tactical choice, for the river provided a firm left flank, but unfortunate in that just inside were the warehouses of the wine merchants, soon discovered by the attackers. The result was that many were quickly out of control and discipline lost.

The British commander, Brigadier-General John Nicholson, was mortally wounded within the first two hours and it required about a week of street fighting to recover the city. Once Delhi was taken, the result of the conflict was in no doubt, but fighting continued in northern and central India for at least another twelve months. The following year, on 1 September 1858, power was passed to the British Parliament and the East India Company ceased to govern in India.

The Mutiny Memorial on the Ridge marks the British line during the months before the attack. It is a typically Victorian gothic structure, but the claim that it owes something to London's Albert Memorial cannot be true, for the Hyde Park monument was constructed more than ten years later. Panels list the regiments of the Delhi Field Force, the engagements fought, the names of the 46 officer casualties – many more died from disease – and the figures of the strengths (Indian and British) of those on the Ridge who were killed and wounded. From the platform, there is the view (the near distance is now obscured by trees) of Delhi as seen by the attacking soldiers: the great mosque, the tall gateway of the Red Fort, the Kashmiri Gate church and the river Yamuna.

Some 180 m (200 yards) north of the Mutiny Memorial, at the side of the road is a 4-m (12-ft) fragment of an **Ashokan Pillar** of the 3rd century BC, one of the two brought to Delhi and set up in his palaces by Sultan Feroze Shah Tughlaq in the 14th century AD. Sultan Feroze Shah was the first of the three great builders of Delhi, after Shahjahan and Lutyens. For a sultan of his period, Feroze Shah was unusual in that, as an enthusiastic antiquarian, he cherished not only Islamic achievements, but also Hindu and Buddhist. He repaired the Qatb Minar as well as the circular Hindu lake of Suraj Kund to the south of Delhi.

The Ashokan Pillar on the Ridge is a fragment, but a specimen of the 3rd century script known as Ashoka Brahmi, a forerunner of today's Devanagiri Hindi script, may be seen. The provenance of the pillar is explained by a plaque at its base.

Opposite is the **Hindu Rao Hospital**. The original house, of which a portion survives, was probably built for a British Resident to the Mughal court in the 1820s. It was acquired by a Maratha nobleman, Hindu Rao, and during the Revolt was occupied by the Sirmoor Battalion of Gurkhas (now the 2nd Gurkhas of the British Army). After the fighting it was used as a military hospital and is now a general hospital.

Within the hospital compound, close to the road, is a portion of Sultan Feroze Shah Tughlaq's 14th century palace, known as **Pir Ghaib**. During the fighting it was called the Observatory Tower; on the roof is a small round sandstone slab for an instrument, with a hole for the plumb-line, used during the 1830s in connection with the Great Triangulation Survey (GTS), when the British first accurately mapped their new territories.

Next along the road is the **Charbuja** (Four Towers) **Mosque**, again one of the remaining buildings erected by Feroze Shah. It is unusual in that the mosque is not on the ground floor but up above.

The Flag Staff Tower: Following the "walk-way" (no vehicles) to the north, and passing the Government of India Seismological Observatory on the left, one comes across the Flagstaff Tower in

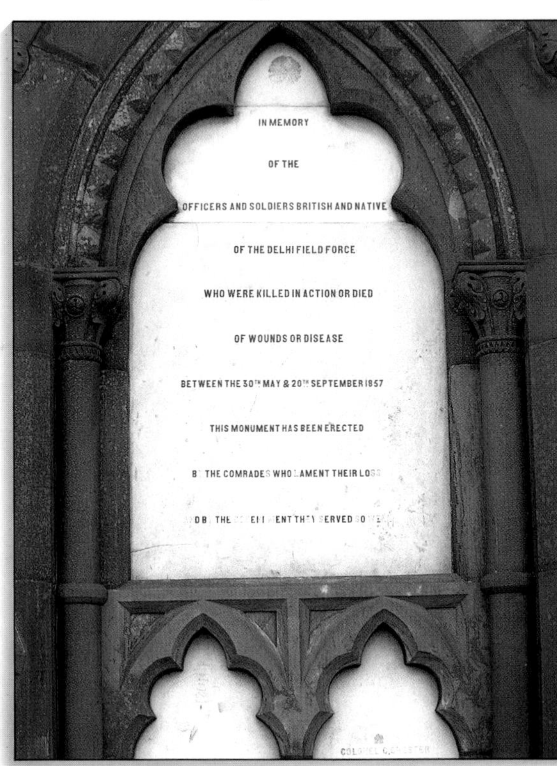

Inscription on a panel of the memorial.

the centre of the road. The association of the Tower with the Revolt lies in the fact that it was here that the Europeans who escaped from the first attacks assembled before moving on to Ambala and Meerut. The origin of the Tower has not been satisfactorily established so far. It is generally believed to have been part of the military cantonment which had lain to the west of the Ridge.

The walk-way down the hill to the left leads to the **Vice-Chancellor's office** in Delhi University. During the visit of King George V in 1911 these grounds were the site of the royal camp. In 1912, today's building was put up as a temporary Viceroy's house while the capital of the Raj was shifted to New Delhi from Kolkata (Calcutta). A modest building compared to the great palace that was later built in the city, about all that it retains of its former grandeur is marble flooring in some of the rooms. It was in the room that is today used as the registrar's office that, in 1922, Lieutenant Lord Mountbatten proposed to Miss Edwina Ashley; the future Countess Mountbatten was a guest of the Viceroy, Lord Reading.

The Coronation Durbar Site: It was several miles to the northwest that possibly the most splendid spectacle of the whole British period took place in December, 1911 the Coronation Durbar, to which King George V summoned the rulers and people of India. Two large semi-circles formed the embankments from which spectators could watch the proceedings; these still stand. The pageantry was so elaborate that Delhi heralds were specially created for the occasion. The King unexpectedly spoke, and made a historic pronouncement:

> "We are pleased to announce to our people that on the advice of our ministers, tendered after consultation with our Governor-General in Council, we have decided upon the transfer of the seat of the Government of India from Calcutta to the ancient capital of India."

British officers after pig-sticking on the Ridge.

In the hugh amphitheatre, not many could have heard his actual words, but within minutes the news had spread – to delight or dismay, according to the point of view. As a royal fiat the change was beyond political argument, but many recalled that Delhi was the graveyard of dynasties. Others prophesied that Bengal as a centre of power was finished. Both points proved to be correct: from its official completion in 1931 to Independence, British New Delhi lasted but sixteen years, while Kolkata's influence on the Government of India, once predominant, has since been eclipsed.

To mollify the Bengalis, it was also announced that the 1905 division of their homeland would be annulled (Bengal was partitioned yet again in 1947). Later, the King and Queen each laid hastily prepared foundation stones for the new capital. The secret of the transfer had been so closely guarded that no planners or engineers had been consulted about the actual site: when the technically qualified team arrived several years later in 1912, their opinion was that the Durbar area was not suitable for the project. The foundation stones were quietly removed and were eventually built into the east walls (beneath the towers) of today's North and South blocks of the New Delhi Secretariat.

In the 1960s some of the statues of British worthies that once loftily overlooked the streets of Delhi were brought to a specially built enclosure within the Durbar site. Some never arrived and just disappeared along the way; some, elsewhere in India, have been accepted as history and remain when they were unveiled.

The most impressive work is the 1936 memorial to King George V which once stood beneath the Lutyens canopy at India Gate. Appropriately for the present site, the King is wearing his coronation velvet and ermine robe, as he did on that day in December 1911, with the train falling 3 m (10 ft) below.

The Ridge as it exists today.

The sculptor was Charles Jagger, who made the nearby statue of Lord Harding, then Governor-General.

Also present are statues of Lord Irwin (later to be Lord Halifax) and Lord Willingdon, both by Reid Dick. Lord Irwin's statue was paid for by public subscription and one can only assume that money was tight, for it is in limestone, rather than marble and has been badly eroded by the Delhi smog. The fourth statue, circa 1935, seems to be that of Lord Chelmsford (there is no inscription), who in 1916 found himself suddenly transferred from his unit in the Simla Hills, where he was a Territorial Army captain, to the Viceregal Palace. The sculptor was M.S. Nagappa of Madras.

Queen Victoria, who sat in bronze majesty on her throne outside Delhi Town Hall in Chandni Chowk for almost 50 years, came here with the others but was slightly vandalised and has now been moved to the Delhi College of Art opposite the Supreme Court.

The centrepiece of the arena is a polished granite column on a high stepped plinth to mark the position of the royal thrones. Amazingly, a bronze plaque in true imperial style is still in position.

The words speak of an age long gone:

> "Here on the 12th day of December 1911, His Imperial Majesty George V, Emperor of India, in solemn Durbar announced in person to the governors, princes and peoples of India his coronation celebrated in England on the 22nd day of June 1911 and received from them their dutiful homage and allegiance."

For those with no particular interest in the British period, the site of the Durbar – not only in 1911, but also previous gatherings in 1877 and 1903 – is a wilderness with no significant monuments on the scale of many to be seen in Delhi; but for others it is a powerful evocation of the pomp, arrogance and folly which marked the height of British colonial rule in India.

Below left, World War II graves in Ridge cemetery. Below right, King George V, forlorn in Coronation Park, once stood under Lutyens' canopy near India Gate.

KC
HAMAN
P.K

THE OLD FORT

The Purana Qila, or Old Fort, was the citadel of the second of the great Mughal emperors, Humayun (1530-40 and 1555-56), and once stood on the banks of the river Yamuna. Its majestic, crumbling walls lie to the east of the Mathura Road. The fort is believed to mark the site of Indraprastha, the magnificent capital built by the Pandava brothers, the heroes of the *Mahabharata* epic. There was a village called Inderpat, a derivation of Indraprastha, actually inside the walls until the British moved it out at the time of the construction of New Delhi. During excavations a kind of pottery called Painted Grey Ware, dating from around 1000 BC, was found in the fort.

Humayun built his capital of Din Panah here. The citadel we see today, however, was the work of Sher Shah Suri (1540-45), an able ruler of Afghan descent, who rebelled against Humayun and forced him to flee the country. During his brief reign Sher Shah reformed the administration and built the Grand Trunk Road, now called Sher Shah Suri Marg, still the country's main arterial route. His successors were not so competent, and Humayun managed to regain his kingdom.

Opposite the main entrance to the fort, on the other side of the Mathura Road, you see the impressive Sher Shah gate, thought to be one of the entrances to the sprawling city of Delhi over which the Afghan ruled. Beside it to the north is the **Khairu'l Manazil Mosque** built in 1561, during the reign of the emperor Akbar. The drive to the main western gateway of the fort is lined by stalls vending tea, snacks and ice cream. The double-storey gate is built of red sandstone, and topped by *chatris*.

Two outstanding buildings remain. The first is the attractive **Qal'a-i-Kuhna mosque**, built by Sher Shah in 1541 on one of the highest points in the fort. The mosque is midway in style between the solid mosques of the Sultanate period, and the graceful ones of the later Mughal period. Nearby is an octagonal pavilion of red sandstone known as the **Sher Mandal**. It is believed to have been the library of Humayun, from where he slipped down the stairs to his death. Surrounded by trees is **Maharani Kunti's temple**, where there is an image of Kunti, the mother of the Pandavas.

From the ramparts you look out over the main railway line between Delhi and Mumbai. To the north are the modern pavilions of Delhi's Exhibition Grounds, and to the south the green expanse of the **National Zoological Park**. Underneath the eastern walls of the fort, by the Pragati Maidan bus stand, is the **Bhairon temple**, popular with Delhiites, who offer libations of whisky to Bhairon, a form of Shiva. This temple reputedly dates back to the *Mahabharata* era, and the main images of Bhairon, the monkey god Hanuman and the Pandava brother Bhima, are rocks painted silver and orange with great eyes. A more modern image of Bhairon shows him holding a human head in one hand and a bottle in the other. At his feet is the black dog which is his mount.

North of the Purana Qila: Pragati Maidan hosts the international trade fair each November, and numerous other fairs throughout the year. It also has a fun fair called **Appu Ghar**, after Appu the Elephant who was the mascot of the Asian Games in 1982. On the other side of the road are the domes of India's Supreme Court.

Near the junction of the Mathura Road and Bhairon Marg, next to the museum, is the shrine of a Muslim saint, known as **Matka Shah**. From the road you can see trees festooned with large, round clay water-pots called *matkas*. The saint's tomb stands here on a small hill which, in the 13th century, was on the banks of the Yamuna. The saint attracted a following and the Sultan

Preceding pages, Purana Qila, the Old Fort built by Sher Shah as his capital. Left, Humayan's tomb seen through the main gate.

Balban is said to have tested him by sending him mud and iron as a gift of food. The saint's prayers turned the iron into chickpeas and the mud into jaggery (sugar derived from date palm sap). The water in his *matka* turned miraculously to milk and all the assembled populace were fed. Nowadays visitors come to the tomb for help and if their wishes are granted they return with a *matka*, chickpeas, sugar and milk as thanks.

At the northern end of the Mathura Road is a major road junction. The turning to the north is Bahadur Shah Zafar Marg, India's Fleet Street. Here are the offices of two of the country's leading dailies, *The Times of India* and the *Indian Express* and their Hindi language publications, the *Navbharat Times* and the *Jansatta*. Here too, in Nehru House, is **Shankar's International Doll Museum**.

Just north of the newspaper offices is a turning into a large parking area by the walls of **Feroze Shah Kotla**, the fifth city of Delhi, built by Feroze Shah Tughlaq (1351-88). Its citadel once lay on the banks of the Yamuna. Unfortunately, little remains of the splendour of Feroze Shah's capital, as much of the more useful stone was carted off in the 17th century to build what is now known as Old Delhi.

Painted figurine in Sundernagar antique shop.

The citadel was made up of two large quadrangles. The northern ruins are set in a pleasant park. You enter through the remains of a huge barbicaned gate. Inside, the most remarkable monument resembles a step pyramid on top of which stands a polished stone Ashokan pillar. This pillar had been set up in Ambala on the orders of the emperor Ashoka (273–232 BC). Feroze Shah ordered that it be brought to Delhi to be a monument for future generations. Ingeniously, a huge bed of silk cotton was prepared, into which the column fell when it was removed from its base, and a carriage with 42 wheels, pulled by over 8,000 men, took it to the banks of the Yamuna from where it was transported to Delhi by boat.

Nearby is the **Jama Masjid**, one of the largest mosques of the Sultanate period, built in 1354. It stands on a base in which there are a number of cells. Amir Timur, the Tamerlane or Tamburlaine of English literature, and an ancestor of the Mughals, prayed in the mosque after plundering the city in 1398. He returned to Samarkand soon after, his caravan loaded down with goods and captives, including skilled craftsmen to help build his capital.

The southern quadrangle of Feroze Shah Kotla is occupied by the village of Vikramnagar. The village appears to have been in its place under the walls for centuries. In fact, most of the inhabitants are refugee families from Pakistan who came to Delhi in 1947 and are still waiting to be given permanent accommodation by the government. To the north of the ruins are the famous Feroze Shah Kotla cricket grounds, where most test matches in Delhi are played, and the Ambedkar stadium.

In the centre of Bahadur Shah Zafar

Marg, just north of the entrance to the ruins and opposite the Maulana Azad Medical College, stands the **Khuni Darwaza**, or Bloody Gate. It was here that Lieutenant Hodson shot dead two sons of the last Mughal, Bahadur Shah Zafar, in 1858.

South of the Purana Qila: **The National Zoological Park**, which covers 75 hectares (186 acres), houses some 1,600 animals and attracts nearly three million visitors a year. The zoo is also a great attraction for migratory ducks and other wild birds. During the winter several thousand pintails, spotbills, common teal and shovelers share the ponds. Between September and November painted storks nest in the trees, while the heronry is active roughly between April and July. The zoo keeps rare white tigers and has been successful in breeding the endangered lion-tailed macaque and brow-antlered deer.

Heading south down the Mathura Road from the zoo entrance you pass **Sunder Nagar market**. During the festival of Divali, you have to fight through the crowds and plead with the staff before you can buy sweets here. There are also several reliable jewellers and craft shops which specialise in antiques, or high quality reproductions.

Further south you come to a historic roundabout at the junction of Lodi Road and the Mathura road, which has in its centre an octagonal tomb with a double dome covered with tiles. This tomb dates from the early Mughal period, and is the only one in Delhi built in a typical Central Asian style. Its name, Sabz Burj, means "Green Tower", but the new tiles fixed on its dome by the Archaeological Survey are bright blue.

The eastern turning from the roundabout takes you to the gates of **Humayun's tomb**, the finest Mughal building in Delhi and architecturally the predecessor of the Taj Mahal at Agra.

Passing through the modern iron gates you enter **Bu Halima's garden**. The southern wall of the garden has steps leading through a stone doorway

Step-well among the ruins of Feroze Shah Kotla.

into an octagonal enclosure with the air of a secret garden. In the centre is the octagonal **tomb of Isa Khan**, a nobleman at the court of Sher Shah Suri. A small, three-domed mosque is attached to it, with some of its original turquoise tiles intact.

At the end of Bu Halima's garden is a large gate, where you buy entrance tickets for the tomb. Beyond is an avenue of banyan trees leading to the tomb's main gate. To the right of the gate is the entrance to a garden in which stand **Afsarwala's mosque and tomb**.

The main gate to the mausoleum, like the one before it, is aligned perfectly with the centre of the monument. It acts as a screen, and your first glimpse inside it is like looking into another world. Humayun's tomb stands on a raised platform and is built mainly of red sandstone. Its symmetrical arches are surmounted by a white marble dome, with *chatris* around it.

The Emperor Humayun's senior widow, Bega Begum, supervised the construction, which was completed in 1565. The emperor's grave lies at ground level in a chamber occupied by bats, and his cenotaph is above in the tomb's main hall underneath the double dome. The last Mughal, Bahadur Shah Zafar, took refuge in the tomb after Delhi fell to the British in 1858.

The tomb stands in a Mughal garden, divided into squares by water channels. To the southeast of Humayun's tomb is the smaller **Barbar's Tomb**. Barbar's identity remains a mystery. There is a pavilion on the garden's eastern wall which once would have looked out over the Yamuna. Now the view is of the railway line. To the south is the turquoise-tiled **Nila Gumbad**, or Blue Dome, a tomb believed to have been built in 1625 for the faithful retainer of a nobleman. To the north is the shiny white dome of the recently built gurudwara, or Sikh temple, **Damdama Sahib**. The gurudwara marks the spot where the last of the Sikh Gurus, Guru Gobind Singh, met the Mughal emperor

Humayun's tomb, the precursor of the Taj Mahal.

Bahadur Shah I in 1707. The emperor wanted to stage an elephant fight between his elephant and the Guru's. But the Guru maintained that a male buffalo of Punjab was as good as any imperial elephant and, the Sikhs say, he was right: the imperial elephant fled in terror from the buffalo.

The road to the gurudwara runs around the northern walls of Humayun's tomb, past the Sundar nursery to the north, and the Bharat Scouts and Guides Training Centre.

Opposite the New Horizon School is a small and peaceful *dargah*, enshrining the remains of a contemporary of Hazrat Nizamuddin. Beside the tomb of this saint is a tree said to be over 750 years old, which, according to local people, produces sugar from its leaves at the height of summer. Devotees eat the leaves of this tree to solve their problems, and tie coloured threads around its trunk. Hence the name of the shrine – the **Patte Wali Dargah** (Shrine of Leaves).

Back on the Mathura road heading south, you pass through the residential area of Nizamuddin. To the east, near the turning to Nizamuddin Railway Station, is the massive square tomb of Abd'ur Rahim Khar Khan-i-Khanan, a poet and general who served the Mughal emperors Akbar and Jahangir, and died in 1627.

West of Humayun's Tomb: Driving westwards down Lodi Road, you pass the Muslim village of Nizamuddin, tall blocks of government buildings, and the huge floodlights of the Jawaharlal Nehru stadium, built for the Asian Games in 1982, to the south. On the northern side of the road is Delhi's Golf Course and Lodi Gardens, named after the Lodi dynasty which preceded the Mughals. During weekends it is invaded by picnickers. Amongst all this activity stand plain stone tombs of the Sultanate period.

To the south, near the Lodi Road, is the octagonal **tomb of Muhammad Shah** (1434-44) of the Saiyyid dynasty.

A couple in Lodi Gardens stroll past the tomb of Sultan Muhammad Shah.

In the centre of the park is the **Bara Gumbad**, or Great Dome, an imposing tomb of a nobleman of the Lodi period.

Adjoining it is a mosque of ashlar stone, decorated with inscriptions from the Quran. About 50 m (160 feet) to the north is a large, square tomb known as the **Shish Gumbad**, or Glazed Dome. It dates from the Lodi period although the occupant is unknown. Sikandar Lodi (1489-1517) is buried in an octagonal tomb which stands in a walled enclosure in the northern part of the gardens, near an ornamental lake. Over the lake is a Mughal bridge, probably built in the latter half of the 16th century.

Along the eastern side of the gardens runs Lodi Estate, site of the India International Centre, a club with a fine library and well patronised bar open to members only. However, the frequent concerts of music and dance held in its auditorium are open to the general public. Northeast of the gardens is **Khan Market**, which sells everything from spare parts for cars to fruit and flowers, Marmite and medicines. It also has several good bookshops which specialise in books on India.

At the western end of Lodi Road is one of the city's main landmarks, **Safdarjang's tomb**. Its bulbous white dome rises above the walls of the extensive Mughal garden surrounding it. The mausoleum is faced with stone removed from Khan-i-Khanan's tomb in Nizamuddin, and it represents the final flowering of Mughal architecture in Delhi. Safdarjang was a powerful nobleman at a time of enfeebled emperors, and played a major role in the civil wars which shook the kingdom during his lifetime. He was also one of the founders of the ruling family of Avadh, who governed independently of the emperor in Delhi and developed the city of Lucknow into a centre of cultural and artistic excellence. Shuja-ud-Daula, Safdarjang's son and successor in Avadh, spent 300,000 rupees on his father's tomb, the last great mausolea to be built in the Mughal capital.

Safdarjang's Late Mughal tomb, at the apex of Lodi Road.

THE LIVING MUSEUM

On the southwestern corner of Pragati Maidan, facing the imposing ruins of the Old Fort, is the 3-hectare (8-acre) site of a living museum of the traditional arts of India. Few other countries in the world have the wealth and variety of arts which India has, and to describe them as crafts is perhaps misleading. Traditionally, Indians never made a distinction: the Sanskrit word *shilpi* means both artist and artisan. The National Handicrafts and Handlooms Museum has a collection of over 20,000 items, from textiles to terracotta, from wall paintings to grass baskets, and from toys to images of the gods. The aim of the museum has been to collect the best examples of Indian craftwork and to serve as a centre for the revival and development of skills.

The museum is in three parts. The main building has galleries housing exhibits from the villages, temples and courts of India, as well as a library and laboratory where older and more fragile pieces are restored. The museum's architect, Charles Correa, has been careful to design a building which harmonises with the exhibits. The walls are mud-coloured, and there are several courtyards open to the sky, surrounded by verandahs with traditional tiled roofs. Outside the temple gallery stands a *rath*, an enormous wooden chariot from western India, on which images of the gods would be drawn through the streets during festivals. In the newly built section of the museum is an entirely wooden *haveli*, a traditional house from Gujarat ornately carved. Among the rarest pieces are huge wooden Bhuta statues, Adivasi deities from coastal Karnataka.

The museum's collection of rare textiles is enlarged by expert weavers who are permanently on the staff and will spend up to eight months recreating saris of traditional design. The museum shop has a fascinating selection of goods for sale, and it is possible to buy from the artisans at work on the site.

Nearby is the festival square, where every month from October to June the museum invites a number of expert workers from different parts of the country to demonstrate and sell their art. In one place you can see miniature paintings of the hill schools from Himachal Pradesh, huge terracotta images from Tamil Nadu, shawls from Gujarat, *ganjifa* or playing cards from Orissa and bamboo-work from Assam. Schoolchildren are invited to learn from the artists and proudly walk off at the end of their visit with what they have made with their own hands. The staff of the museum make a photographic record of the techniques, tools and art of the visiting craftspeople.

The third part of the museum consists of a village complex, where villagers have built examples of their own traditional houses and shrines. There is a small building typical of Kullu in the Himalayas. There is a hut from the Andaman Islands, and a round thatched home of the Banni community in Gujarat, complete with a multi-storey hen house. Peacocks meander past the semi-circular hut of the Toda peoples of the Nilgiri Hills, who for years have tended their sacred buffaloes on the high downs.

The museum also has open-air theatres, where performances by rural artists are organised and you can hear the music of village and Adivasi India. The museum's publications provide you with a visual record of the variety of traditional Indian arts.

As part of the project to record and preserve India's traditional arts and crafts, the museum has an excellent reference section containing over 15,000 items. This is open to use by visiting researchers, craftspeople and designers.

Right, singer performing at the Crafts Museum.

NIZAMUDDIN

The modern, middle-class residential area of Nizamuddin has in its western half a medieval village known as the Nizamuddin *basti*. Twisting narrow lanes run between old houses which are rapidly being built upon to accommodate a rising population. The bazaar is crowded with stalls selling fruit, prayer mats and beads, the white caps which Muslims wear, perfume or *itr*, antimony or *surma* for the eyes, sticks for chewing to clean teeth, and Islamic literature. Small restaurants with rows of shiny pots on stoves do a roaring trade in *biryani*, mutton curry and *tanduri roti*. It is like a piece of Old Delhi in New Delhi. But the Old Delhi we know today was only founded in the 17th century; Nizamuddin's village is much older. It has grown up since the 13th century when Hazrat Nizamuddin, one of the greatest of India's Muslim saints, chose the area to live and work in.

His shrine, or *dargah*, now draws tens of thousands of visitors every year, especially to the two festivals or Urs which mark the anniversaries of the passing of the saint and of Amir Khusrau, one of the most talented poets and musicians of his age and a devout follower of Hazrat Nizamuddin. The great Muslim festival of 'Id marking the end of the month-long Ramadan fast, often falls in the same month as the Urs of Hazrat Nizamuddin; Amir Khusrau's falls in Shavval, the 11th month of the Muslim calendar. Before the Urs, fairground stalls are set up on the northern edge of the village. *Parathas*, a kind of Indian bread almost a metre (3 ft) wide are fried in great iron pans to be eaten with semolina *halva*. The biggest crowds come at night to hear the music of the *qavvals*, who sing *qavvalis*, particularly those composed by Amir Khusrau, in praise of God, of the Prophet, and of the great saints – Hazrat Nizamuddin and Amir Khusrau.

The *dargah* has two entrances, one to the north, and the main one to the south. The route to the latter gives a flavour of the *basti* atmosphere. Take the turning into the main bazaar by the Nizamuddin Police station on the Mathura road. Past the taxi stand on your left, the road quickly becomes more crowded with customers for the restaurants and stalls, pilgrims and students of a modern six-storey Islamic college, or *madrasa*. The *madrasa* adjoins the large Bari or **Bangle Wali** mosque. Opposite, the *basti*'s most comprehensive Islamic bookshop stands on the corner of the alley which leads to a branch of the famous Karim's restaurant. Beyond the alley you see a medieval stone doorway on your left. Enter it and you find yourself in a walled yard, with a roofed hall on your left which is used at festival times. There are a few crumbling tombs – some of the many in this area, as devotees of Hazrat Nizamuddin down the centuries have wished to be buried near his shrine. In the right hand wall of the courtyard is a gate which leads through to a finely carved marble pavilion, the **Chaunsath Khamba**, or Hall of 64 Columns. The hall is surrounded by a latticed marble screen and covered by a roof of 25 domes. Inside is the marble tomb of Mirza Aziz Kokaltash, carved with floral decorations and marked with the date 1033 AH (1623-24 AD). Mirza was the son of the wet nurse of Akbar, perhaps the greatest of the Mughal emperors. The nine other tombs in the pavilions probably mark the graves of members of his family.

Returning to the main bazaar, you come to the modern **Ghalib Academy**. Ghalib (1796-1869) was a poet of enormous sensitivity, humanity and humour who belonged to the court of the last Mughal emperor and lived through the troubled period of the Mutiny or First War of Indian Independence, the defeat of the rebels, and the vengeful treatment of Delhi's inhabitants by the victorious British. He is considered one of the greatest Urdu poets and the Academy has a library with many of his works, including translations. The watchman there keeps the key to the compound south of the Chaunsath Khamba, site of the poet's modest marble tomb, which is generally covered with strings of roses left by admirers. From his tomb, you can see to the north the dome of the Lal Mahal, or Red Palace, a 13th century building which has been renovated and turned into a family home.

Ignoring lanes swerving off north and south, and passing some of the *basti*'s numerous buffalo meat shops, you realise you are approaching the *dargah*. Lines of stalls sell strings of red roses, incense, packets of small white sweets and *chadars*, cloths decorated with gold tinsel, to offer at the tombs of the saints. The lane widens, flanked by meat shops and restaurants, before you take the plunge into a tunnel of flower-selling stalls which winds to the gate of the *dargah*. At several corners there are shoe-keepers who will look after your footwear, forbidden inside the shrine. Just before the main entrance, there is a stone doorway through which you can climb to the well-proportioned domed tomb of Ataga Khan, the father of Mirza Aziz Kokaltash, and husband of Ji Ji Anga, a wet nurse of the Emperor Akbar. Ataga Khan was an important courtier but met an untimely end in 1562 at the hands of Adham Khan, son of Maham Anga, another of the emperor's wet nurses.

When you enter the main courtyard of the **dargah**, the atmosphere becomes more peaceful. Most visitors come on Wednesdays and Thursday. You can still see *bishtis*, water carriers, filling their traditional goatskins from taps. This is where **Hazrat Nizamuddin** (1236-1325) worshipped for many of his 90 years and where he is buried. He was a member of the Chisti order of Muslim mystics or Sufis and the spiritual successor of Shaikh Farid Shakarganj. As an earlier mystic put it,

Supplicants at Hazrat Nizamuddin's shrine.

"The Sufi is like the earth on which every foul thing is thrown and from which only fair things come forth." The Chisti order used, and still use, music to help reach a state of spiritual ecstasy. Unlike some orthodox Muslims, they do not believe that this is "unIslamic". The saint and his followers had no possessions but relied entirely on God for sustenance. During his lifetime Hazrat Nizamuddin attracted a huge number of devotees – laymen and disciples, Hindu and Muslim, who gave up the world to follow him. He refused gifts of land, and spent gifts of money on the poor. He is said to have wept "because of the worldly prestige given to him which did not please him at all, and if at any time he received valuable gifts, he wept all the more and intensified his spiritual endeavour". He understood and shared the sorrows of the ordinary people with whom he preferred to live closely. To them he was a holy man and a worker of miracles. The size of his following unnerved several of the seven Sultans of Delhi through whose rule he lived; firstly, because the state's power was not entirely stable, and secondly because the saint mistrusted rulers. However, the Sultans who were hostile to him never lived long enough to do him harm.

After his death Hazrat Nizamuddin's tomb became a shrine, and the position of Pir, or spiritual head, became hereditary rather than a reward for spiritual effort. The present Pir traces his ancestry back to the sister of Hazrat Nizamuddin (the saint remained celibate), and to the Prophet himself. Over the centuries the rules of poverty gradually slackened. The austere path of the Sufis is difficult to follow. Some 200 families, descendants of the saint's sister and disciples, and of servants of the shrine, still depend on the *dargah* for their livelihood. It comes mainly from the donations of visitors, Hindu as well as Muslim, who revere the saint and believe prayers at his shrine can achieve

Contrasting architecture of the later Chisti tomb at Fatehpur Sikri

wonders. The donations also provide for the upkeep of the shrine, and on request will be used to feed the poor.

The courtyard of the *dargah* has numerous tombs, and around it are the offices of various descendants of the saint's followers and family. A margosa tree shades the red stone screens of the tomb of Amir Khusrau, Hazrat Nizamuddin's most celebrated disciple. A poet, he wrote in Persian and in the local language of the time, an old form of Hindi. His Hindi poetry is still popular to this day, and sung at the *dargah*.

Further to the middle of the courtyard are marble screens surrounding two sets of tombs. In the eastern enclosure, nearest the entrance to the *dargah*, are the tomb of the Mughal emperor Muhammed Shah (1719-48), and those of two brothers of the last Mughal, Bahadur Shah Zafar and Azam Shah. In the further enclosure is the grave of the talented daughter of the emperor Shahjahan, Jahanara (d.1681). Shahjahan had built the Taj Mahal as a tomb for her mother, but her simple tomb is filled with earth. An inscription reads:

"Let naught cover my grave save for the green grass: for grass well suffices as a covering for the grave of the lowly."

To the north of these graves is the tomb of the saint himself, surmounted by an onion dome with a gold pinnacle, and surrounded by verandahs and finely carved marble screens. The basic structure of this tomb dates from the 16th century, but many changes and additions were made later, notably the floral paintings on the exterior. According to tradition, women are not allowed inside the tomb. However, many sit on the verandahs reading the Quran, peer through the marble screens, or tie threads or pieces of cloth to the screen – symbols of requests made to the saint. If their wish is granted they will return to offer decorated *chadars* to cover the tomb, and offer money to feed the poor. Inside, male devotees with covered heads offer prayers, flowers, and incense. Outside, musicians sing *qavvalis* or religious songs.

If you approached by one of the servants of the *dargah* asking if you would "Sign the book", this is a request for a donation, and some small gift of money is customary.

To the west of the tomb is a large mosque, which also serves as a dormitory during festivals. It was built in 1325 by a son of Sultan Ala-u-ddin Khilji, one of the saint's admirers, and has a lotus bud fringe to its great arches. Muslims pray here throughout the day as well as at the five prescribed times.

To the north of Hazrat Nizamuddin's tomb is a passage which leads to a large *baoli*, or stepwell. The well was built during the reign of Sultan Ghiyas-ud-din Tughlaq (1320-25), and is fed by several springs. Legend has it that it was built at night by workers who were building Tughlaqabad during the day, after the sultan had forbidden them to work for anyone else during the day. It

Offering incense – a practice adapted from Hindu rituals.

is believed that bathing or drinking the water will treat incurable diseases, although the water now looks very unhygienic. A passage running north from the well leads to the northern entrance to the *dargah*.

There are several buildings from pre-Mughal times worth seeing in the *basti*. The most notable is the **Kali Masjid**, a fort-like mosque built by the prime minister of Sultan Feroze Shah Tughlaq in 1370-1371. This mosque stands on the south-eastern edge of the village. It is in use and has recently been given a new floor of polished marble. Massive stone pillars support the domed roof of a verandah which runs round the edge of the courtyard, and two covered ways which cross the courtyard, dividing it into four equal parts. Although most of the village population is Muslim, near the mosque's main eastern entrance live members of the low-caste Valmiki community. They are named after the author of the Hindu epic, the *Ramayana*. There is a small Valmiki temple around the back of the mosque, with a statue of the sage sitting on a leopard skin, writing the *Ramayana*.

To the north of the village is the Bara-Khamba or Twelve-pillared hall, a square building with a central chamber and with three arches on each side. It was probably a tomb. To the west, completely hemmed in by houses, and divided into a number of different living compartments, is an extremely ruinous but very fine early octagonal tomb belonging to the Khan-i-Jahan Tilangani, the prime minister of Feroze Shah Tughlaq.

A lane runs round the western edge of the village. To the west you see a new pink Hindu temple, decorated with colourful concrete images of the gods, and a night shelter for the destitute. Along this lane on the eastern side is a new and spotlessly clean *dargah*, containing the tomb of another mystic, Inayat Khan Sufi, who has a large following of devotees in Europe and the United States.

Below left, *qavvalis* (devotional songs) are sung before the tomb of the saint. Below right, bookshops sell Islamic literature.

Eating The Muslim Way

Close by the Jama Masjid in Old Delhi, and down a narrow lane in Nizamuddin are Karim's restaurants, owned and run by a family among whose ancestors were chefs to the Mughal emperors.

Originally from Saudi Arabia, they settled in India where they specialised in preparing meat dishes cooked with curd, *ghi* and spices for their royal patrons. In 1857, at the time of the First War of Indian Independence, the family fled Delhi, along with thousands of others, and lived for more than 30 years in a village in what is now Uttar Pradesh. In the 1890s Haji Karimuddin, the great-grandfather of the present owner, returned to Delhi with two great ambitions: to bring this royal food to the the rest of the population, and to win fame and fortune. In 1913 he opened the original Karim's in Gali Kababiyan, Matia Mahal bazaar, a stone's throw from the Jama Masjid in Old Delhi, and succeeded in both ambitions. In 1974 Karim's opened in Nizamuddin, the only genuine branch of the Jama Masjid restaurant.

Rumali roti and _masala chops_: delicious food from Karim's.

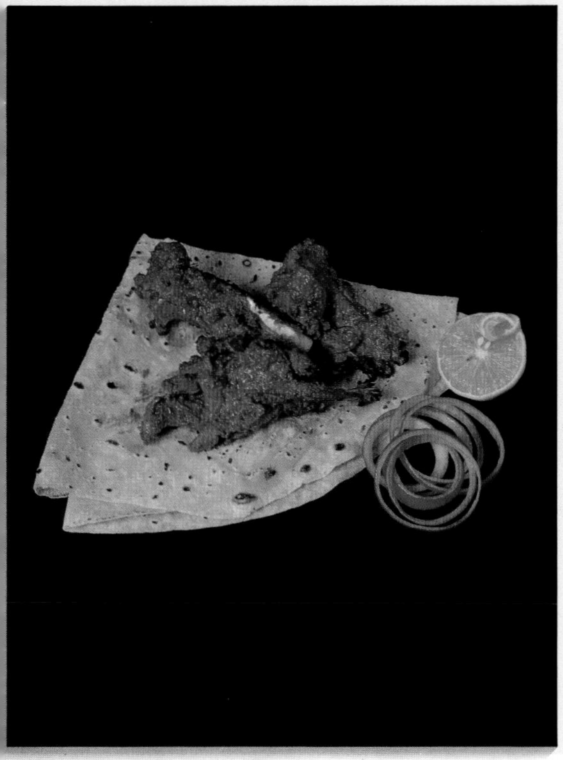

Wasimuddin, who runs the restaurant, explains that the family recipes are still a closely guarded secret, kept even from the cooks in the restaurant's kitchens. The women in the family mix and grind the spices at home – 32 different ones go into the special *garam masala* alone. The spice mixtures are then given ready-made to the cooks. The women also make Karim's celebrated *khir*, a preparation of milk and rice covered with edible silver foil and set in earthenware dishes, which give the sweet a unique flavour.

Over half the restaurant's sales, says Wasimuddin, are made up of the *tanduri* specialties, cooked in huge charcoal-fed *tandurs*, or ovens. On request he will roast a whole goat, but most customers are satisfied with *tanduri ran*, or leg of lamb (as cooked goat is known), and *tanduri* chicken. The kebabs include *tanduri burras*, lamb chops, and *sikh kebabs*, minced meat on skewers. *Sikh kebabs* were invented, according to Wasimuddin, for an emperor who had toothache and couldn't chew his meat. Another large *tandur* is used to cook *nans* and *tanduri roti*, made of leavened dough. The cook uses iron rods to retrieve the bread a few seconds after it has been slapped on the inner wall of the hot *tandur*.

Among the Mughal delicacies Wasimuddin says were favoured by royalty are the *Akbari Murgh Masala*, a fragrant chicken dish cooked with curd, *Makhani Murgh-e-Jahangiri*, chicken cooked with butter and select spices, and *Jahangiri Qorma*, a rich mutton curry. A lighter dish is the *Badshahi Badam Pasanda*, a universal favourite, which consists of mutton escalopes chopped and cooked with almonds, curd and a secret combination of spices. *Nargisi Kofta*, named after the nargis or narcissus, are mutton balls stuffed with eggs. The *Shahi Murg-Do-Piyaza* is especially low in chillies and suits the stomachs of visitors new to India. Among rice dishes are chicken and mutton *biryanis*. The food, by modern standards, appears rich, but Wasimuddin maintains that, because of the choice of spices and careful cooking, it is easy to digest. You can wash down your meal with *jal jira* (cumin water), *lassi* (yoghurt) or syrupy *sherbet*.

Karim's also serves an excellent creamy black dal and several vegetable dishes, but these cannot match the variety and taste of the meat preparations.

Karim's is closed on Mondays. During the Muslim month of fasting, Ramadan, it opens when the Muslim community eats – after dark and before dawn.

THE CITIES OF THE SOUTH

In the triangle enclosed by the Ridge and the Yamuna river lie, not the conventional "seven cities" of Delhi but as many as fifteen different Delhis. But a map showing the successive cities of the Delhi area has little consonance with the modern map. The pressure on urban land has drastically changed the landscape, so that to identify the boundaries needs imagination. Of these, the first four are in the south, and the next three are further north, on the river, Delhi 8 and 9 were the British Civil Lines, in the far north, and Lutyens' Delhi, centred between the oldest Delhis and Shahjahanabad.

Until the 1960s, Delhi was informally categorised as "Old" and "New", to distinguish the older cities from the currently settled one. Today "Old" and "New" persist in official terminology, but the average citizen uses the terms "North", "West", "South", "East" and "Central" – an indication of the urban sprawl. In this Greater Delhi many old townships have been swallowed up. They have certain common features – a cluster of old monuments, with an adjacent village settlement; in most cases the fields of the villages have been taken over for housing estates, so that both monument and "urban village" are hemmed in by modern "colonies". Lord Curzon's enthusiasm led to many of the major monuments being "protected" and their environs landscaped, but many of the smaller buildings have disappeared or are quite hidden.

Preceding pages, colourful *tazias* carried in procession during the Muslim festival of Muharram. Left, the *dargah* in Mehrauli, visited by Hindus and Muslims alike.

A local saying lists the three things necessary for setting up a town – *badshah, badal, dariya* – a king, clouds and a river. The Yamuna was a useful means of transportation, the clouds brought the rains which filled the storage tanks necessary for Delhi's arid climate, and the kings used the landscape of Delhi to site their cities and its rock to build their palaces. In the 13th century the Il-baris occupied the city of Prithviraj Chauhan on the Ridge (it continues to be called Qila Rai Pithaura) and contributed some beautiful pieces of architecture, to be seen in the Qatb Minar complex. Alauddin Khilji (1290-1316) built a new palace at Siri, in the plains. The Tughlaq dynasty, in a span of less than a century, built three fort-palaces – Tughlaqabad, Jahanpanah and Feroze Shah Kotla.

This chapter introduces you to the four southern cities – Mehrauli and the Qatb Minar complex, Siri, Tughlaqabad and Jahanpanah. The French traveller Rousselet who visited Delhi over a century ago strongly recommended that the Qatb Minar should be saved till the end, but the order of viewing will obviously depend on the visitor's convenience.

The surviving buildings are relics of urban cultures where beautiful gardens, cool and colourful interiors, elaborate ritual and a vibrant cosmopolitan culture contributed to make Delhi the rival of Baghdad and Isfahan. Though so much has been lost, the well built and intelligently ventilated structures and the painstaking artisanship speak for themselves.

Mehrauli–Qatb Minar: About 11 km (7 miles) from India Gate, Mehrauli has been continuously inhabited since the 12th century, if not earlier. Until 60 years ago, Mehrauli was separate from Delhi, a half-day's tonga-ride away. Its mango groves, hills and fields made it a pleasant summer resort for the city dwellers, although most of the groves and fields have now disappeared. Fortunately, the monuments are protected, and this is the Archaeological Survey's showpiece in Delhi; some sections have been landscaped by the Delhi Development Authority. Development is bringing piped water from the river to Mehrauli, but the best potable water you can get is from one of the old wells which are dotted about on the hillside. This area has to be explored in three sections – the Qatb Minar complex, the village of Mehrauli, and some monuments on the Mehrauli–Gurgaon Road.

The Qatb Minar complex: The significance of these monuments, quite apart from their sheer beauty, is that they number many "firsts". Qatb-ud-din Aibak was anxious to proclaim the political victory of Islam in North India, and he speedily did this by demolishing many Hindu temples and using their dressed and carved stone to lay out the first mosque in India – the **Quwwat-ul-Islam** (Victory of Islam) **mosque** – where the columns and the three arches of the prayer-hall's screen bear the stamp of local craftsmen in the manner of their ornamentation. This is seen even more exquisitely in the wavelike effect obtained by using slabs of varying shades of sandstone, in the walls of Iltutmish's tomb in the north-west corner of the complex. Though bereft of its dome, this is noteworthy for being the first known example of the use of the squinch, the technique for laying a dome on a large frame.

In each of the dynasties that ruled Delhi, there was invariably one great builder. For the Il-baris it was Iltutmish, who added many distinctive touches to structures begun by Qatb-ud-din. Ala-u-ddin Khilji added a gatehouse, the **Alai Darwaza**, for the mosque. This is a perfectly proportioned structure, though in photographs it looks squat alongside the Qatb Minar. In it we get the true arch, the shallow dome, the dramatic combination of white marble and red sandstone, geometrical carvings and "lotus bud" fringes – all features to be found in later buildings. Bishop Heber found the words to describe the total effect: "They built like giants, and they finished like jewellers".

The **Iron Pillar** is one of the more puzzling elements in the mosque courtyard. Its inscription proclaims it to be of the 4th century, but does not explain how it came to be where it is. No one has been able to explain how it has

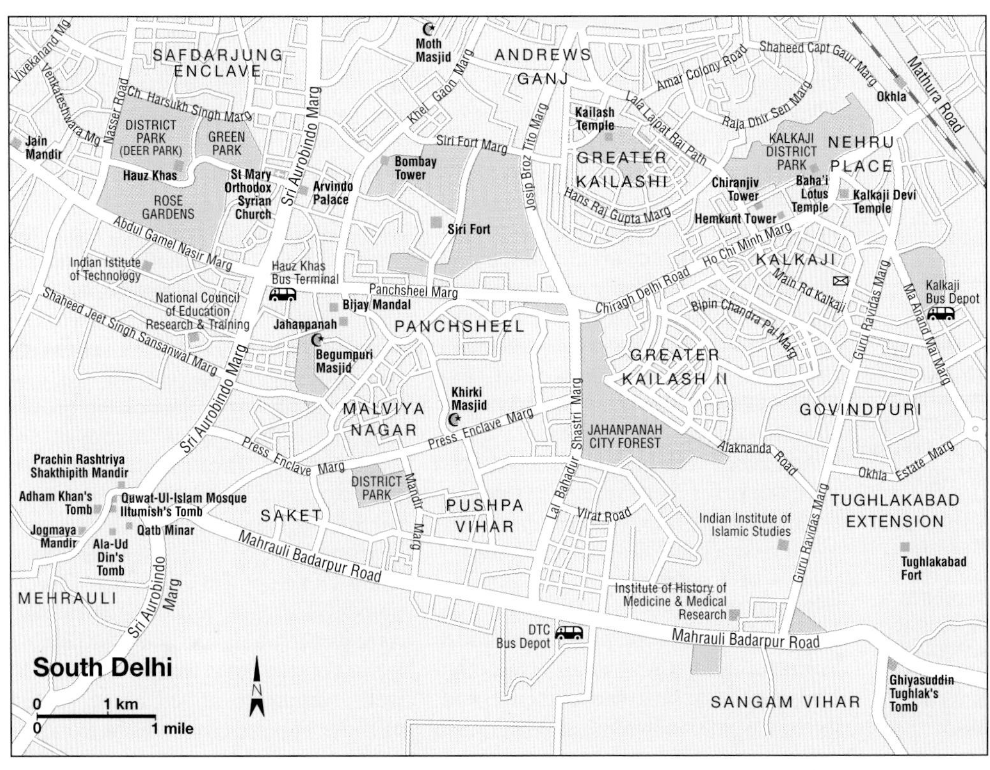

remained free of rust. It tantalises the visitor with the popular belief that the person who can encircle it with their hands held behind their back will have their wish granted (it is now fenced off).

The **Qatb Minar** is also a puzzle: watchtower or minaret of the mosque? It is the joint effort of many individuals – Qatb-ud-din built the first storey, the rest being added by Iltutmish and modified by Feroze Shah Tughlaq who carried out some necessary repairs. The cupola he installed was damaged by earthquake, and a British engineer raised a new one. This was criticised by a later Governor-General, and was accordingly removed; it now stands as a pleasant little canopy on the lawns. Despite being the product of so many hands, the Minar has a remarkable aesthetic integrity, with its rounded and angular flutings and exquisite stalactite-pendentive brackets to support the balconies. Thomas Metcalfe's daughter Emily has delightful descriptions of picnics on the top storey; later visitors were only allowed as far as the first storey. At present no one is allowed into the Minar, because the staircase is judged to be unsafe.

West of the complex is the tomb of Ala-ud-din Khilji, and a *madarsa* (school) established by him. Southeast of the Minar, outside the Qatb complex, is the dilapidated tomb of Quli Khan, which in the 1840s Thomas Metcalfe converted for his own use by extending each of its octagonal sides to make a room. He also felt called upon to contribute to the built landscape of the area by constructing two pyramidal towers near the entrance, a *kos minar* and the towers of a Gothic palace on the further rocks.

Mehrauli: Reached by taking the road to the left as one leaves the complex, Mehrauli is a linear village which, among other things, has a major wholesale vegetable market. At its northern end is the massive octagonal building which is the **tomb of Adham Khan**, a general in the Mughal army in the 16th century; the tomb was built by emperor Akbar, who had himself sentenced Adham Khan to death. If we walk down the village street, on the left is the **shrine of Bakhtiyar Kaki**, a Muslim saint of the early 13th century, whose resting-place has been renovated from time to time. Many of the rulers of Delhi are also buried nearby. Adjacent to the shrine is **Zafar Mahal** (named after the last Mughal emperor Bahadur Shah, whose pen-name was "Zafar"). This three-storey sandstone building of the 18th century, in some ways resembling the entrance-way of the Red Fort, is a reminder of the Mughals' habit of spending some time every year in Mehrauli. Along the busy street one can glimpse the occasional arch or dome that proclaims a period building; many of these are being "renovated" and enlarged beyond recognition. At the far end of the village, on the right, is **Jahaz Mahal** (Ship Palace), so called because it is on the bank of a large tank, the **Hauz**

The Qatb Minar.

Shamsi. While the Hauz dates back to Iltutmish, the Mahal is of the 16th century. On the left side of the street is a *jharna* (spring), the overflow from the tank. Early in the month of October, Mehrauli celebrates its own festival, the Phul-walon-ki-Sair (Flower-sellers' Procession) which originated in the 16th century. The highlight is a procession of people carrying decorated floral fans blessed at the shrine of Bakhtiyar Kaki and at the Hindu temple of Jogmaya near Mehrauli village; these are brought to the Jahaz Mahal for a formal ceremony.

Sultan Ghari, Jamali-Kamali: South of Mehrauli, at a distance of 5 km (3 miles) along the Mehrauli–Gurgaon Road, is a little cluster of ruins on the left. In the midst of these is the tomb that Iltutmish built for his son, who died 4 years before him. Apart from its ornate *mihrab* on the western wall, this bears little resemblance to the tomb of Iltutmish in the Qatb complex. This structure has a quiet austerity, with its domed bastions of mellow golden sandstone, its colonnaded enclosure and octagonal tomb-chamber.

Returning to the Qatb area from Sultan Ghari, you reach a massive modern Jain statue on a rocky hill on the right. On the left, a signpost points to the **Jamali-Kamali tomb**, which is set back from the road and not immediately visible. This large 16th century mosque was built by a Sufi poet whose pen-name was "Jamali". The first-floor platform of the mosque affords a superb view of the surrounding area. In an enclosure next to the mosque is the tomb of Jamali, designed by him to frame his verses in a rich ornamentation of blue, white and red. Near the mosque is a well laid-out park, and the curious might speculate about the structures covered by the undulating slopes. Further north is a large roofless building, the **tomb of the emperor Balban**.

Tughlaqabad Complex: From the Qatb complex take the road to the left, but instead of going past Jamali's mosque,

Ancient iron pillar before the Ala'i Darwaza.

take the road on the left. After about 8 km (5 miles), you will come to the massive walls of the Tughlaqabad fort. Ghiyas-ud-din Tughlaq had this built as a defensive outpost, but it was hardly used. Legend ascribes this to the fulfilment of a curse of the saint Nizamuddin; the emperor had turned down his request for masons to build a shrine, and he had prophesied that the royal fort would remain uninhabited. With most of its buildings gone, the desolation today is even more striking. The visitor now enters it from a small gate on the southeast, but when it was inhabited, it was approached by a gentle gradient from the northwest, where lay the adjoining city (now a village). Entrance halls in the southwest led to the palaces and up to the high point of the citadel on the east. Deep water-storage tanks, passages with cubicles let into the sides, and subterranean passages, make the fort a delight for the adventurous. However, it is wise to visit the fort as part of a large group, because a number of attacks on visitors have been reported.

The fort was connected by an embankment to a smaller fort to the south; **Adilabad** was built by Ghiyas-ud-din's successor, Muhammad. Like the larger fort, it is so ruined that it is hard to imagine it as having once contained palaces. One can only wonder at the massive building activity under the Tughlaqs in the Delhi area alone. That this was not always utilitarian and austere is borne out by the **tomb of Ghiyas-ud-din**, enclosed in a heavy stone wall, which suggests that it also doubled as a fortified outpost. This structure was an island, set in the vast body of water that lay south of the fort. The tomb is perfectly preserved. Like the Alai Darwaza, it relies for dramatic effect on a combination of sandstone and marble. It marks a point of departure in its sloping sides. From the ramparts of the stone walls one gets a pleasant view of fields and forts. It is a quiet place in

Ruins of Tughlaqabad, the third city of Delhi.

comparison to the Qatb complex, with long spells of silence broken only by the chatter of monkeys and the rustle of banyan leaves.

Siri and Jahanpanah: Ala-ud-din Khilji's citadel on the plains to the northeast of Mehrauli was called Siri. Located between present-day Khel Gaon Road and Tito Road, this was a round fort, serviced by a huge water reservoir, the Hauz Khas, and by an elaborate system of channels linked to the river, which can still be seen today. Sections of the tall walls of Siri are to be found behind the houses to the north of Panchsheel Road and south of Siri Fort Road. Little remains of Khilji buildings apart from a mosque in the village of Shahpur Jat, south of the Asian Games Village campus. A great deal is buried under the ground, and the exact location of Ala-ud-din's famous 1,000-pillared hall will perhaps remain a mystery.

Muhammad Tughlaq planned to link Rai Pithaura and Siri by a defensive wall, which would also enclose his own city, called Jahanpanah (Refuge of the World). As with Siri, we can identify sections of this wall along the Saket road linking Tito Marg and Aurobindo Marg. Unlike Siri, the citadel of Jahanpanah survives. **Vijay Mandal** (south of Sarvapriya Vihar, across from the Panchsheel Club) has a dramatic set of high arches which indicate the entrance. Within the complex, the ground indicates two levels, the first one being the base of a spacious platform with traces of posts which must have held up a canopy. Higher up, there is a suggestion of chambers to the south, and colonnaded rooms leading to an octagonal structure with a flat roof over which also a canopy was fixed. The king is supposed to have reviewed troops from this vantage point.

To the south of Vijay Mandal is the impressive **mosque of Begumpur**, reached by walking through Begumpur village. This is supposed to have been one of the many mosques built by Khan-e-Jahan Telingani, the minister of

Wayside performer beside the tomb of Jamali-Kamali, a 16th-century poet and mystic.

Feroze Shah Tughlaq. It has a resemblance to the mosque at Kalu Serai (about 1 km/half a mile southwest of Vijay Mandal), that at Nizamuddin, Masjid Kalan near Turkman Gate in Shahjahanabad, and the Khirki Masjid: all these are built of stone and rubble, most of them multi-domed with sloping sides. Begumpuri Masjid is so hemmed in by the village that its grandeur cannot be viewed from a distance. Its stately flight of steps leads to an interior dominated by an arresting central arch with soaring minarets.

On retracing our steps to Sarvapriya Vihar, it is worth going the short distance down the curving road from Panchsheel to Malviya Nagar, to look at **Lal Gumbad**. This is thought to be the tomb of the saint Kabir-ud-din Auliya, but because of its proximity to Vijay Mandal, it has been suggested that Muhammad Tughlaq built it for himself. Covered in dull red sandstone, with a minimum of marble, it bears a certain resemblance, because of its sloping sides, to Ghiyas-ud-din's tomb.

From Panchsheel Club, travelling eastward to Tito Marg, a right turn at this junction and another right turn at the point where it joins Saket Road brings you to **Satpula**. This ruined structure is all that remains of a weir built to regulate the flow of water into a large reservoir which fed the channels that criss-crossed the Delhi area. On top of the bridge was a school. Near Satpula is the little village of **Khirki**, in which is the mosque of the same name. The name Khirki (window) refers to the stone lattice windows of this interesting mosque, unusual in being enclosed. Its cloistered courtyards are reminiscent of a medieval monastery.

The Baha'i Lotus Temple: To the east, near the colony East of Kailash, is the striking new Baha'i temple. The Baha'i faith is a monotheistic religion, based on the scriptures of three 19th-century Iranian mystics, Bab, Baha'u'llah and 'Abdu'l-Baha. The nine-sided, lotus-shaped temple – its design is symbolic

Tomb of Adham Khan, Mughal general executed by his foster-brother Akbar.

HAUZ KHAS VILLAGE

Hauz Khas Village, like so many others in Delhi, is an old settlement. As Delhi expanded, and village fields became housing estates, the villages became swallowed up. Hauz Khas Village is somewhat different. It is not adjacent to housing estates, but to two large parks, both of which are home to herds of deer. What also makes Hauz Khas unusual is its array of chic boutiques selling designer clothing, expensive restaurants, and "antique" and interior design stores.

The origins of this concentration of fashionable outlets can be traced back to the late 1980s, when a group of Delhi's fashion designers relocated their studios and opened shops in the village. The "ethnic chic" of the village appealed to Delhi's rich and middle classes, and soon Hauz Khas had more designer boutiques that buffaloes. It has remained a fashionable location but what is left of the original village atmosphere is by now rather contrived. That said, Hauz Khas is still very pleasant, surrounded as it is by greenery and with the ruins of the *madrasa* and tomb of Feroze Shah Tughlaq. It is also one of the best places to check out the latest styles of Delhi's top designers.

The 14th-century *madrasa* in Hauz Khas.

Of all the various types of shops on offer, the most numerous, and best, are the designer boutiques. These sell mostly *shalwar kamiz* (the long flowing top and loose trousers traditionally worn by Muslim women) and *lehenga* (a combination of long skirt, blouse and jacket worn by women from western India) in expensive silks, muslins and printed cottons, many with stunning appliqué. Expect to pay anything up to Rs15,000 for the most expensive outfits. Among the more interesting designs are those by Ritu Kumar, whose shop **Ritu's** is at E4 Hauz Khas Market. **Nasreen Qureshi**, orignally from Lahore but now living in Delhi, sells elegant *shalwar*, **Neelam Jolly's** has traditional designs that might appeal to Western visitors, and, for a wide selection of different designers' work, try **Marwari's** who maintain a constant turnover of stock. Many of the boutiques also sell accessories, including delicately decorated traditional shoes and bags. One boutique branching out into interior design is **Expressionist Designs**, whose ground floor is given over to the clothes of Delhi-based designer Jaspreet. For ethically sourced and beautifully embroidered clothes visit SEWA (Self-Employed Women's Association), a Gujarati organisation which promotes women's rights. They are at M1 Huaz Khas.

Hauz Khas is also the location for some excellent restaurants. Perhaps the most atmospheric of these is the **Park Balluchi**, within the Deer Park itself. Its design resembles a large greenhouse, from which you can look out on to the surrounding trees and grass. The award-winning food consists of beautifully prepared non-vegetarian Mughlai dishes. The other restaurants of Hauz Khas are within the village. The **Village Bistro Complex** contains the **Mohalla** and **Khas Bagh**, which serve North Indian dishes, the **Kowloon** Chinese restaurant, and the rooftop **Top of the Village**, which looks out over the *madarsa*. Traditional dance performances are staged very evening on the roof. Also part of the complex is **Le Cafe**, selling Western food. Next door to Le Cafe is the **Baujee ka Dhaba**, a restaurant specialising in dishes from the Northwest Frontier.

Behind the restaurants is the **Village Gallery**, displaying works of local and visiting artists. All in all, a great deal has been squeezed into a very small area – a tribute to the planning of village lanes rather than to modern innovation.

of unity and purity – was built between 1980 and 1986. The basic structure is made of concrete clad in brilliant white marble. Visitors may enter the temple (closed on Mondays) but they must remove their shoes and remain silent when inside.

Hauz Khas: If you go north on Aurobindo Marg from the Qatb, you come to a large redbrick church embellished with a white cross, which separates Green Park from the Safdarjang Development Area. If you turn left at the church and some 500 yds (457 m) on you reach, on the right, the beautifully landscaped Deer Park, on the left a wooded area with pleasant walks. In front is **Hauz Khas Village**; if you pick your way through the village, you reach the entrance of the monument. Small and well-kept, this is a green island of peace in which to relax for half an hour.

The name Hauz Khas (Great Tank) derives from the spacious reservoir that in the 13th century Emperor Ala-ud-din Khilji had constructed to supply water to the people of Siri. After you enter, turn right and look out and down at the steps leading down to the ground. Centuries ago, these steps were the ghat that led to the tank. Timur, who camped here before gathering his forces to attack Ferozabad in 1398, was amazed by the expanse of the tank: an arrow shot from one bank, he declared, could not reach the opposite shore. The Hauz, repaired carefully by Feroze Shah Tughlaq some years before Timur's invasion, became the cool setting for a *madrasa* (high school/college). The classrooms, ranged along two storeys in an L-shape around the tank, must have made this a very pleasant university. In Feroze Shah's reign Delhi was among the major intellectual centres of Islamic culture, with many *madrasas.*

That Feroze Shah had a special attachment to this place is suggested by the fact that he wanted his own mausoleum to be here rather than in Tughlaqabad where the earlier Tughlaq

Urban sprawl engulfs the village of Begampur and its fine Tughlaq mosque.

rulers were buried. His tomb, to the west in the complex, has lost its white-lime facing but has a pretty marble-and-sandstone string course, and an attractive stone railing.

Lodi Delhi: The Sayyid and Lodi rulers did not build any citadel in Delhi, but the area from Hauz Khas to Siri and the modern Khel Gaon Marg has many scattered building of that period. Some Sayyid and Lodi monuments further north were enclosed by the spacious Lodi Gardens, marking the southern boundary of Lutyens' Delhi. These are awesomely sturdy stone buildings, with striking details in marble and sandstone. Some have tantalising fragments of the original blue tiles on the exterior, and traces of their original colours in the stucco relief work in the ceilings. The Dadi-Pothi (Grandmother-Granddaughter) tombs between Hauz Khas village and the Free Church, and the Nili Masjid (Blue Mosque) on the other side of Aurobindo Marg and across from the Church, are a few of these. A right turn off the road from Aurobindo Marg to Panchsheel Colony leads to **Chor Minar**, a tower with the holes in the sides from which it is said the decapitated heads of criminals were displayed.

Some interesting monuments are tucked away in the two sections of South Extension, on both sides of Mahatma Gandhi Marg (Ring Road).

South Extension Part One: Turn left from the Mahatma Gandhi Road going east, just before the Market; the second turn to the left brings you to **Kale Khan's tomb**, on raised ground inside an enclosure. This memorial to Mubarak Khan, a nobleman of the Lodi court, belongs to the genre of square tombs seen in the Hauz Khas area and in the Lodi Gardens. The ceiling has a bold geometric design in black and white, a precursor of the elaborate geometric patterns in Mughal buildings.

If you walk a few yards north, you will reach another enclosure with two remarkably well-preserved buildings of the same vintage. **Bade Khan's tomb** is

The Baha'i Lotus Temple.

large, about 22 sq. m (26 sq. yds), with its bulk cleverly underplayed by a *trompe l'oeil*, which creates the impression of a double-storey building by means of sunken arches. The ceiling decorations and the sandstone pendentives are striking. A comfortable staircase, wider and with more shallow steps than are usually found in monuments, leads to the roof where three of the four corner *chatris* are in perfect condition and offer a vantage point for a wonderful view. The other structure, **Chote Khan-ka-Gumbad**, has some blue tiles on the exterior, and rich stucco decorations in the interior, far more elaborate than in any other contemporary building. Due west of these two tombs, next to Kidwai Nagar Market, is the uncovered marble **tomb of Dariya Khan**, the son of Mubarak Khan. This is set on a vast three-tier platform with *chatris* on the four corners.

South Extension Part Two: If you take the road skirting the eastern end of the market, and walk on past the rows of houses, you reach the village of **Masjid Moth**. The lovely mosque after which the village is named dates back to the Lodi period. Legend has it that the Sultan Sikander Lodi gave a *moth* (handful) of grain to his minister Miyan Bhuwa; this prudent gentleman sowed the grain and, many years and many harvests later, had saved enough money to build the mosque. It is entered from a beautiful sandstone gateway, more akin to Mughal gateways than to anything from the previous period; it is set off by bands of white marble with inscribed verses which look as it they were etched yesterday. The mosque has three domes, which mark it as a forerunner of Jamali's mosque in Mehrauli and of Sher Shah's mosque in the Purana Qila, both built within a few decades of this one. The stucco work, the lotus designs and medallions, the ornamental elements in the walls and arches, were to be elaborated into the wealth of carving and designs that reached their high point in Sher Shah's mosque.

Tughlaq remnant opposite the IIT now serves as a *madrasa* (theological school).

THE WILDLIFE OF DELHI

Delhi, despite being a crowded capital city, has a rich variety of birdlife and most of the commoner Indian birds are to be seen in its environs. The riverain tract along the Jamuna, the dry scrubland forests of the northern Ridge and the swampy marshes of the Sultanpur Jhil south of the city offer a wide range of bird habitat. According to the 1908 *Imperial Gazetteer*, at one time Delhi also had foxes, blackbuck, Indian gazelles, crocodiles and even leopards, but now there are only a few jackals and Nilgai left. However, the birdlife is still abundant and the green areas which surround Delhi's historic monuments like the Lodi tombs, Humayun's tomb, Surajkund and the Tughlaqabad fort have a thriving population of birds. In winter the Delhi Zoo turns into a small bird sanctuary as many migratory species fly in to winter on its artificial lakes. From October to March, Pintail Ducks, Barheaded Geese and Shovellers can be seen swimming here along with the resident Spotbill Ducks and Painted Storks.

Migratory birds also come in large group to the Sultanpur lake, which is an hour's drive from Delhi. This shallow but expansive lake has hundreds of Greylag Geese, Demoiselle Cranes and Pintail Ducks visiting it regularly every winter. There are Gadwalls, Mallards and a few Brahminy Ducks as well, floating languidly around the lake. One has to get here quite early in the morning to be able to see the birds, since many of them fly away later to feed in the fields around the lake. The reedbeds that encircle the lake shelter many resident waterbirds and their nests. There are always a few Pond Herons (Paddy Birds, as they are also known), standing here on guard and nearby Pied Kingfishers catching their fish by hovering above the water. Gliding a few feet above there may be a Marsh Harrier, scanning the lake for prey. There are always many River Terns, Blackwinged Stilts and Common Sandpipers feeding here, along with groups of Spoonbills, Avocets and White Ibis. The grove of acacia trees growing in the middle of the lake sometimes hides a large Nilgai or a herd of Sambar in its shade.

Left, Sarus cranes favour open countryside such as Sultanpur.

While Sultanpur is a good place to find migratory ducks and waterbirds, the flowering trees that line the avenues of Delhi also teem with birds. The Silk Cotton, a tall tree with large scarlet flowers, will often harbour Rose-ringed Parakeets, Redvented Bulbuls, Mynas and Purple Sunbirds in its branches once it begins to flower around the end of February. The Gulmohur tree also has bright orange-red blossoms but they only appear in the burning sunshine of May to last till the end of July. The golden yellow flowers of the Indian Laburnum and the pink and white flowers of the Pink Cassia appear a few weeks before the summer starts but the fragile blossoms fade away quickly once the sun becomes too strong. The flowering trees attract many insects and butterflies, and the insect-eating birds follow in their wake. The tiny Greyheaded Flycatcher, the arrow-lake Small Green Bee-eater and the olive green, dummy White-eye all fly around the trees looking for insects. The glossy Black Drongo with its forked tail and the black-masked Rufous-backed Shrike can also often be seen hunting here. The fawn-coloured Hoopoe with zebra markings on its wings stays on the ground mostly, and digs out worms with its curved beak. Its smart crest feathers are usually kept neatly folded back and are sometimes fanned out suddenly as if the bird were surprised. The drab brownish-grey Jungle Babblers hunt on the ground too and move around the undergrowth in groups of seven or five. They are called "seven brothers" in Hindi while in English the popular name for these noisy, querulous birds is "seven sisters". The Red-wattled

Lapwing runs hurriedly to and fro on the lawns insistently calling out, "Did-you-do-it" as it looks for food on the ground.

The old Neem and Mango trees with their crowns of dense green foliage often have Goldenbacked Woodpeckers and Mahratta Woodpeckers scuttling up and down the tree trunks, picking out insects from the bark. The elegant Magpie Robin is a common bird that can be seen in every garden, along with the Indian Robin, as they fly around the shrubs whistling melodiously. The Koel begins to call usually when the summer season starts, and continues to do so for the next two or three months. Its cousin, the Pied-crested Cuckoo, arrives in Delhi just before the monsoon rains, and both these birds are said to dupe crows by laying eggs in the crows' nests. The small green Coppersmith can be heard all through the summer months as it calls out in metallic, monotonous notes. This fruit-eating bird is seen on Pipul and Banyan trees which have ripe fruits on them. The Golden Oriole, one of the most beautiful birds of India, can sometimes be glimpsed on fruit trees, but mostly stays hidden in the foliage. The Green Barbet calls out so loudly and tunelessly from the tree-tops that one has to notice it. The Tailor-bird too has a loud call, surprising coming from such a small bird. It uses its sharp beak to stitch up a leafy cover for its nest. It stars as the "Darzee" in Kipling's famous story *Riki-tiki-tavi.*

The Ridge is a vast area of scrubland forest preserved right in the heart of Delhi, and this rocky terrain has more than a hundred bird species in it. There are narrow paths leading into the forest from the main Sardar Patel Road, and once inside you can follow the horse tracks which run like a maze through the acacia trees. The most common bird on the Ridge is the peacock and many large families walk around the bushes. The rocky ground is full of rodents, and the Indian Hare can be seen scampering along the dry grass.

Birds of prey find this a rich hunting ground and Tawny Eagles, Black-winged Kites, kestrels and Pariah Kites can be seen scouting for prey on the Ridge. The thorny bushes of the forest have wild berries on them and the Pied Bushchat is in evidence, along with the smallest of all migratory birds, the Bluethroat. When the Flame-of-the-Forest flowers in March, its orange flowers attract nectar-feeding birds like bulbuls, parakeets and barbets. The harsh cry of the Tree-pie can be often heard on the Ridge, and the bird will glide through the trees, trailing its long black tail. The large Grey Hornbill is a resident too, and there are quite a few nests with plastered up walls in the trunks of old trees. The grasses and low bushes that cover the ground have large flocks of White-throated Munias flitting about collecting seeds, and there are usually some Red Avadavats amongst them. The acacia tree may shelter a pair of dozing Spotted Owlets. Their larger relative, the Great Horned Owl, might be found in a rocky hideout nearby. In winter many Black Redstarts come down from the mountains to live on the Ridge, and very often Scarlet Minivets fly there too.

The Ridge has an uneven terrain with many low-lying areas and crevices where water collects during the rains. Bee-eaters gather here to catch winged insects. The White-breasted Kingfisher and the Small Blue Kingfisher sit patiently on branches above the muddy pools to pick up tadpoles and insects.

During the summer months, the Ridge becomes very dry, and most birds fly into gardens nearby to drink water from hose pipes. There are large numbers of monkeys on the ridge too, and they usually stay around trees like the Jamun, Pipul and Neem. The monsoon rains change the vegetation of the Ridge and for a short while the dry, brown landscape turns into a green forest. Now birdlife becomes even more varied since the rich fertile ground brings many more species to the Ridge.

Right, Nilgai, "blue bull", the largest antelope.

कान्हबिलोकनिकाजसुनांनिफिरेमिसगांनिकेनंदद्वार ॥१३॥

کانهه بلوکن کاج سجان پھرے مس ٹھان کی نند دوارے

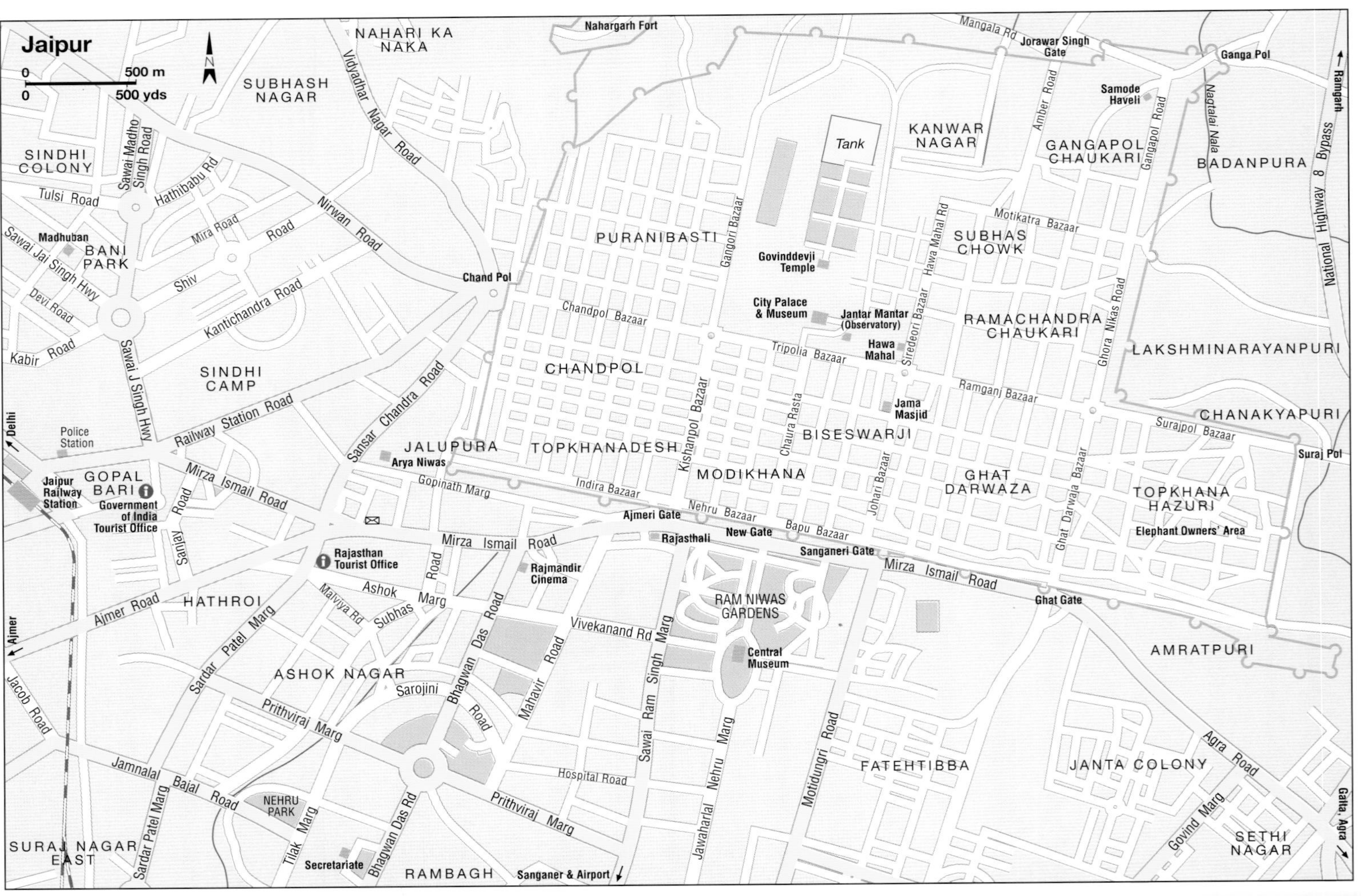

Jaipur
0 500 m
0 500 yds
N
NAHARI KA NAKA
Nahargarh Fort
Mangala Rd
Jorawar Singh Gate
Ganga Pol
Rangarh
SUBHASH NAGAR
Vidyadhar Nagar Road
Samode Haveli
Nagtalai Nala
National Highway 8 Bypass
SINDHI COLONY
Sawai Madho Singh Road
Hathibabu Rd
Tulsi Road
Tank
KANWAR NAGAR
Amber Road
GANGAPOL CHAUKARI
Gangapol Road
BADANPURA
Mira Road
Road
Nirwan Road
PURANIBASTI
Gangori Bazaar
Motikatra Bazaar
Hawa Mahal Rd
SUBHAS CHOWK
Madhuban
BANI PARK
Sawai Jai Singh Hwy
Govinddevji Temple
Shiv
Chand Pol
Devi Road
Kantichandra Road
Chandpol Bazaar
City Palace & Museum
Jantar Mantar (Observatory)
Siredeori Bazaar
RAMACHANDRA CHAUKARI
Ghora Nikas Road
LAKSHMINARAYANPURI
Kabir Road
Sawai J Singh Hwy
Tripolia Bazaar
Hawa Mahal
SINDHI CAMP
CHANDPOL
Ramganj Bazaar
Sansar Chandra Road
Jama Masjid
CHANAKYAPURI
Railway Station Road
Chaura Rasta
Surajpol Bazaar
Delhi
Police Station
JALUPURA
TOPKHANADESH
Kishanpol Bazaar
BISESWARJI
Suraj Pol
Arya Niwas
Johari Bazaar
MODIKHANA
GHAT DARWAZA
TOPKHANA HAZURI
Jaipur Railway Station
GOPAL BARI
Government of India Tourist Office
Mirza Ismail Road
Gopinath Marg
Indira Bazaar
Nehru Bazaar
Ghat Darwaja Bazaar
Ajmeri Gate
Bapu Bazaar
Elephant Owners' Area
Sanjay Road
Mirza Ismail Road
Rajasthali
New Gate
Sanganeri Gate
Rajasthan Tourist Office
Rajmandir Cinema
Mirza Ismail Road
Ashok Marg
Ghat Gate
Malviya Rd
Subhas Marg
RAM NIWAS GARDENS
Ajmer Road
HATHROI
Bhagwan Das Road
Vivekanand Rd
Ajmer
Sardar Patel Marg
Central Museum
AMRATPURI
Mahavir Road
Sawai Ram Singh Marg
ASHOK NAGAR
Sarojini Road
Jacob Road
Prithviraj Marg
Motidungri Road
Agra Road
Jamnalal Bajal Road
Hospital Road
FATEHTIBBA
JANTA COLONY
NEHRU PARK
Jawaharlal Nehru Marg
Galta, Agra
Sardar Patel Marg
Tilak Marg
Prithviraj Marg
Govind Marg
SURAJ NAGAR EAST
Bhagwan Das Rd
SETHI NAGAR
Secretariate
RAMBAGH
Sanganer & Airport

JAIPUR – THE RAJPUT CITY

In 1947, the map of India was a melange of swathes of pink "British India" interspersed with irregular blotches for the "princely states" – the former, territory directly administered by the British, the latter, that which had escaped conquest. Though colonial rule kept a firm control over their political activities, it did not blur their cityscape. Sidney and Beatrice Webb, travelling in India in 1912, pronounced on the pleasing individuality of these small states, and the contrast they provided with the formless towns of British India. Today the difference is diminishing, as all towns face problems of spreading urbanisation. The royal capitals have lost their symbolic role, but their commercial activities have expanded. In many, as in Jaipur, a strong local pride helps them to retain their individuality. This is aided by the tourism industry; when exploited sensitively, one of the best allies of intelligent conservation.

All the towns of Rajasthan are "picturesque"; Jaipur has the added interest of reflecting Sawai Jai Singh's fascination with the cosmic order. (Similarly planned towns have existed at other times and places; St Petersburg and other European towns were built at about the same time as Jaipur.) Jai Singh's city was planned on the *mandala* model of the nine-square grid, different from the Mughal cities where axes radiated from the citadel at one side. Controls were exercised on the facades and height of buildings, as were applied later in the avenues of Delhi.

The cities of Rajasthan have come to terms with the challenges of living in a harsh climate with techniques perfected over centuries. The palaces of Jaipur, Amber, Samode, and Alwar are man-made oases, where the searing heat has been combated with breeze-catching balconies and *chatris*, the sunlight with carved *jali* filters, the sandy soil with gardens. Today, modern technology has attempted to transform the desert by releasing the water of the Punjab rivers into Rajasthan via the Indira Gandhi canal.

Driving near Jaipur will show how the hills are threatened – reckless quarrying in recent years has chipped away at their forms. Conservation has in the last quarter century slowed down another form of depredation – the elimination of forest cover and wildlife. In a wide arc to the east of Jaipur is a range of beautiful sanctuaries for birds and animals – Siliserh, Sariska, Ranthambore and Keoladeo Ghana. In the last of these, large stone slabs detail how many birds were slain and by whom; the list comes to an abrupt end in the middle of the 20th century. Today a belt of tiger country and tranquil stretches of water link the imperial cities of the Yamuna plain with the towns of the desert, at the entrance of which stands the gateway city of Jaipur.

Preceding pages: the battlements of Nahagarh fort look over the expanding city of Jaipur; bridgegroom on horseback passing Hawa Mahal; mid 18th-century paintings from Jaipur – folio from the *Sarasa-rasa-grantha* (left) and portrait of Sawi Jai Singh by Sahibram (right).

THE CITY OF SAWAI JAI SINGH

In a land of forts and palaces, temples and mausolea, the city that stands out for its unique design and layout is Jaipur, the "Pink City". Built in the 18th century, it symbolises the dreams and desires of a visionary king, Jai Singh, and his accomplished architect-builder-courtier, Vidyadhar.

Jai Singh was anointed ruler of Amber in February 1700 at the tender age of 12 after his father Bishan Singh died in distant Afghanistan. Jai Singh was a precocious child possessing an intimate knowledge of politics, religion, literature, mathematics and astronomy. He obtained the title *Sawai* from the crafty old Mughal emperor Aurangzeb when he was barely 15. How he was given the title has not been precisely recorded, but popular legend has it that the distrustful emperor had not wanted the young ruler to live in Amber and despatched him to fight against the Marathas in the Deccan. When Jai Singh procrastinated, Aurangzeb purnished him by reducing his rank and despatched the imperial mace-bearers to fetch him. When the boy was brought before the old emperor, the story goes that Aurangzeb gripped his prisoner's hands to reprimand him and demanded to know what Jai Singh proposed to do to protect his life and kingdom. The lad replied fearlessly that he expected to be protected by the emperor, who was holding his hands in much the same way as a bridegroom reassures his bride at the time of the wedding. The bemused emperor appreciated this unexpected wit and, remarking that the Rajput boy-king was "more than one", restored his rank and bestowed on him the title *Sawai*, meaning one-and-a-quarter. All the Kachchwaha rulers have been addressed as such ever since.

Preceding pages, Jaipur dealer in antique textiles displays one of his treasures. Left and right, Jai Singh's astonishing astronomical observatory with its sculpturesque forms.

Life for Sawai Jai Singh became increasingly trying after Aurangzeb's death in 1707. The new emperor Bahadur Shah was not well disposed towards him as he had openly supported the cause of Azam Shah, Bahadur Shah's younger brother, in the war of succession. He was consequently deported from Amber, which was handed over to his younger brother Vijay Singh. The injured pride of the fallen Rajput strengthened his determination. Within less than a decade he had not only become the well entrenched ruler of a stronger, larger and more prosperous Amber, but also the leading light amongst all the Rajput rulers in the area. He assumed the role of king-maker and helped install Muhammad Shah Rangila on the Mughal throne in Delhi.

At last Jai Singh had the time and means to concentrate on his own affairs, to pursue his own avocations and interests. Scholars, lawgivers, poets, painters, astronomers and artisans from all over the country came to work for him. Amber, never too propitious for Jai Singh, was proving too cramped and

inadequate for his growing needs. Water was always a scarce resource there. He envisaged a new city which would bear his name; fortunately, he did not have to search far for an architect to translate his ideas into concrete reality. A Bengali Brahman who worked as a minor revenue official, Vidyadhar Chakravarti, had already demonstrated his skill by making a series of ingenious alternations to Amber, Jaigarh and Nahargarh which ensured a round-the-year water supply. Vidyadhar soon came up with a blueprint for a large, spacious and beautiful city south of Nahargarh ridge.

The foundation of the city was laid on 18 November 1727 with a religious ceremony performed by the principal court preceptor and renowned scholar Jagannath Samrat. Within five years, the hillocks, scrubby jungles, marshes, sand dunes and five little villages that had comprised the area had been transformed by Vidyadhar into a spectacular city with straight, wide roads, ordered rows of houses and shops, beautiful buildings, temples and open spaces, all secured by strong fortifications. The city was named Sawai Jaipur after the Maharaja. Even after 260 years of use and despite the neglect of recent years, it retains much of its original charm and functionality.

As Sawai Jai Singh wanted to live near the temple of his personal deity Govinda Deva, Vidyadhar constructed the Chandra Mahal (Moon Palace) complex with its seven storeys and multiple courtyards on the southern edge of the large *charbagh*-type landscape garden, Jai Niwas Bagh, which housed the modest towerless temple of Govinda Deva. The palace complex with its public buildings, astronomical observatory, *zenana mahals* (harems), 36 ateliers and state departments and 52 offices occupies the central sector comprising one-seventh of the rectangular city. Divided into seven unequal rectangular sectors called *chaukris* (from *chauk*, square), the city

Elephant-back polo.

is arranged in a grid pattern with criss-crossing avenues, roads, lanes and by-lanes. An equal number of shops of uniform size, shape and facade lines either side of each of the seven main roads or *bazars*. Large *havelis* (mansions) with impressive gateways and facades were constructed in the earmarked residential sectors for prosperous citizens, traders and feudal lords (*thakur*s). Trade and commercial centres, markets, factories and religious establishments were allotted specific areas in keeping with Vidyadhar's plan. Rigid control was exercised from the very beginning to curb encroachments and haphazard growth. This remained true till the merger of the state of Jaipur with the Indian Union in 1949. Additions and alterations earlier made by successive rulers, specially by Sawai Madho Singh I, Pratap Singh, Ram Singh II, Madho Singh II and Man Singh II, had been planned with the utmost care in keeping with Vidyadhar's original layout.

The most important part of the city is the Palace quarter, known as the City Palace. The approach from the east is through **Hawa Mahal Bazaar**, **Sireh Deorhi** (Victory Gate), **Naqqara Pol** (Drum Gate), **Jaleb Chowk**, or **Dundubi Pol**, and from the south through **Tripolia** (Three-arched Gate), **Chandni Chowk**, **Rajendra Pol**, **Mubarak Mahal** and **Singh Pol**. Portions of the palace are open to the public as these were given over to the Maharaja Sawai Man Singh II Museum in 1959 (open 9am–5pm). As the **Tripolia** and **Rajendra Pol** are for the members of the royal family, visitors use the **Atish Pol** (Stable Gate) and **Gainda-ki-Deorhi** to enter the palace. The building that first strikes the eye is the beautiful marble and standstone **Mubarak Mahal** (Welcome Palace) constructed in 1895–1900 by Sawai Madho Singh II to receive foreign visitors. It was used later as the **Mahakma Khas** or Cabinet Office and these days houses the **pothikhana** (manuscript store) and offices of the Museum on the ground floor, and the **toshakhana** (textile store) on the first floor. This building is the most attractive example of the mixed Rajput and Indo-Saracenic style evolved by the British State Engineer Sir Swinton Jacob in the later 19th century.

The textile gallery exhibits a fine selection of court costumes and rich textiles from the royal wardrobe of Jaipur. There are Mughal embroidered screens, coverlets, throne carpets, Kashmiri *pashmina* shawls and *shahtush* wraps, tie-dyed and block-printed materials and *odhnis* (scarves) from Jaipur, silks and brocades from Banaras, Aurangabad, Bengal, Gujarat and Chanderi. The salmon-pink padded dress (*atamsukh* or soul-delighter) of Madho Singh I is possibly the most impressive garment because of its gigantic proportions. The king is said to have weighed 225 kg (500 lbs) and stood 2.1 m (7 ft) tall. His pyjamas are vast enough to leave no doubt about his

Parrot in the Pink City.

girth, but his legendary height remains questionable. The other eye-catching exhibit is a gold-and-black Divali festival outfit of one of the Maharanis of Sawai Ram Singh which has several kilograms of gilded *zari* and *gota* appliqué decoration. Jaipur is still famous for this craft and no high-caste Rajasthani wedding or festival is complete without the bride and other women wearing clothes decorated in this way. A small but interesting selection of Mughal glass, ritual objects, musical instruments and decorative artefacts from the stores of the family are also displayed here.

To the left of the Mubarak Mahal is an exhibition hall made by rebuilding an old *rasoda* (royal kitchen) complex. Long ago, vegetarian and non-vegetarian dishes, snack and savoury items, preserves and pickles, sherbets, betelnut and accompanying *masalas* were prepared here in separate units for the Maharaja, his family and his male and female retainers.

Next to it, near the magnificent marble-inlaid Singh Pol (Lion Gate), is the way to the *silehkhana* (armoury). A number of weapons, daggers, swords, spears, firearms, shields and body armour selected from the old state armoury and the personal collections of former rulers are on view here. These are the rooms where once the *dhrupad* singers and *kathak* dancers of the Jaipur **Gunijan khana** (department of music and dance) practised and performed. This collection of weapons includes two inscribed swords from the personal armoury of emperor Shahjahan, a Persian imperial sword and a heavy (5 kg/11 lbs) curved sword belonging to Raja Man Singh. Dozens of daggers, knives (*katara*) and swords with rare, intricately carved handles of jade, crystal, agate, ivory, silver and gold, as well as a unique turban-shaped gold-damascened helmet are some of the highlights of the exhibition.

The huge brass-plated doors of the imposing Singh Pol lead into the

Women dancing in the private apartments of the City Palace.

Sarvatobhadra or **Diwan-i-Khas** (private audience hall) courtyard. A pair of caparisoned elephants, each carved out of a single piece of white marble, stand on either side of the marble and *pietra dura* gateway. The Singh Pol with its enormous brass doors is one of the highlights of the city. The star exhibit of this place, however, is a pair of sterling silver vessels (*gangajalis* or containers for holy Ganges water) standing under the scalloped salmon-pink arches of the Sarvatobhadra. With a capacity of 8,180 litres (1,800 gallons) each, these are thought to be the two largest silver objects in the world. The story behind them is that Maharaja Madho Singh II was eager to visit London to attend the coronation of Edward VII in 1902. Being an orthodox Hindu, he had to overcome the taboo against undertaking a voyage. A brand new ocean liner was therefore chartered for him, in which he sailed with the family deity installed in a temple built on board. To avoid ritual pollution during his journey and stay, he carried with him these silver vessels filled with the holy water of the river Ganga, in which he bathed every day.

Guard of the Peacock Gate in the City Palace.

To the right of this pink-and-white painted courtyard is the **Sabha Niwas**, now converted into the Art Gallery. Originally built as a venue for holding important durbars and ceremonies, it contains fine cut-glass chandeliers. Rare Mughal floral carpets, hand-written manuscripts, colourful miniatures, gold-and-silver thrones, painted and ivory-inlaid howdahs and mirrored miniature shrines are on view here. The most important art treasures of the Museum, the Emperor Akbar's profusely illustrated Persian *Ramayana* and *Mahabharata* (*Razm-nama*), are displayed only on special occasions.

A part of the collection of carriages, palanquins, chariots and buggies from the old **Baggi khana** (the garage for carriages) has been arranged in sheds constructed around the Sabha Niwas. The most remarkable carriage, the Indra-viman, a monstrous double-storeyed contraption drawn by four large elephants, still lies in its garage outside the Naqqara Pol.

Across the Sarvatobhadra courtyard the beautiful white marble **Ridhi-Sidhi Pol** leads to the courtyard facing the ground floor of the Chandra Mahal, called **Pritam Niwas** (Hall of the Beloved). Four magnificent gateways adorn two sides of this enclosed courtyard where music and dance parties used to be held on full moon nights, watched by the royal women from behind the *jali* screens of the upper storey.

The painted northern verandah of Chandra Mahal opens onto the sprawling **Jai Niwas Bagh** with its rows of fountains, monkeys and flocks of peacocks. The temple of Govinda Deva in the centre is visited by devotees chanting hymns in praise of Lord Krishna. On festive days like Holi, Divali, Annakut and Janamashtami (Krishna's birthday), devotees can number hundreds of thousands. Each of the upper storeys of Chandra Mahal, nowadays used privately by the royal family, contains a different kind of decor, from the traditional paintings of **Sukh Niwas**, blue arabesques of **Chavi Niwas** to the gold-and-glass ornamentation of the **Shish Mahal**. These are finally topped by the open three-arch **Mukut Mahal**. Beyond the palace, to the left, is the **Zenana Deorhi** meant for the royal women who lived in purdah, totally shut off from the gaze of all but their own menfolk. Suites, open halls, latticed corridors, temples, ateliers and other facilities actually cover an area which is more than that of the main section.

Just outside the Gainda-ki-Deorhi, to the right, is **Jantar Mantar**, the astronomical observatory of Sawai Jai Singh. Beyond this, a little further to the east, stands the **Hawa Mahal**, the Palace of the Winds. Sawai Pratap Singh (1778-1803), well known as a poet, composer and devotee, constructed this extraordinary edifice in 1799 for the benefit of his queens and their numerous maids and retainers so that they could watch the grand processions in the bazaar below, unobserved from behind the 953 latticed windows. This five-storey, gently tapering pink stone structure is unique in several respects – in its jewel-like intricacy and in its planning, such that the faintest whiff of breeze is caught by the projecting windows to cool and refresh the onlookers sitting behind them (hence its name, *hawa*, "cool air").

Other important buildings found in this bazaar are the **temple of Ramchandraji**, built by one of the Maharanis of Sawai Ram Singh II in 1845, the **Town Hall**, built some years later and now used as the Vidhan Sabha (Legislative Assembly) for the entire state of Rajasthan, a rare temple to Kalki, the tenth incarnation of Vishnu, and the **Ram Prakash theatre** down the road.

Below, Flower seller in a Jaipur bazaar. Right, veiled Muslim women and escort marvel at the brass Chakra Yantra.

JANTAR MANTAR

"Jantar Mantar" is derived from the Sanskrit **Yantrasala**, literally, storehouse of machines; its scattered futuristic structures are an assemblage of complex astronomical instruments designed and constructed by Sawai Jai Singh in his pursuit of unravelling the mysteries of the universe.

Sawai Jai Singh was interested in astronomy and astrology from his early years. After studying all the available contemporary works in Sanskrit, Arabic and Persian with his preceptor, the renowned scholar Pandit Jagannath Samrat, he became interested in instrumentation. Noticing the defects in the brass astrolabes, sextants and sundials collected by him, he decided to design his own instruments based on his personal observations. The metal instruments made by him were too heavy and had limited application; the resourceful Jai Singh went on to design and construct gigantic instruments of stone and masonry to help him in his task of revising the planetary tables. He declared later in the preface of his comprehensive work, the *Zij Jadid Muhammad Shahi*, that as no one had paid attention to this since Ulugh Beg, the Timurid ruler of Samarkand and astronomer, he, would undertake this task.

Accordingly, five observatories were constructed in Delhi, Jaipur, Mathura, Varanasi and Ujjain. The Jaipur observatory is the largest among these and almost intact. All the 13 instruments designed by him as well as three large metal ones are still to be seen here. Instruments of note in the Jaipur observatory are:

Nari Valaya Yantra: This is an instrument which can determine local time, ante and post meridian. It is a hemispherical sundial which consists of two cylinders with a diameter of 3 m (10 ft), and an axis parallel to the earth's and in the meridian.

Samrat Yantra: This is an equinoctial sundial of gigantic proportions (the largest in the world) designed to measure local time, meridian pass time, zenith distance, and the declination and altitude of the celestial spheres with greater precision. It consists of a 27-m (90-ft) high wall topped with a domed *chatri* in the shape of a triangle, the 44-m (146-ft) long hypotenuse of which is the gnomon pointing towards the north pole at an angle of 27°, equivalent to the altitude of Jaipur. This is flanked by two quadrants of 15-m (50-ft) radius with graduations in hours, minutes and seconds where the shadow of the gnomon travels about 4 m (13 ft) an hour.

Rashi Valaya Yantra: This is a group of 12 instruments which appear to be smaller versions of the Samrat Yantra. They represent the 12 zodiac signs. Though they are not of much use in serious astronomical research, traditional astrologers and almanac-makers find them serviceable.

Jai Prakash Yantra: This is a multi-purpose instrument invented by Sawai Jai Singh, an armillary sphere, consisting of two marble bowls sunk into a rectangular sandstone platform. The concave hemispheres represent the celestial sphere. The rim of the bowls represent the horizon which is graduated in 360°. It displays the relationship between the local and the equatorial system of coordinates.

Ram Yantra: Consisting of two complementary cylindrical structures of huge proportions found at the western end of the observatory, this is used to calculate the azimuth and altitude of celestial objects at any time of day or night.

Diganshа Yantra: This is a huge compass of unique design consisting of three concentric constructions round a pillar-like structure in the centre. It is used for calculation of azimuth of the sun and other celestial bodies.

Amongst the metal instruments designed and made by Sawai Jai Singh two are of great significance, the **Kranti Valaya Yantra** and the **Yantra Raj**. The former is a combination of two graduated frames, one resting on a masonry base inclined to the plane of the equator by 23° and another rotating frame inclined to the ecliptic. The Yantra Raj is the most ambitious of Jai Singh's metal instruments. It is a huge astrolabe marked with the stereographic projection of the heavens upon its surface. This is the largest astrolabe in the world.

EATING OUT IN JAIPUR

Surprisingly for such an overwhelmingly Hindu state, Rajasthan has a strong tradition of non-vegetarian cookery. This may, in part, be due to the favourite sport of the ruling Rajputs, hunting or *shikar*, and many of the non-vegetarian recipes evolved in the royal kitchen – the *rasoda*. Recipes were sometimes exchanged among the princely families of the region and the other states of the country. Some of the princes, such as the Maharaja of Sailana, were expert cooks. Attention was paid to prescribing the appropriate food for daily meals as well as for special occasions.

Though *shikar* is restricted today, the Rajputs have maintained their tradition of non-vegetarian food to the extent that even their vegetarian dishes are said to have the flavour of meat dishes. Mutton dominates their food: the meat of lamb or goat is prepared in a variety of curries, barbecued and roasted in the traditional Indian style or minced to make *kima* or *kebabs*. Rajput cuisine also includes chicken, fish, pork, rabbit in the permitted season, as well as partridge and sand grouse. Of the extensive list of dishes, the most savoured preparation is the *sulla*, which was found easy to cook at home as well as on the battle field. This consists of marinated pieces of lamb, skewered and grilled over charcoal in the traditional style.

By and large the food is rich and hot, with a strong flavour of onion, garlic, red chilli powder and aromatic spices. However, a special white curry seasoned with yoghurt and cashewnuts excludes chilli powder and turmeric. *Safed mas* or meat cooked in the white sauce is a ceremonial delicacy.

Vegetarian food is patronised by the leading business community, the Jains. Since vegetables could neither be grown nor imported due to the scarcity of resources, the traditional vegetarian menu was dominated by *dal*, split gram or chickpeas, and in particular by yellow gram. The flour of yellow gram is used for curries like *kadhi* or *gatta*. Dry balls of ground gram provide another interesting curry – *mangodi ka sag*. Today the irrigation of previous desert tracts of Rajasthan has enabled the cultivation of a wider variety of vegetables, which has greatly extended the range of preparations.

Away from the lavish vegetarian and non-vegetarian cuisine, everyday food for the majority of people is simple. The daily diet consists of buttermilk and *bajre ki roti* or millet bread, eaten with onions and a chutney of red chillies and garlic. At best the meal includes *ker-sangri* (the vegetable of a thorny shrub), a simple potato curry referred to as *jhal*, and a fried bread made of white flour.

A dish relished by both rich and poor is *dal bati churma* – gram, baked bread balls and a sweet made of crushed bread. It is usually eaten outdoors. For the rich, who have evolved a number of

Rajasthan's *sullas* are grilled over charcoal braziers.

variations, it marks special occasions like the picnics held during the monsoon. But those who stick to the basic preparation see it as an al fresco dish to take to work or to a fair.

Any kind of Rajasthani food is best eaten at home since, unlike other more cosmopolitan areas, eating out is not part of the city's life-style. Of the luxury hotels, the best food in town is said to be served by the **Jai Mahal Palace Hotel** of the Taj Group. The food there includes non-vegetarian specialities like chicken and mutton *sulla* and, for vegetarians, *gatta* curry and *ker-sangri*. The **Rambagh Palace** too has a pleasant restaurant and a wonderful bar. Another well known restaurant is **Niro's**, on M.I. Road, which was founded in the 1930s. Although it does not serve traditional Rajasthani cuisine, the Mughlai, Continental and Chinese food is fairly good. The *durg* or fort at Nahargarh has a restaurant which is worth visiting during the tourist season – more for the spectacular views it affords of the city than for its food, which (though good) often comes after a long delay.

Robust millet bread, *bajre-li-roti*, is a Rajasthani staple.

The Walled City's favourite eating place is the LMB, short for Lakshmi Mishthan Bhandar, a restaurant which started as a sweet shop in Johari Bazaar. In 1954 the celebrated sweet shop started an exclusive vegetarian restaurant, and in 1965 expanded into a hotel – all under its well-known banner.

LMB's vegetarian food is of the orthodox Brahmans: all preparations are made in *vishudh ghi* (clarified butter) and even onion and garlic are excluded from the ingredients. Its Rajasthani specialities include two gram flour curries, *kadhi chokhanwali* and *gatta*. Among the variety of breads served is *missi roti*, while LMB's savoury *dahi bara*, made of yoghurt, is justly celebrated.

The most famous offerings of LMB are its sweets. Two of the most popular sweet specialities are *ghewar*, a festival sweet traditionally made for the Tij festival, and *ras malai*, a preparation of cottage cheese balls cooked in milk flavoured with saffron and served sprinkled with chopped pistachio nuts. Outside, beside the sweet shop, is a fast food counter which serves hot snacks like *alu tikia* and *samosas*.

The secret of LMB's success is said to lie in the purity of its ingredients. "From wheat to red chillies, all ingredients are ground on the premises", explains the manager,

Perhaps the best place to sample the traditional vegetarian food of Rajasthan is the **Chanakya Restaurant** on M.I. Road. Their Rajasthani *thali* comes with all the staples of *khadi*, *gatti* and *dal batti*. This food is very different from the Indian dishes served up in restaurants in the UK and elsewhere abroad, relying heavily on different *dals* and lots of *ghi*.

For streetside snacks, head further down M.I. Road to **Lassiwala**, said to serve the best *lassi* (yoghurt drink) in Jaipur, served in small, unglazed earthenware bowls.

THE GLORY OF AMBER

Nestled amidst the hills of the Kalikhoh range, the narrow valley of Amber provides an ideal refuge to its inhabitants. Not much of its early history is known, though many nearby sites have yielded archaeological objects, including prehistoric tools. The name Amber is probably derived from Ambikesvar, a manifestation of Shiva whose temple is situated here, or from Amba Mata, a manifestation of the Mother Goddess. In medieval literature the place is called Ambavati.

It was during the occupation of the Mina peoples that the Kachchwaha Rajputs appeared on the scene in the 12th century. They claim their ancestry from Kusha, one of the twin sons of Lord Rama. They call themselves Suryavanshis, or descendants of the Sun God. During the 11th century, the Kachchwahas lived in central India in a place called Narwar, near Gwalior. In 1128 their chief Dulha Rai married Maroni, the daughter of the Bargujar chief of Dausa, not far from Amber. Facing internecine struggle, he had to leave his native state and wander in search of a new home. Dulha Rai and his queen came to Amber in around 1150 and settled there, seizing it from the Minas. For the next six centuries, until they moved to the newly built city of Jaipur, Amber remained the Kachchwaha capital. Subsequently, the fortifications of Amber were completed by Rajdev in the 13th century; his grandson Kuntaldev founded Kuntalgarh, and his great-grandson Narsinghdev built the temple of Narsingh which is still intact. Other rulers and their queens built various tanks, temples and fortified structures whose remains are no longer traceable.

Preceding pages, Amber reflected on Moatha Lake. **Left**, tourists being carried up to Amber on elephant-back. **Right**, Jaigarh's famous cannon, known as Jai Van, the Voice of Victory.

Much that remains in Amber, both within the fort-palace in the town and in the adjoining areas, belongs to the period when the Kachchwahas came into prominence, from the beginning of the 16th century onwards. Prithviraj ascended the Amber throne in 1503 and ruled until 1527. He fought under the banner of Rana Sanga against Zahir-uddin Babur, the founder of the Mughal dynasty, in the battle of Khanua in March 1527. Before his death he allotted nine principalities (*thikanas*) to the sons of each of his nine wives from different clans: Nimera, Sanganer, Samriya, Chomu and Samod, Achrol, Diggi, Surothe, Bagru and Kalwar. These nine, along with three others (Banskhoh, Nidar and Watka) formed the Bara Kotri or Twelve Chambers of the Kachchwaha house. Their rulers formed the highest aristocracy of Jaipur. Most of them have played important parts in the history of Amber and Jaipur. All these places have impressive forts and *havelis* (mansions) worth visiting.

The Kachchwaha Raja who formed an alliance with the rulers of Delhi and Agra, with Sher Shah and the young

Mughal emperor Akbar, was Bihar Mal. He gave his daughter in marriage to Akbar to forge a lasting bond with the powerful Mughals. In return, the Kachchwahas were given important positions in the Mughal court as well as key military and administrative assignments in different parts of the empire. After Bihar Mal his successors Bhagwan Das and Man Singh continued the same policy and assiduously maintained cordial relations with the imperial power centre. Raja Man Singh became one of the celebrated "Nav ratans" (Nine Jewels) of Akbar's court – a great distinction at the time.

As a direct consequence of Amber's cordial relationship with the Mughal empire, its prestige, position and prosperity increased exponentially. Raja Man Singh built a spacious and beautiful palace in the fort of Amber and a landscaped garden called Dilaram Bagh on the Moatha Lake, as well as other buildings and temples. He brought the black basalt image of Jessoresvari, the Mother Goddess, from the private temple of Raja Pratapaditya of Jessore in Bengal and installed it in his own temple adjoining his new palace. Worshipped as Shila Mata, a manifestation of the fierce goddess Kali, it attracts a large number of devotees from all parts of India throughout the year. To this day, only a Bengali priest descended from the priests Man Singh brought from Bengal can conduct the worship of the deity. (Interestingly, Vidyadhar Chakravarty, the architect of Jaipur, came from one of these families). The temple was beautifully decorated with green and yellow marble by Sawai Man Singh II in 1939, who also donated a pair of silver doors carved with figures of ten different manifestation of the Mother Goddess as described in Hindu religious texts. Artistically they represent the last phase of the Jaipuri style of metal-crafting.

Much of Raja Man Singh's palace

The Aravallis, reinforced with stone ramparts, guarded the wealth of the Rajput kingdoms.

stands intact behind the ornate buildings erected by Mirza Raja Jai Singh half a century later. Man Singh built twelve suites of rooms for his twelve queens on the four sides of a spacious open court which led to a beautiful pavilion in the middle. Traces of blue tilework on the rooftops and paintings on the walls of his living rooms reflect the elaborate decorations made under his orders, which are described in great detail in the biography written by his court poets. Remains of similar paintings are also to be seen in the *chhatri* of his grandfather Bihar Mal on the northern part of the town, as well as in a nearby structure, **Maqdum Shah-ka-Maqbara**.

Raja Man Singh was a great builder as well as a connoisseur of the performing and decorative arts and of literature. Since he served as Akbar's governor in various parts of the country from Kabul to Bengal and Lahore to Burhanpur, it was possible for him to bring artists, craftsmen and scholars from these places to work for him. He started many ateliers for arts and crafts in Amber including gold enamelling (*minakari*), paper making, block printing and ceramics. These craft traditions still flourish in Amber and Jaipur.

Most of the magnificent structures standing in the Amber palace can be traced to Mirza Raja Jai Singh, who ascended the Amber *gaddi* at the age of 12 in 1621 and ruled for 46 years. Being close to the emperor Aurangzeb, he rose to the pinnacle of power and glory as the commander of 7,000 troops, a rank never before given to any one outside the imperial family.

Amber is approached from the north via a narrow circuitous road through the hills, protected by high serpentine walls. Crossing the small, densely inhabited town, one gets a breathtaking view of the yellow palace complex built atop a low hill with its reflection in the placid waters of Moatha Lake below. The steep path to the **Singh Pol** (Lion Gate) of the palace used to be traversed

Ganesh Pol, the main entrance to Amber Palace.

on horseback or on elephants which still convey visitors from the base of the fort to the first courtyard, **Jalebi Chowk.** Steps lead up to an open courtyard with the spectacular red standstone **Diwan-i-Am** (Public Audience Hall) in front. This closely resembles the Mughal Diwan-i-Am of Agra and Delhi; the Mughal emperor, in fact, had been irked by its construction as no courtier was expected to copy the works of the emperor. Jai Singh had to give an undertaking that he would never formally hold court in the Diwan-i-Am.

To the right is the huge double-storied entrance to the inner courtyard called **Ganesh Pol** (Elephant Gate). Beautifully decorated with polished plaster reliefs and painted floral motifs, the upper part of the scalloped doorway has a painting of the elephant-headed Ganesh, the god of victory and good omens. Galleries run through the upper storey with screens in stone so that the purdah-bound royal women could observe the functions and processions below without being seen themselves.

A small but elegant *charbagh* type landscaped garden fills the inner courtyard, with the **Sukh Niwas** (House of Pleasure) to the right and the **Jai Mandir** (House of Victory) to the left. The former was used in hot weather as a resting place for the ruler since it has an elaborate system of fountains and cascades to keep it cool. Its embellishments are said to have been the most beautiful of all the Rajput palaces. Some of its ivory-inlaid sandalwood doors and carved and painted window-panes still survive.

The king must have spent the evenings in the garden where sets of unusually shaped carpets (now on display in the Art Gallery of the Maharaja Sawai Man Singh II Museum), evoked spring with their vivid colours.

The **Jas Mandir** (House of Glory) combines the finest elements of Mughal architecture and interior decoration in a Rajput setting. Decorated with convex

Meditative watchman at Amber Palace gate.

mirrors on stucco reliefs of flowering plants and arabesques, paintings and coloured glass, the Jas Mandir is also Jai Singh's masterpiece. From its windows, which overlook the valley, it is possible to get a bird's-eye view of the **Dilaram Bagh** amidst the waters of the Maotha Lake, and the forest-covered hills of Kalikhoh beyond it. The upper floor of this building had verandahs on three sides which provided space to hold lavish open-air parties and music and dance performances. Rooms, passages and halls were decorated with superb cloth furnishings, screens and spreads and were used by all the inmates and their countless retainers.

Unlike many other ancient and medieval towns in India, Amber was not entirely deserted in spite of the foundation and steady rise of Jaipur a short distance away. The beautiful *havelis* built by important courtiers and nobles did suffer from disuse and neglect, but enough remains to bear witness to its past glory. These provide evidence not found elsewhere of urban architecture in medieval Rajasthan. The most important landmark of Amber town is the **Jagat Shiromani** temple, built in memory of Jagat Singh, the eldest son of Raja Man Singh, who died at a young age. Also known as the Mira Bai temple for its association with the celebrated queen and saint-poet of Chittaurgarh, it is an impressive structure made of marble and red and grey sandstone. The beautifully carved marble gateway with two stone elephants standing guard on either side of the arch leads to an open assembly hall and a spacious sanctum. The temples of Narsingh Avatar, Ambikesvar Shiva, Surya and Jain Tirthankara occupy vantage positions in the old town. A small but impressive mosque known as **Akbari Masjid** was also constructed here in the 17th century. Of all the reservoirs and stepwells, the large 17th century **Panna Mian-ki-Kund** with its central pavilion is specially arresting.

ali screen,
as Mandir.

The *chatris* of different rulers stand somewhat forlornly outside the city wall. Some of these contain traces of paintings. Although many of the rulers of Amber died outside the city, most of them had traditional memorials built for them. Temples to Surya and Shiva and a recently built Jain temple were erected on the other side of Sagar, a large man-made lake in the northwest corner of Amber. In the small **Archaeological Museum** at the foot of Amber palace, Mauryan relics, sculptures, terracottas and coins discovered at Bairat and other nearby sites are on display.

The fort which dominates the western horizon of Amber is **Jaigarh** (Victory Fort). A small fortress known as **Chilka-tola** (Kite Castle) previously stood here and was rebuilt by Vidyadhar with extensive additions and alterations in 1725. In order to overcome the perennial problem of water shortage, Vidyadhar constructed an elaborate network of masonry channels and aqueducts for the collection and storage of every drop of rain that fell on the ridges of Kalikhoh. The water was collected in a hugh open tank and distributed to three huge covered *tankas* (tanks) for storage. The inner walls of these tanks were carefully plastered to prevent seepage. This arrangement assured adequate drinking water even in years of drought. A small palace with the usual **Diwan-i-Am, Diwan-i-Khas, Sukh Niwas** and **Zenana Mahal** was constructed, along with a high tower, a large armoury, magazine, gun foundry, barracks and several temples. The fort was so closely guarded by a contingent of brave Minas that no one dared enter its massive gates except the ruler and the Prince-Regent. The treasure of the Kachchwaha house is said to have been housed here under their guard; traditionally, each newly installed ruler would be conducted blindfolded into the secret vault and permitted to choose one object from the hoard for himself. In 1976 the Indian authorities spent six months in a fruitless search for the treasure. Jaigarh is open to visitors who may see the deserted fort including the enormous **Jai Van**, the second largest cannon in the country, and the gun-foundry complete with moulds, kilns and implements – the only one of its kind surviving in India.

At the top of the southernmost hill of Kalikhoh stands **Nahargarh** (Tiger Fort) which was to be a watchful sentinel guarding the newly-built city of Jaipur. Traditionally the place is associated with a powerful local chief, Nahar Singh Bhomia. Sawai Jai Singh built a small fort here in view of its strategic importance, and as a retreat for his queens. Two temples, **Garh Ganesh Mandir** and **Charan Mandir**, were constructed along the Jaigarh–Nahargarh ridge. Sawai Ram Singh made extensive additions in the middle of the 19th century with twelve well-appointed suites for his twelve principal queens. The fort offers a magnificent view of the city, specially during sunrise and sunset.

Right: Amber's Shish Mahal. Below: saffron is a favoured colour for turbans.

A Crafts Bonanza

"The main streets are the principal Bazaars; on each side, under the arcades of the palaces, temples and houses, are the shops of the artisans who are seen working almost in the open air at their trades: the tailors, shoemakers, goldsmiths, armourers, pastry cooks, confectioners, coppersmiths...", wrote Victor Jacquement, a guest of the Governor General of India in 1832, in his *Impressions of Jaipur and Amber*.

Few other cities can offer the range of opportunity to encounter so many artisans practising skills centuries old, and for this the credit must go to the art-loving rulers of Amber and Jaipur. They not only invited craftspeople to the city from as far as Iran, but provided the environment in which to develop and refinine their arts. Jaipur's founder, after completing his palace, concentrated his treasure on building shops and bazaars and luring traders, bankers and craftsmen from Delhi, Udaipur and other regions to settle down in Jaipur.

Over the years the crafts of Jaipur have become major earners of foreign exchange and have had an impact on the city's economy. Rambling through the bazaars of Jaipur is an education in the variety and diversity of Rajasthan's hand-made goods.

The oldest and busiest market of the walled city is **Johari Bazaar**. Laid out between **Sanganeri Gate** and **Bari Chaupar** (the main square of the city), the market has temples, vegetable sellers and grocers side by side with emerald dealers. It is the main shopping area for the local people as well as an internationally known centre of the lapidary trade. Most of the leading dealers of precious and semi-precious stones are located either in Johari Bazaar or its by-lane, **Gopalji ka Rasta**. Gems and jewellery are one of the major export industries of the country, and the contribution of Jaipur's artisans here is immense. The country imports the raw material which is then hand-cut, polished and re-exported. Almost all of the country's cutters and polishers live in the walled city of Jaipur. Employing traditional tools, they achieve perfect angles, and their dexterity turns the least promising rough stones into gems worth thousands of rupees. An outlet of the wholesaler is popularly known as a *gaddi*, named for the mattress on which one sits cross-legged in the traditional Indian manner. One of the best outlets for fine jewellery is the **Gem Palace** on M.I. Road, established in 1852. The Kasliwal brothers who run the shop have a list of clients that runs from Hollywood stars to Parisian fashion houses. They have opened a small showroom/museum above the shop, in a beautiful room decorated using traditional techniques.

Inlay of gems in gold jewellery in the style referred to as Kundan has been exclusively practised in Jaipur. One of the best-known dealers is located in

Left, traditional textile techniques adapted to contemporary styles. Right, miniature-artist at work.

Haldiyon ka Rasta, another by-lane of Johari Bazaar: the dazzling shop of Bhuramal Rajmal Surana is romantically housed in a medieval mansion. Closely linked with Kundan is the art of enamelling which travelled from Persia via Lahore. Of the five Sikh enamellers brought to Jaipur by Raja Man Singh I in 16th century, the descendants of one continue to practise the art in a narrow lane – **Jadiyon ka Rasta**. Sardar Kudrat Singh is a master craftsman of the art of enamelling and has several international awards to his credit. The artist is willing to display his pieces at his place of work – which happens also to be his home.

Another art which flourished in Johari Bazaar is tie-dying. Though the artists practise their craft in their colonies some distance away, Johari Bazaar itself is the major outlet for their creations. A large portion of the market is occupied by dealers in tie-dyed textiles. The Rangrez, the traditional Muslim community of Jaipur dyers, have included various techniques in their creations but they are famous for *laharia* – the striped tie-dye – and *mothra*, a criss-cross pattern, both customarily worn for the monsoon festival of Tij.

Also on Johari Bazaar is **Rana Saree**, a family business which has been dealing in fabrics for over 250 years. This is an excellent place to find *zardosi*-work saris – silk saris elaborately embroidered with gold and silver thread.

Passing through the square of Bari Chaupar offers a vivid glimpse of local life: flower sellers, shops of attar, and dealers in traditional silver jewellery and block printed textiles throng the area. On one side, under a banyan tree, are wayside shops selling simple but beautiful bangles, local shoes and rustic jewellery. There are tailors here who can stitch traditional dresses within hours of order. A road from the square leads to the **Ramganj Bazaar**, known for the hand-crafted slip-on shoes called

Below left, puppets for sale. Below right, tie-dye craftswoman at work.

juti. A fascinating range of traditional shoes from all over Rajasthan is available here. The most comfortable are made of camel hide. From this road the settlement of the dyers can be approached, if one is interested in witnessing the intricate process of tie-dying.

Past the square, all around **Hawa Mahal** is the tourist market. Shops have sprung up like mushrooms with the advent of tourism. Here, you can buy embroidery, gems and jewellery, *jutis* and curios, but tourists should be on guard against poor quality and over-priced goods. Ahead, a labyrinth on the right of **Subhash Chowk** unfolds the world of carpets and *durri* weavers. Jaipur is an exporter of a large number of carpets and rugs. An outlet with a good reputation for quality is **Maharaja Carpets** based in Samode Haveli.

Jaipur markets are overflowing with miniature paintings on paper, silk and ivory, predominantly reproductions of old masterpieces. A careful eye is required to differentiate the painting of a skilled miniature artist from one produced in the mass production factories. Some painters excel in painting on ivory, but with the worldwide restriction on ivory they are switching to the traditional medium of paper. These can be seen at **The Collection Painting School** on Mount Road, and at the **Friends of the Museum Master Craftsmen and Artists** in the City Palace (this is also a good place to see traditional tie-dyed fabrics and hand-made paper).

A more contemporary view of Rajasthani life can be seen in the paintings of **Jaya Wheaton**, who can be contacted at C80 Subhas Marg. Her work is distinguished by the use of just one or two complementary colours.

There are particular crafts which are identified with particular areas of the walled city. The Silawats or marble sculptors have been practising this art since the inception of Jaipur in the lane named after them, **Silawaton ka Rasta**, also referred to as the Khazne Walon ka

Below left, Rangrez dyeing *lahariya*. **Below right,** embroidered *jutis*.

Rasta. The craftsmen have excelled in sculpting single marble slabs into images of the deities of Hindu pantheon, adhering to the principles laid out in the ancient canons. One of the principles requires them to abandon the unfinished statue if it should undergo any damage. Hindu temples all over the country and overseas have installed statues carved by the Jaipur Silawats. Today they make statues to order as well as intricate marble arches, balconies and wall panels. One of the best places to see marble carving is **Shashi Arts and Crafts**, a family-run business that has been producing work in the same *haveli* for over 150 years.

Turning lac bangles is another colourful craft of Jaipur. The lac bangle makers, known as Manihars, inhabit **Maniharon ka Rasta**. Lac bangles are of great significance in the life of Rajasthani people: women are given special bangles on auspicious occasions such as marriage and childbirth. Some of the bangle makers here also make designer jewellery for the export market.

Certain other crafts patronised by the former rulers of Jaipur flourish beyond the walls of the city. These include block printed textiles, blue pottery and paper making. Near the airport lies the village of Sanganer, well known for its block printed textile and hand made paper. It also has a blue pottery factory.

The ceramics artist Kripal Singh Shekhawat was largely responsible for reviving the art that was brought to Jaipur by Sawai Ram Singh II. His creations, adhering to traditional skills and shapes, are on sale at **Kripal Kumbh** on Shir Marg in Bani Park. Other outlets for blue pottery, also interesting, are the **Blue Pottery Art Centre** on Amer Road, and **Neerja International** on Bhawani Singh Marg.

The ensemble of crafts of Rajasthan has been presented under one roof by the government-sponsored emporium **Rajasthali,** just off M.I. Road – this is the *only* government-approved store. You can shop there at a fixed price.

Jaipur blue pottery ceramic beads.

ANOKHI

Among the shopping highlights for a visitor to Jaipur is the fabric and furnishings store called **Anokhi**, meaning "unique". On Tilak Marg, opposite Udyog Bhawan is an unpretentious low building – behind the simple white door are the garments, furnishings and accessories sold under the Anokhi label, that are handsome, comfortable and innovative enough to have created a worldwide clientele. What distinguishes Anokhi the firm, however, is not just its classic prints and designs, but its commitment to encouraging traditional craft skills. With outlets in major cities all over the world, Anokhi is a business enterprise which helps craftsmen to use their skills in the creation of contemporary products of high utility and aesthetic value.

The story of the creators of Anokhi is also singular. Jitendra Pal (John) Singh met Faith Hardy in the swimming pool of the Rambagh Palace in the summer of 1968. John, educated at the Doon School, Delhi University and Oxford, was setting up a poultry farm in Jaipur after quitting his job on a tea plantation. Faith, the daughter of a quondam Bishop of Nagpur, had come to India from England to learn and work with traditional textile crafts. They married and started a discotheque which they optimistically named "The Fertile Egg".

***Anoki* fashion show in Samode palace.**

In 1970, they came under the influence of a spiritual mentor and their lifestyle underwent a transformation. They turned vegetarian and John sold his hunting guns, chicken farm and discotheque. He decided to supply his energy and attention to creating an organised and stable business based on the work Faith was doing in a small way with block-printers and tailors.

A firm called Registan was registered in June 1970 and its label chosen. Over time, the firm evolved its policy: to provide craftspeople with design input, finance, quality control and marketing, blending modern management with traditional skills, without disrupting their autonomy and way of life. In Faith's words, "Anokhi has consistently sought to create an environment, a relationship between the market and the design product, skill and tradition. In this, traditional textiles have their place and value. But they must be supported by contemporary prints and designs which can create excitement and hold interest in a demanding and fast-moving world market".

The discreet image of the Anokhi shops and the absence of "hard-sell" enhances Anokhi's image. Beginning with garments, Faith and John added furnishings and accessories to their range so that their printers, weavers and dyers could be kept in work all year round. Anokhi's commercial expansion has gone hand in hand with the increase in the company's other activities. It set up the Digantar Trust which runs a free school, a health centre, a free veterinary clinic, and sponsors activities ranging from cycle polo to motorcycle racing.

John Singh is deeply involved with the conservation of Rajasthan's cultural and natural heritage. His experience on his farm outside Jaipur has led him to an involvement with propagating sustainable agriculture and the greening of barren lands. In addition to ensuring their goods are ethically sourced, the couple have also used their business to help during humanitarian crises. For instance, in 1988 they organised a sale of goods for one of the most effective relief projects in Barmer District, during the worst drought of the century.

Note: Anokhi's garments and furnishings are sold at shops in Jaipur, Delhi and in Mumbai.

JAIPUR BEYOND THE WALLED CITY

It is curious that the fame of the walled Pink City has overshadowed the Jaipur that lies beyond the city walls. From the point of view of tourists, it is an interesting mix of historical monuments and signs of modern development. The first attempt to move beyond the walled city was made by Sawai Ram Singh II (1835-80). Of the four major public works undertaken by him, three were located outside the city walls: the Ram Niwas Garden, the Museum and Mayo Hospital. He also converted Kesar Garden, 3 km (2 miles) south of the old city, into his hunting lodge, renaming it Rambagh.

After the death of Maharaja Ishwari Singh in 1750, Jaipur remained virtually without any contact with the world outside. When Maharaja Ram Singh came to the throne in 1854, he decided to extend his reach to the world beyond Jaipur State. As a member of the Imperial Legislative Council he spent some time in Kolkata (Calcutta), the political and intellectual capital of British India, and was struck by the city's rich and lively culture. Fired with enthusiasm, he decided to emulate it: he set up new departments of education, medicine and public works in his administration and hired the services of British officers to modernise his state. Sir Swinton Jacob, designer of many important buildings, was appointed as the Chief Engineer of the State. Gas lighting was introduced, and certain buildings as well as the road from Sanganeri Gate to the railway station were illuminated. The Maharaja also promoted the construction of schools, colleges, hospitals and a museum.

Ram Singh decided to take up the construction of the **Ram Niwas** as a famine relief project in 1868, with the failure of the monsoon that year. The garden was designed on the lines of the Eden Gardens of Kolkata. Within its precincts a zoo was set up, which is among the oldest in the country. A beautiful bandstand marked the centre of the park where on every Monday evening the State Band performed, attired in ceremonial garb. The total cost of the project at that time is said to have been about 400,000 rupees.

What draws a visitor to the garden today is the majestic **Albert Hall**. A few years after the Ram Niwas Garden was laid out, the Maharaja decided to add a Durbar Hall and a museum on the lines of the Victoria and Albert Museum. Sir Swinton Jacob designed the building in the Indo-Saracenic style, combining Oriental arches with late Victorian proliferation. On 6 February 1876, the Prince of Wales and future King Edward VII laid the foundation of the building, which was completed and opened as a museum only ten years later, in the reign of Maharaja Ram Singh's successor Madho Singh. Today it is the Central Museum managed by the State Department of Archaeology and houses an interesting and, in parts, eccentric (for instance, the small models of "the amusements and vices of man") collection of paintings, carpets, ivory, brassware, textiles and other objects. The Persian 17th century garden carpet woven in Kirman is regarded as one of the finest carpets ever created. Apart from the collection within, Jacob's building itself is a treasured piece of colonial architecture. The huge garden has been reduced to less than half of its original size and now houses the main theatre of the city, **Ravindra Rang Manch**, along with an open-air theatre and the art gallery of the Lalit Kala Akademi.

Further down the road stands the **Takht-e-Shahi**. Designed like a Scottish castle on the low hill of Moti Dungri, it offers an excellent view of the city. In 1975, Indian tax officials seized a part of the fabled treasures of the Jaipur royal family from its secret vaults. Its commanding view has been obscured by a modern marble temple.

Under Maharaja Ram Singh, railway lines were laid connecting Jaipur with Agra, Mumbai and Delhi. The trunk road between Agra and Ajmer via Jaipur and Bharatpur was completed, and many other metalled roads were laid and provided with wayside facilities for travellers.

Ram Singh's successor Madho Singh II completed many public works initiated by him. The main achievement of his reign was the construction of the much debated irrigation dam at Jamwa Ramgarh, which dragged on for 25 years. Over the years the reservoir has proved to be an important source of water for the city. Madho Singh could not, however, match his predecessor's zeal for progress. To the end of his reign Jaipur continued its medieval rituals: the gates of the walled city were closed at 11pm. and nobody could leave or enter till they opened at daybreak. It was only in 1923 that an order was issued to keep the Chand Pol on the west open through the night for the convenience of passengers, since it was on the way to and from the railway station.

Kishan Pol: imposing gates once controlled access to the medieval city.

Man Singh II was a minor when he came to the throne and received his full powers only in 1931. His accession fostered the growth of the city outside the city walls – mostly southwards – which became a prestigious area when the Maharaja took up residence in the Rambagh Palace. Initially it was difficult to induce people to build houses in the area; it was almost a wilderness, and many older citizens remember spotting big game in the area. It required infrastructure development in terms of roads and other civic amenities as well as ridiculously low-priced plots to lure people out of the walled city. With Sir Mirza Ismail as the Prime Minister of the state, the development of the new city received added momentum.

Among the important buildings built by Man Singh were the new Maharaja College near the Ram Niwas garden, Lady Willingdon Hospital (today the S.M.S. Hospital) and Sawai Man Singh Guards Barracks, today the Secretariat of the Government of Rajasthan.

Mirza Ismail Road, popularly abbreviated to M.I. Road, is the high street of the new city with showrooms of car agencies, consumer products and banks interspersed with bookshops and eateries. Originally known as the Hawa Sarak, the existing road was developed by Sir Mirza Ismail. It runs just along the southern wall of the city, from Sanganeri Gate in the East to close by the railway station in the west.

There are some interesting buildings on the road, such as the Government Hostel, built as a Dak Bungalow for travellers taking the trunk road to Ajmer and for a while used to house the state secretariat. Later it was converted into a hotel and further remodelled on a palatial scale at, what was then, a huge cost of 150,000 rupees. A resident British officer recorded in 1909 the advent of tourism: "Carriages and elephants [for Amber] are supplied by the Managers, and English speaking guides are always available".

On the north along the road to Amber is the Man Sagar Lake, with the picturesque **Jal Mahal** in its centre. It was constructed by Sawai Madho Singh I based on the Jag Mandir and Jas Mandir on Lake Pichola at Udaipur where he grew up. About 4 km (2 miles) to the west of the main road lies Gaitore, the burial ground of the rules of Jaipur. The *chatri* (mausoleum) of Sawai Jai Singh is expectedly the finest of all the *chatris*. This large, delicately carved marble memorial was constructed by his son and successor, Sawai Ishwari Singh. Ironically, his own *chatri* is not to be found here; he died by committing suicide when Marathas came to invade the city in 1750, and was cremated hurriedly outside the northwestern corner of Jai Niwas Bagh. The *chatris* of the Maharanis of Jaipur are to be found near the spot where the road to Ramgarh Lake branches off from Amber Road.

The rulers of Jaipur and their principal courtiers constructed garden houses along the Agra road outside the southeastern corner of the city. The most notable is the terraced garden, **Sisodiya Rani-ka-Bagh** made for the queen who belonged to the Sisodiya clan of Sawai Jai Singh. The garden houses of Vidyadhar, the architect of the city, and his son Muralidhar, were also built in this area. Beyond these gardens lies the holy spring of **Galtaji** and on the top of the hill, a small temple of the Sun God, the only sun temple in this part of India. Several large temples dedicated to Lord Krishna, Shiva and Hanuman were built along the road to the Galta spring.

Jaipur is geared up for its fast-growing tourism industry. It has many hotels, of varying standards. Some of the best are in old buildings like the Rajmahal Palace (the former residency of the British representative in the state) and the Jai Mahal Palace, that have been taken over by the Taj Group of Hotels, which also manages the Rambagh Palace Hotel. Many of the Thakurs, Rajput nobles, have started offering accommodation in their stately mansions, including the Narain Niwas owned by the ex-rulers of Kanota, and Samode Haveli, run by the same family who own Samode Palace.

One of the more recent landmarks of the new city is the marble **temple of Laxmi Narain** built by the Hindustan Charitable Trust of the country's leading industrial group, the Birlas. (Many of India's top industrialists hail from Rajasthan.) Some find the temple exquisite, while others see it as an eyesore since it is built next to the "Scottish castle" of Man Singh. The temple is certainly a testament to the skill of Jaipur's marble carvers.

Another local landmark is the Rajmandir Cinema on Bhagwan Das Road. One of India's most opulent cinema halls, this is an excellent place to introduce yourself to modern Bollywood movies. Book one day in advance as it is usually full.

The 18th-century Jal Mahal on Man Sagar Lake, a pavilion for duck shooting.

RAMBAGH PALACE HOTEL

In the heart of the new city stands the legendary Rambagh Palace Hotel in an estate of 15 hectares (36 acres). Although India's prestigious hotel chain, the Taj Group of Hotels, took it under its wing only in 1972, royal hospitality has been a tradition from its inception in 1887.

The palace originated from a garden created in 1835 by Kesar, a *badaran* or hand-maiden of Maharani Chandrawati, the mother of Sawai Ram Singh II. The garden with its 4-room pavilion became known as Kesar Bagh, the garden of Kesar, and was later turned by Maharaja Ram Singh into a hunting resort. Since the Maharaja had restricted hunting within a radius of 16 km (10 miles) around the city, except for members of the royal family, game was available in abundance. Kesar's garden was renamed Rambagh. It became a personal guest house of the Maharaja, initially with 26 rooms. On his return from a tour of England in 1902, Madho Singh II decided to give the mansion a new look with the help of Sir Swinton Jacob, the designer of the Albert Hall museum in Jaipur. It is said that the Rambagh was the only private residence in the world to have its own polo field.

Soon after the death of Maharaja Madho Singh in 1922, a special school was set up at the Rambagh Palace for a short while for his 11-year-old successor with the aim of him secluding from "the intrigues of the harem" – in other words, keeping the young heir firmly under British tutelage. Sir James Roberts started the school and tutored the young Maharaja himself, along with 22 other children of distinguished families. Three years later, Rambagh was made the official residence of the Maharaja, again to segregate him from the "undesirable" atmosphere of the City Palace.

Moving to the Rambagh Palace proved to be lucky for Man Singh. Two events of importance took place there. His eldest son Bhawani was born in 1931, the first direct heir in the family after nearly 100 years. The following year brought another memorable event which added a romantic chapter to his life. He had invited the Maharani of Cooch-Behar to stay at Rambagh when she went to Ajmer to visit her son at the Mayo College. Man Singh escorted her two daughters on sightseeing tours. It was at that time that, dazzled by the 13-year-old younger princess, the twice-married Man Singh decided to make her his Maharani when she grew up. The young princess was Gayatri Devi, who went on to play an important part in the politics of the new state of Rajasthan.

Man Singh took a keen interest in making the Rambagh Palace a luxurious residence. A new dining hall designed in London was added in 1936. Lalique fountains were brought in from Paris in 1940, when Man Singh married Gayatri Devi. They occupied refurbished adjoining suites: these are now the Maharaja and Maharani suites, the most prized of all the rooms available in the hotel.

Until 1957 the family continued to live at the Rambagh Palace. Then came a series of changes brought about by India's new democratic rulers after Independence and the integration of the princely states. Much against the wishes of his family, the Maharaja decided to turn his spacious residence into a hotel.

Over the last 120 years, the Rambagh Palace has developed from a 4-room pavilion to a 26-room royal guest house, and finally to a 110-room palatial hotel. Popular with filmstars and fashion models, it is predictably opulent, with the Polo Bar and its marble fountain, the manicured gardens, lavish suites and the finely decorated Oriental Room.

The Rajmata's cavalry in the Rambagh Palace gardens.

Sanganer, Bagru and Samode

The people of the town of Sanganer (16km/10 miles south of Jaipur), are almost wholly engaged in traditional crafts. Its location close to the river Saraswati, now mostly dry, encouraged crafts like paper-making and hand-block printing, which need an abundant supply of water. Sanganer is also known for its hand-painted pottery, screen-printed textiles and its Jain and Krishna temples.

Legend says that the town was established by Sanga Baba about 1,500 years ago, and that hand printed fabrics have been produced here for more than 1,000 years. The **Sanghiji temple** of the Digambara (literally, "sky-clad", i.e. naked) Jain sect was reputedly established by Dyuta Ram Sanghi about 1,000 years ago. All twenty-four Tirthankaras are installed in this Jain temple where there is a small bas-relief of the original chief priest beside the inner portal.

Painted figures in Rajput dresses near the tops of columns in the first courtyard seem to be later additions. On the exterior is depicted the romantic story of Dhola-Maru (Dulha Rai and Maroni). Also in white marble is a **Kirti Stambha** (Pillar of Fame), in front of the **Krishna temple**.

All the stages of the production of handmade paper can be seen in workshops in Sanganer, especially in the **Kagazi mohalla** (Paper Precinct) area. The large establishment of Salim Kagazi on Gramodyog Road can show the processes and a wide variety of papers, some of which are unique. At other places, craftspeople paint designs on notepaper, attach pressed leaves and flowers to envelopes and shape stiff paper cones into loudspeakers. About 50 families here are engaged in handmade paper manufacture, and to preserve their trade secrets they avoid marrying outside the community.

Preceding pages, richly embellished Durbar Hall of Samode Palace. **Left**, rural sewing bee: decorating tie-dyed veils. **Right**, screen-printed fabric drying on racks.

In recent years a trend has appeared among hand-block printers of moving away from traditional techniques to screen printing. This is because of the much higher levels of output they can achieve with the new technology, using the same amount of time and labour. The old craft may well die out with the passage of time. The screen printing industry produces fabrics, spectacular on their own and even more so when seen draped on drying racks a few floors high – hundreds of metres of brilliantly coloured cloth.

The hand-block printed fabrics are no longer purely traditional, having encompassed modern materials. The designs with traditional motifs, however, continue to be intricate and beautiful, and the process can be seen in workshops in the **Chippa mohalla** and the Training Centre near the bridge. Places to buy these fabrics are mostly along the main road. The handpainted pottery of Sanganer mostly has floral motifs in blue, pink and white.

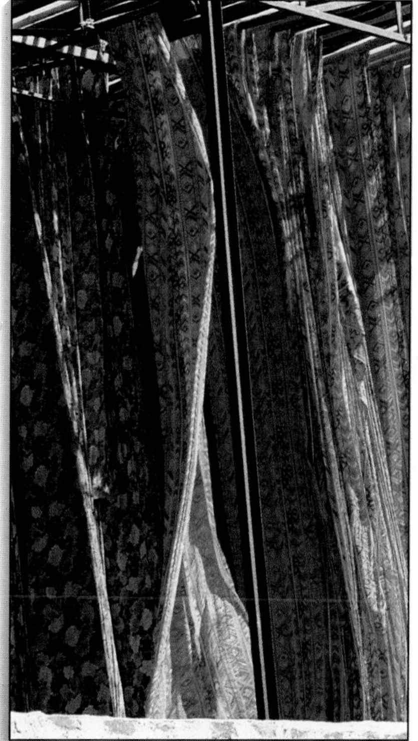

Sanganer was also the scene of a dramatic episode of feudal intrigue, which contributed to the primacy of Jai Singh as the ruler of Amber and thus to the establishment of the city of Jaipur. Vijay Singh, the half-brother of Jai Singh, had presented him with a list of demands which revealed his ambition to seize the seat of power at Amber. A parley was arranged between the two brothers at Sanganer. Just before the meeting, a messenger arrived from the palace in Sanganer summoning both brothers to the presence of the queen mother. The message said she wanted to see them and witness their reconciliation. The queen mother's command could not be disobeyed: the brothers met in Sanganer and embraced, and Jai Singh offered to meet all of Vijay Singh's demands. At the door of the queen's chambers Jai Singh paused to take off his dagger, saying "Brother, what is the occasion to bear arms here?" Vijay Singh, not to be outdone, followed suit. As he entered, the door closed behind him, and Vijay Singh found himself a prisoner. It was a plot hatched by Jai Singh and his Wazir. The entourage of the queen mother was a host of Bhatti solders in disguise. No more was ever heard of Vijay Singh. Jai Singh went on to establish Jaipur city and become its most accomplished, scholarly and renown ed ruler.

Bagru, which is about 35 km (20 miles) from Jaipur on the road to Ajmer, lies west of Sanganer and is famous for its hand-block printed fabrics made in the traditional manner, with vegetable dyes and natural colours. It is a small market town where about fifty families of Chippas, traditional hand-block printers, are involved in this activity.

The wooden printing-block is the most ancient mechanical device used for the patterning of cloth. In Rajasthan, legend tells us that Sawai Jai Singh (1699–1743), founder of Jaipur city, invited craftsmen and artisans of many skills to his newly built capital. It was on account of his patronage and that of

Vegetable dyes are used on fabrics.

subsequent rulers that textile printing in the region became so important.

It is possible to watch the various steps in the making of hand-block printed cloth. A typical finished piece of cloth may have gone through the following stages, with frequent washing in between to remove the substances used at each stage: preparation of the raw cloth – soaking, boiling and beating by hand; tanning and block printing with the mordant (which aids dye penetration); curing in the sun; dyeing in a copper pot, set into an earthern platform over a wood fire (this dye bath, enhanced with the flower locally known as *dhawda*, produces fast colours on those areas which have been printed with mordant); block printing with "resist paste" to reserve portions of the pattern in their original colour; dusting of the printed surface with sawdust to prevent smudging; immersing in the indigo vat; removal of the resist paste (sometimes repeatedly); application of yellow dye, made from pomegranate and turmeric, to produce green on blue areas; immersion of the cloth in alum solution to fix the yellow; and curing of the fabric for at least fifteen days.

Until recently, the blocks were rarely larger than 7.5 cm by 10 cm (3 inches by 4 inches), but nowadays most blocks measure about 15 cm by 20 cm (8 inches by 6 inches) to accommodate larger and bolder patterns and meet the exigencies of present day socio-economics. All pressing and registration is done by hand and eye, and an experienced printer may complete 15 m to 20 m (49 ft to 65 ft) of a six-colour design in a day.

Knowledge and expertise is handed down within the family. All the printing activities are commonly clustered around the central courtyard of the house and one can trace the whole process by climbing up the various floors.

Bagru prints are known for their inky black (*syahi*) and ochre colours. The black colour is prepared from rusted iron (old horseshoes, nails, etc) and jaggery, while the ochre is prepared

Hand-made paper, Sanganer.

from alum, gum and *geru* (a kind of red earth). The creamy yellow colour is made from turmeric and pomegranate skin. The resist paste, *dabu*, is derived from rusted wheat, earth, slaked lime and gum.

Bagru was also the site of a battle between the invading Marathas and the rulers of Jaipur in August 1748. The battle, which raged for six days, was often stopped by rain. Ishwari Singh, the Maharaja of Jaipur, was driven into Bagru fort and was compelled to make terms with the enemy. The fort, in spite of being in the town, and the only "sight" in Bagru, is mostly empty.

Twenty-eight miles (42 km) northwest of Jaipur is the impeccably preserved palace-turned-hotel of **Samode**. Snugly sited amongst protective hills crowned with forts, the palace is the grand culmination of an uphill drive through a series of gates. Since its debut in the film of *The Far Pavilions*, it has become a favourite location for filmmakers. This is a mixed blessing: at times the palace is entirely taken over by film crew and barred to visitors.

Samode was the seat of one of the feudatories of the Jaipur kingdom. The family traces its lineage back to the illustrious Prithviraj Singhji of Amber (1503-28), a prince of the Kacchwaha Rajputs. The lords of Samode were loyal to the Maharaja of Jaipur and many served as ministers to the king. These faithful warriors were honoured with the hereditary title of "Rawal Saheb", and their descendants still live in Samode.

Spatially the palace is a progression of courtyards of increasing height and opulence. The first courtyard with the lawns and the old stables forms the entrance. A charming feature is the decoration done in the local style by the Jaipur artist Jaya Rastogi.

The grand stairs at the western end lead to the next courtyard which has the family temple and some private rooms. The third courtyard, reached by yet another imposing staircase, is the most

Block printing, Sanganer.

interesting, with playing fountains and glimpses of mirror inlay work and miniature paintings in the rooms around. On the floor above, adjoining the terrace which overlooks the courtyard, is the Sultan Mahal. Beyond the silver sofas and the arches set with mirrors, is the splendid room where no surface escapes decoration with mirror and intricate painting. The sense of exuberant opulence is overwhelming and the visitor can spend several hours here studying the miniatures of scenes of life from past ages. These were done in the late 18th and early 19th centuries.

A similar pleasant assault on the senses is the **Shish Mahal** (Hall of Mirrors) in the Durbar Mahal, which lies along the south side of the palace. The magic of the place is best experienced by candlelight. The last courtyard is architecturally completely different. With its mostly pure Hindu architectural elements, it seems to be the oldest part of the palace. The other areas show the progressively greater influence of the style of architecture made fashionable by the Mughals. The Durbar Mahal, which was built about a century ago, would not have been out of place in any Mughal palace.

A recent addition to the palace is a magnificent marble swimming pool, on one side of which is an outdoor jacuzzi. Four kilometres (3 miles) away is Samode Bagh, a garden retreat with luxury tent accommodation, of the same high standard as the Palace and the family *haveli* in Jaipur.

A candlelit dinner by moonlight on the roof of the palace is definitely worth experiencing for anyone staying at Samode. Rooms 114 and 116, which were specially redesigned for the Anokhi festival in 1988, are of particular interest. During the day the nearby forts of Sheogarh and Mahr may be interesting hiking destinations. The small village of Samode, which lies below the Palace, also produces traditional tie-dyed fabrics, lac bangles and the ubiquitous miniature paintings.

Samode Palace exterior.

AROUND JAIPUR

While Jaipur itself provides a number of sights and opportunities for tourists, it is possible to take advantage of its proximity to many interesting places which are easily accessible by train or road. These may be visited either en route to Jaipur from Agra and Delhi or on excursions from Jaipur.

The **Sariska National Park and Tiger Reserve** lies 34 km (21 miles) south of Alwar, on the road to Delhi. It used to be the exclusive hunting preserve of the rulers of Alwar. In 1955 it became a sanctuary and since 1979 has been a designated a Tiger Reserve. The National Park covers 800 sq. km (309 sq. miles) of forested Aravalli hills.

Amongst Sariska's archaeological features, the ruined temples of **Nilkanth**, 32 km (20 miles) away, date back to the 9th and 10th centuries. There is the **Kankwari fort** on the plateau of the same name, from the Mughal period. The Sariska palace was completed in 1902 as a royal hunting lodge and is now used as a hotel.

The park has a good network of roads which branch out into forest tracks accessible by jeeps. The animals are most easily seen at the artificial waterholes that have been constructed in this dry region. Ungulates such as **sambar**, **chital**, **chinkara**, **nilgai** and **chausingha** populate this area. Predators include **tiger**, **leopard**, **jungle cat**, **hyena** and **jackal**. These are somewhat difficult to spot, emerging mostly at night, but tiger sightings are possible during the day. Many bird species inhabit the area, including a variety of **shrikes**, **grey partridge**, **golden-backed woodpecker**, **peafowl**, **owls** and the **crested serpent eagle**.

Siliserh Lake, lying 13 km (8 miles) from Alwar, used to water the gardens in Alwar via a still visible aqueduct. It has a picturesque water palace at its edge, from where pleasant evenings can be spent watching the birds at dawn and sunset. Paddle boats can be hired for excursions on the tranquil lake.

Alwar city itself is replete with palaces, gardens, museums and a nearby fortress, the **Bala Qila**. Extending 5 km (3 miles) along a steep cliff, it offers a spectacular view of the city below; the ruined town of **Ravana Devra** lies at the bottom of the cliffs. The Bala Qila is accessed by a rough track and police permission is required to visit it (obtainable from the City Palace Superintendent of Police).

The magnificent **City Palace** lies in the heart of the old city. It now houses Alwar's district government in the rooms of the former armoury, treasury and library. Its five massive gates were once kept closed at night to allow tigers to prowl outside and protect the city. The splendid Durbar Hall may be visited with permisson. The extravagance of Alwar's former rulers is evident from the exhibits found in the **Museum** located on the top floor of the

Left, street scene in Alwar before a modern temple. Right, Siliserh Palace, overlooking a 19th-century reservoir.

palace. Rare manuscripts, weapons, *objets d'art* and miniature paintings are amongst the exhibits.

Visible from the City Palace museum is the **Musi Maharani ki Chatri**, a cenotaph regarded as a fine example of the prevalent Indo-Islamic style and named after the mistress of a former ruler who performed *sati* here. The **Vinay Vilas Mahal** and the **Company Bagh** have some of the finest gardens in Alwar. Both gardens were once watered by the now disused Siliserh aqueduct.

Other sights worth seeing are the old **Railway Station** and the 16th century Mughal **Fateh Jung Gumbad**, both of which contain examples of local stone tracery. The **Vijay Mandir** palace is a former royal residence, and offers a glimpse into the lifestyle of the erstwhile princes.

Near the exit to the road to Jaipur stands the **Moti Dungri fortress**, built by Jai Singh, an eccentric but popular ruler of Alwar. The fortress sits on a hill which once was the location of a palace called Landsdowne. This was inexplicably dynamited by Jai Singh, and a park now occupies its site.

On the way from Jaipur to Agra, the visitor can tour the towns of Deeg and Bharatpur, as well as one of the world's most important bird sanctuaries at Bharatpur. This area has a distinct cultural identity, being mainly populated by the Jats, a predominantly agricultural community who speak a dialect of Hindi known as *Braj Bhasha*. In the 18th century, Jat rulers such as Badan Singh ruled a kingdom which extended between Delhi and Agra, east of the Yamuna river. They warred with the Mughals, Marathas, Rajputs and British, defeating all and temporarily occupying both Delhi and Agra.

Deeg, 86 km (54 miles) from Agra, is approachable from Alwar via Milakpur. The main attraction in this small, dusty agricultural town is its **Fort**. The walls of this immense citadel tower 28 m (85 ft) above a moat 17 m (50 ft) broad. The fort has twelve bastions, the largest

The tank and cenotaph of the Alwar Palace complex.

being **Lakla Burj**, still mounted with cannon. Deeg is famous for the palace and gardens laid by Badan Singh and his son Suraj Mal during the first half of the 18th century.

The largest building, **Gopal Bhawan**, overlooks a tank called **Gopal Sagar**. It is flanked by two pavilions shaped like pleasure barges. Central to the garden is **Keshav Bhawan**, a pillared pavilion with an ingenious system of 500 fountains, which sprayed coloured water on special occasions. Other buildings include **Suraj Bhawan**, made of marble, and **Purana Mahal**, which displays a collection of wall paintings.

Bharatpur, 51 km (32 miles) from Agra, contains the once impregnable **Lohagarh Fort**, which successfully resisted a four-month-long British siege in 1805. It contains three palaces, of which one is now a **museum**. Their architecture demonstrates Rajput and Mughal influences, but in a more austere form. The museum contains a good archaeological collection, including a late Gupta sculpture of Shiva and Parvati from the 8th century and a 2nd century red sandstone Shiva *linga*. There are also two towers, **Jawahar Burj** and **Fateh Burj**, built to commemorate victories against the Mughals and the British respectively.

Keoladeo Ghana National Park, or the Bharatpur Bird Santuary as it is popularly known, lies 5 km (3 miles) from the fort. In area the park covers a mere 29 sq. km (11 sq. miles), of which one third lies submerged during the monsoon; but it has a variety of grasses, trees and aquatic plants which support millions of insects, crustaceans and fish. These in turn provide food for the indigenous **painted storks, spoonbills, cormorants,** various **herons** and **egrets** and other water birds which breed in the season from August to November. By early October the first migrants, such as **ducks**, **geese** and **waders**, arrive from northern and central Asia. These are followed by raptors like the **steppe eagle**, **golden eagle**, **osprey** and **harrier** and by the rare **Siberian crane**. They remain until March, feeding mainly on sedge tubers. The cranes failed to appear for several years – possibly due to hunting on their migration route – but some four breeding pairs have reappeared as regular visitors. Animals ranging from **nilgai** to **rhesus macaque** also inhabit the park.

About 160 km (100 miles) south of Jaipur, situated amidst the Vindhya and Aravalli hills, is **Ranthambore National Park**. A Project Tiger reserve, it covers 411 sq. km (158 sq. miles) of forest. Ranthambore's landscape has a fort, temples and tanks dotted all over the park; this mixture affords stunning images, such as of **tigers** resting inside ruined temples.

Other predators and scavengers usually found here are **leopard**, **caracal, hyena** and **jungle cat**. In addition to the usual varieties of **deer**, you can find **marsh crocodile, monitor lizard**, **sloth bear**, **wild boar** and others.

Bharatpur: green bee-eater.

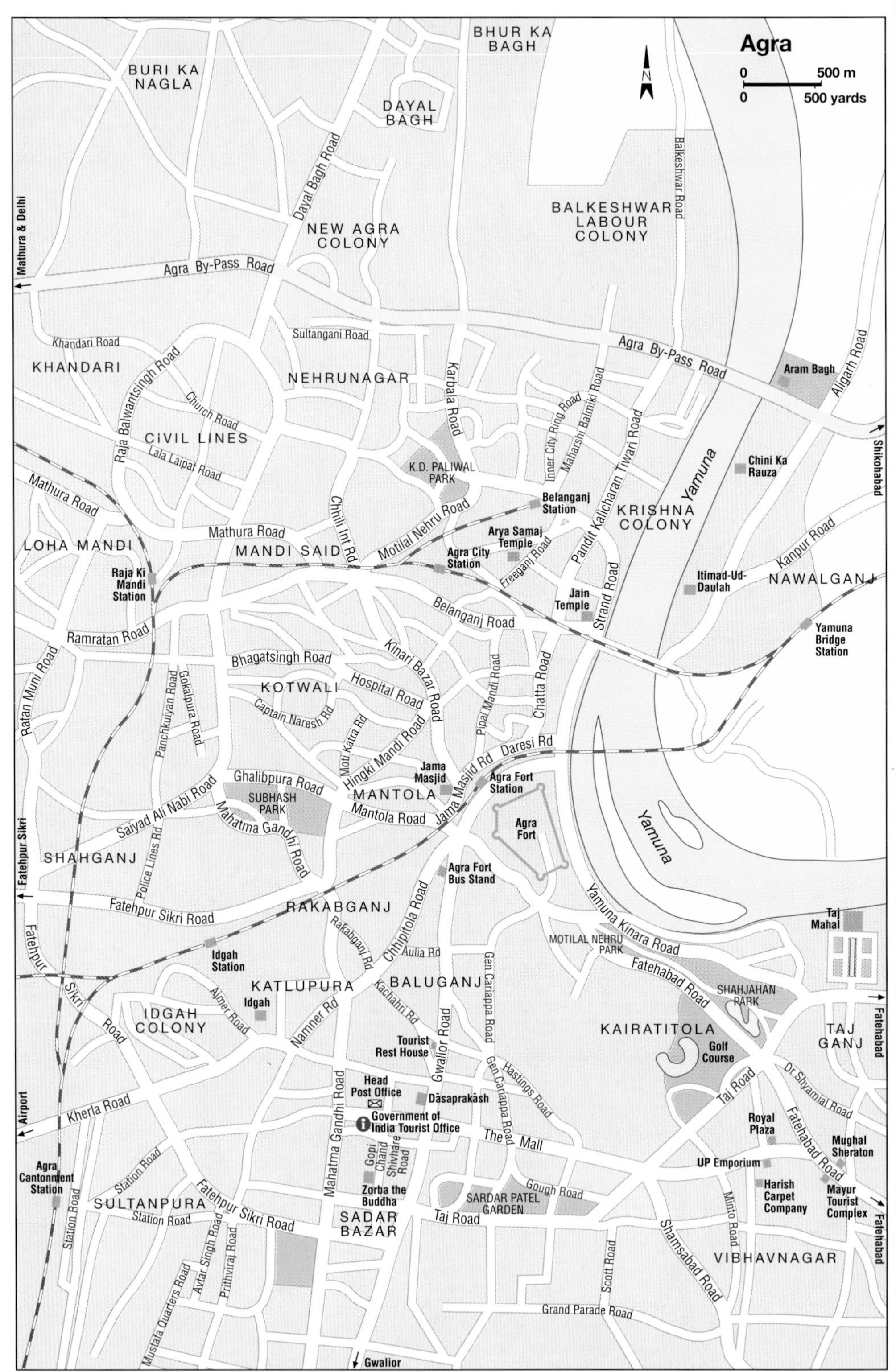

Agra
0 500 m
0 500 yards
BHUR KA BAGH
BURI KA NAGLA
DAYAL BAGH
Dayal Bagh Road
NEW AGRA COLONY
BALKESHWAR LABOUR COLONY
Balkeshwar Road
Mathura & Delhi
Agra By-Pass Road
Sultangani Road
Khandari Road
KHANDARI
Raja Balwantsingh Road
NEHRUNAGAR
Karbala Road
Aram Bagh
Aligarh Road
Church Road
CIVIL LINES
Lala Lajpat Road
K.D. PALIWAL PARK
Inner City Ring Road
Maharshi Balmiki Road
Pandit Kalicharan Tiwari Road
Yamuna
Chini Ka Rauza
Shikohabad
Mathura Road
Chilli Int Rd
Motilal Nehru Road
Belanganj Station
KRISHNA COLONY
LOHA MANDI
MANDI SAID
Arya Samaj Temple
Agra City Station
Freeganj Road
Kanpur Road
Raja Ki Mandi Station
Itimad-Ud-Daulah
NAWALGANJ
Jain Temple
Strand Road
Belanganj Road
Ramratan Road
Yamuna Bridge Station
Ratan Muni Road
Bhagatsingh Road
Kinari Bazar Road
Pipal Mandi Road
Chatta Road
Panchkuiyan Road
Gokalpura Road
KOTWALI
Hospital Road
Captain Naresh Rd
Moti Katra Rd
Hingki Mandi Road
Daresi Rd
Jama Masjid Rd
Jama Masjid
Agra Fort Station
Ghalibpura Road
SUBHASH PARK
MANTOLA
Saiyad Ali Nabi Road
Mahatma Gandhi Road
Mantola Road
Agra Fort
Yamuna
Fatehpur Sikri
SHAHGANJ
Police Lines Rd
Agra Fort Bus Stand
Chhipitola Road
Yamuna Kinara Road
Fatehpur Sikri Road
RAKABGANJ
Taj Mahal
Rakabganj Rd
Aulia Rd
MOTILAL NEHRU PARK
Idgah Station
Gen Cariappa Road
Fatehabad Road
Fatehpur Sikri Road
KATLUPURA
BALUGANJ
SHAHJAHAN PARK
Fatehabad
Idgah
Kachahri Rd
Ajmer Road
IDGAH COLONY
Namner Rd
Gwalior Road
KAIRATITOLA
TAJ GANJ
Golf Course
Tourist Rest House
Hastings Road
Airport
Head Post Office
Dāsaprakāsh
Taj Road
Dr Shyamlal Road
Kherla Road
Government of India Tourist Office
The Mall
Royal Plaza
Agra Cantonment Station
Station Road
Mahatma Gandhi Road
Gopi Chand Shivhare Road
Mughal Sheraton
UP Emporium
Harish Carpet Company
Mayur Tourist Complex
Zorba the Buddha
Gough Road
SULTANPURA
SARDAR PATEL GARDEN
Station Road
SADAR BAZAR
Taj Road
Minto Road
Shamsabad Road
Station Road
Avtar Singh Road
Prithviraj Road
Scott Road
VIBHAVNAGAR
Mustafa Quarters Road
Grand Parade Road
Gwalior

AGRA – CITY OF THE MUGHALS

Like Delhi, Agra is an urban settlement of great antiquity. It would have remained just another small town on the Yamuna but for the fact that two major Muslim dynasties chose to make it an alternative capital. While the Lodis built some impressive edifices in Delhi in the early 16th century, their capital remained the small fort in Agra. It was here that the Mughals (an English derivation from the word "Mongol") set up court, and who continue to evoke a vivid picture of an urbane culture, exquisite taste and great wealth – from which point "Mughal" becomes "mogul" and gets lost in Hollywood.

It was Babur's grandson Akbar who made Agra into the city the world came to know. At a time when Europe was riven with religious dissension, Akbar had gathered about him men of culture and genius and sought to create a universalist religion. His fort in Agra, built on the foundation of the Lodi fort, and his complex of palaces atop the hill near the village of Sikri, are the beautiful shells of a once vibrant court. These sites alone would merit a visit to Agra and Fatehpur Sikri, even without the attraction of the exquisite tomb commissioned by Shahjahan for his consort, the Taj Mahal.

Akbar's son Jahangir and grandson Shahjahan continued to live in Akbarabad (as Agra was named by Jahangir). *Mandis* (wholesale markets) and bazaars proliferated, and Agra became a great entrepôt of trade as well as a magnet for craftsmen and artists. The carpets, footwear, marble artefacts and kites for which Agra is still famous are traditions handed down for centuries. After Shahjahan impulsively moved the capital back to Delhi, Agra lost some of its lustre but its wealth remained to attract the Jats from Bharatpur, who in the 18th century plundered the Fort to furbish their own palace in Deeg. The Marathas also, shortly after, captured the city with the help of French mercenaries. In a manner parallel to the history of Delhi, Agra was then conquered by the British and in the early 19th century became one of the major military outposts of the East India Company. Agra's old cemeteries rank as some of the most interesting in India.

Agra and its historic buildings are today threatened by the pollution and environmentalists see the oil refinery in Mathura as more sinister than the Jat invaders of an earlier age. North of Agra is the ancient city of Mathura (the resonance with the temple town of Madurai in Tamil Nadu led historical records to refer to these as the "northern and southern Mathuras") sacred for centuries as the birthplace of Lord Krishna. Here, too, efforts are underway to cleanse the river and repair the ghats. It is hoped that the alarmed voices of conversationists will be heard and that the cultural wealth of this area will be preserved.

Preceding pages: the luminosity of the Taj enhanced by a monsoon sky; Taj silhouette at sunset – a hazy cluster of shapely domes and turrets; stately colonnades of the Diwan-i-Khas, Agra Fort.

THE TAJ MAHAL

A number of colourful stories about the Taj Mahal were given currency during the period of British rule in India. Most of these took the line of attributing this magnificent creation to European architects – flying in the face of authentic contemporary evidence, both written and inscribed on stone that the Taj was conceived by the emperor Shahjahan and designed by his chief architect.

A monument to love, the Taj has immortalised the name of the emperor's devoted wife, Mumtaz Mahal, the "light of the palace" and unquestionably of his heart. Mother of his 13 children, she was again in labour when she died on 28 June 1631, while he was campaigning in the Deccan. According to an account in a guide published in 1854, the empress had a premonition of her death when she heard an unborn child cry out from her womb. "When a child dies before its birth," she told the emperor, "the mother always dies; therefore I must prepare to take leave of this world". She made him promise never to remarry, and "to build over [her] such a beautiful tomb as the world never saw".

This touching tale is at least in part corroborated by the fact that Shahjahan never remarried and that he magnificently fulfilled the vow to build for her a beautiful tomb. The body of the empress was brought to Agra and laid in a temporary grave in a garden by the river until the vault was completed.

Shahjahan assembled many highly skilled Indian artisans, and some from neighbouring Islamic countries, for his project. The *mimar-i-kul* or chief architect was Ustad Ahmad of Lahore, and the master mason was Muhammad Hanif of Baghdad. A long-standing canard that the architect was Geronimo Veroneo was originally propagated by one Father Manrique, though the Italian had died in obscurity in Agra some 15 years before the Taj was completed. Another attribution to Austin de Bordeaux, a French jeweller who died in 1632 (a year before construction commenced) is even more preposterous. Apart from positive evidence provided by various corroboratory sources, Ustad Hamid's gravestone mentions three of his principal undertakings: the Taj, the Agra Fort and the Jama Masjid in Delhi.

The great Mughal works were invariably undertaken by a number of technical experts whose sole aim was to comply with their imperial master's wishes and faithfully execute his decisions on style, form and decoration. Akbar's personal stamp on his buildings in Agra, and even more so in Fatehpur Sikri, strikingly illustrates the way the great Mughal buildings were created. There was no single overall architect. The usual arrangement was that an Amir, a high-ranking noble, would be appointed as superintendent. In the case of the Taj there were two, as the supervision of the practical tasks entailed constant attention. The actual designs were coordinated by the *mimar-i-kul*, but the inspiration for the Taj was the emperor's own.

The detailed plans drawn up by the *mimar-i-kul* and his assistants were lost, probably in the turbulent 18th century. A work of this kind is no chance masterpiece. It could not have been carried through unless the plans were both detailed and definitive. Discord instead of perfect harmony would have been the result. One of the original drawings was last seen in Agra in 1916 in the possession of a descendent of an architect in Shahjahan's service. Tragically, that also is lost, and with it some of the unresolved mysteries of the Taj.

A single example will illustrate the way individual tasks were in all probability assigned. Amanat Khan Shirazi, the calligraphist of the Persian inscription encircling the soaring gateway to the mausoleum, would have arranged with the architect to be given a precisely dimensioned band for his

Preceding pages: honeycomb design on marble *jali*; motif on dado panel of the Taj. **Left**, front view of the Taj Mahal: one of the world's best known images.

work to enhance the effect of the arch. For his part, the calligraphist resolved the problem of perspective in relation to these dimensions, and ensured that the lettering appeared uniform in size from the level of the terrace instead of diminishing as the inscription reached the top. Amanat Khan, with pardonable pride, added his own name to his individual creation.

Without constant coordination of design and execution between Muslim architects and perfectionist Hindu craftsmen who cut the pieces and then put them together, it would have been impossible to have wrought the many masterpieces of Mughal architecture. The synthesis achieved in the Taj is essentially Indian. Though the predominant design is Persian, its harmony is such that no element should be viewed in isolation from the whole.

The choice of the site is itself an artistic decision. Shahjahan knew Agra well, the course of the river and contours of the landscape. From his marble palaces in the fort he must have judged that the bend in the river about a kilometre (half a mile) downstream would give him at least a partial front view. Had it been placed anywhere closer, he would have seen only the walled side of the garden, and further beyond the bend would have been too distant, too isolated from the imperial ambience of the fort. A major decision naturally followed: to leave the northern facade open to the river.

The character of the mausoleum was already determined in advance by the circumstances of the empress' death. In the first place it had to be a Rauza, or tomb set in a garden, and not a plain Charbagh, or rectangular garden. Most important of all, the place was an Urs, a place of pilgrimage, for the empress had died in childbirth, thus becoming a martyr. Then, as now, prayers were said at the tomb and recitations from the Quran repeated constantly in the cenotaph chamber. The effect achieved by the architect is uncanny. Standing beside

The main gateway to the tomb, from the Charbagh.

the cenotaph and hearing the murmured prayers, or the call of the attendant as it rises to the full height of the inner dome and reverberates back to the listener, serves to illustrate the tombs wonderful acoustics.

A tomb serves yet another purpose, that of a Baradari or festival hall. On the very first anniversary of the empress' death, Shahjahan arranged a celebratory feast in the garden where a temporary grave had been made. According to the *Badshah Nama*, costly marquees were put up and guests entertained with a superb feast. We are told that the seats were assignedaccording to rank and that learned Ulema (members of the clergy), sheikhs and *huffaz* (those who recite the Quran from memory) were also present. Shahjahan could not always be present personally, initially because he moved to Delhi and ultimately because he was incarcerated in his fort palace by his son, Aurangzeb. But expenses were provided in his absence for the continuance of alms-giving and other pious duties.

The architect then set himself to prepare a plan embodying the conception of his master, the emperor, which also served the other purposes required as Rauza, Urs and Baradari. Thus the main features fell into place, starting with a forecourt for shops and assemblies and proceeding through the imposing gateway set in its northern wall into the garden laid in the form of a *charbagh*. The design of the garden contained the formal features of water channels and footpaths crossing at right angles, with a raised pool in the centre.

The forecourt is largely functional, though not obstrusively so. Entering through the old builders' *qasba* (precinct) of Tajganj brings the visitor directly to second feature – the magnificent three-storey gateway of Persian design. An imposing central apsed entrance is set off by pairs of recesses, one above the other, ending in octagonal corner towers crowned by matching *chatris*. An elegant coronal breaks the skyline, while slender

Women in the entrance gardens.

minarets, rising along the external corners, flare out in fluted finials. The apsed entrance is framed by marble bands, inscribed in black slate with Quranic texts. This facade is repeated on the side facing the tomb. The gateway opens out into a vaulted chamber, decorated with a network of white stucco on a red background.

From the gateway an axial water channel leads to an elevated marble pool in the centre of the garden. This is the **Hauz-i-Kauser**, with four water channels radiating from it to divide the garden into four large quarters. These are further divided into sixteen parts in all. The east-west channels flows towards **naubat khanas** (balconies) from which musicians played for the weekly Urs and to salute the emperor's arrival. Traditionally, the garden was laid with flowers specially favoured by the Mughals, such as dahlias, which were Akbar's favourite, narcissi, fritillaries, crocuses and tulips. Fruit trees were massed at the deep ends. The present garden, consisting principally of lawns, shrubs and flowering trees, is more suitable for an age when the monument is visited by thousands of people every day. A map of the traditional garden may be seen in the small museum near the western **naubat khana**. A magical effect is created by the fountains as the tomb in the distance seems to float above the spray.

The central elevated marble pool is a symbolic feature in the **Bagh-i-Adan**, or Garden of Eden. A full view of the monument is presented before the visitor moves on to the foot of the plinth. Here they may become aware of the magnitude of the engineering problems which confronted the designers. The height of the plinth, at 5.5 m (18 ft) is appreciably lower than the 6.7m (22 ft) of Humayun's tomb in Delhi. Aesthetically, the Taj plinth is distinctly more pleasing, though the Delhi tomb needed to be lofted above the extensive Charbagh. Besides, a higher plinth for the Taj would have added enormously

Visitors admire low-relief carving and stone inlay on exterior.

to the weight of the main structure resting on foundations vulnerable to river action. Judging from the floods of the 1924 and 1978, when the terrace stood clear of high water, the range of potential problems arising from the location of the site was studied with scrupulous thoroughness. Moreover, a higher elevation would have created distortions of perspective for the emperor as he arrived at the river front on the royal barge. Although aesthetic considerations were paramount, their application was based on thoroughly sound engineering.

The mausoleum is a square 57 m (186 ft) each way, with chamfered corners, the whole structure rising to a height of 32 m (108 ft) along the top of the parapet over the entrance. Resting on a drum, the dome sweeps upwards till the height at the tip of the finial is 72 m (237 ft). From base to tip the finial alone is 9 m (30 ft). The terrace is a square of 95 m (313 ft), laid on a platform extending the full length from the mosque at the western end to the **mihman khana** (guest house) balancing it in precisely the same form to the east.

The subdued elegance of the four minarets, detached from the funerary chamber and yet integrally related to it, cannot be missed. The architect has subordinated them to the tomb by finishing them at about the level of the maximum bulge of the dome. Each of the three storeys is marked by cupolas held aloft by eight columns. In contrast to the white marble of the mausoleum which is relieved by floral inlay, the joints of the plain marble blocks in the minarets are countersunk and lined with black slate.

The arrangement of forms in the mausoleum and their dimensions are the architect's crowning achievement, related as these features are to the elegaic beauty of the minarets. Here the mingling of Indo-Persian elements is even more evident in the octagonal *chatris* placed at the four chamfered corners. Crowding has been deftly

The Taj combines mass and delicacy.

avoided by setting them apart from the dome, each demonstrating its own validity. This arrangement is best appreciated from a short distance. The visitor should remember to view them from the Hauz-i-Kauser.

Advantage should also be taken of the slow walk up the water channel towards the tomb to appreciate the soaring entrance and the decorations on the white marble surfaces. These also serve the purpose of moderating the intensity of reflected sunlight. A narrow staircase leads you to the terrace. Stand there for a minute, facing the imposing gateway, to absorb the detail. The inner roof of the arch is decorated with flowing inlays. Quranic inscriptions executed by Amanat Khan Shirazi set off the main arch, which is reproduced in miniature in the screened entrance.

When you re-emerge from the chamber, do not fail to circle the tomb slowly, so that you can assimilate the skill with which the architect has handled the problems of space, arrangement of forms and surface decoration. Outside as well as inside, the white marble is broken by inlays of coloured stone and raised reliefs in the marble itself. Decorative purity and consistency is maintained throughout.

Small though significant architectural touches will become apparent as you move around. On either side of the main entrance, elegant columns with black and yellow chevron tesselations run upwards along the outside corners to open in lotuses, each crowned with its own miniature dome. The recesses on either side are surmounted by lower parapets, permitting views of the corner *chatris* before a closer perspective cuts them off. This attention to seemingly minor detail is one of the outstanding features of the Taj. The conventional Persian plan is just the guiding formula for an inspired composition.

The southern facade is repeated on the other three sides, without entrance doorways. As you move to the northern end, the intimate relationship of the

Morning mist in the village of Tajgunj.

empress' tomb and the once wide flowing river will become apparent.

An altogether different range of experiences awaits the visitor in the **Aina Mahal**, or glass palace, where the cenotaphs symbolise the mortal remains buried in the mortuary chamber below. Here, the designers have created an atmosphere of solemnity by a combination of architectural features, filtered light and subdued sound. The hall itself is drawn upwards 24 m (80 ft). Rectangular rooms at the four corners with interconnecting passages create a sense of undefined space while recitations from the Quran, gently intoned by the *huffaz* performing religious duty at this place of pilgrimage, circulated the passages and rise to the dome above. Shadowless light, filtered through double marble screens fitted with milky glass, is the third element.

In the centre of this unconfined space lie the cenotaphs, surrounded by an octagonal screen of great beauty. It consists of single pieces of fretted marble set in marble frames decorated by intricate pietra dura inlay. This masterpiece alone took 10 years to make. It replaced a gem-encrusted golden rail fabricated by the jewellers who created the emperor's Peacock Throne. It is said that the rail was removed because it was an invitation to theft. However, there is little doubt that the gaudy decoration was out of place and that the marble screen harmonises with the atmosphere far more successfully. Flowing marble reliefs and inlay discreetly decorate the interior of the Aina Mahal. The shouts made by the *khadims* (attendants) rise and fall, echo and circulate through the passages for 13 seconds.

Near the entrance a ramp leads down to ground level. This is where the bodies were laid, the empress in the centre and the emperor by her side. Shahjahan's son Aurangzeb allowed him a larger memorial befitting his station, but Quranic texts are absent; it is engraved in Nastaliq script with the date of his death and all his high-

Mirrored in the Yamuna.

sounding names and titles. The empress' grave is inscribed with the 99 names of God in highly stylised Naskh. In the mortuary chamber a lantern held aloft intensifies the solemnity.

The consummate artistry of the designers and decorators is lavished on the memorial stones. Agate, lapis, bloodstone, carnelian, jade and other stones are cut and laid in floral arabesques and carpet designs with great precision. One poppy in the octagonal screen is made of 31 pieces, and as many as 64 have been counted in the large flower on the outer side.

During the reigns of subsequent Muhgal emperors, the interior of the tomb was transformed with sumptuous carpets and decorated, according to the French jeweller Tavernier, with "chandeliers and other ornaments of the kind, and there are always some mullahs there to pray". The French physician Bernier confirmed that "nothing can be conceived more rich and magnificent".

The essential beauty of the Taj is in no way diminished by the lack of luxurious ancillaries. Rather, it stands out in greater purity, reflecting the transient mood of the sky, the play of light and shade and the sudden monsoon storm. In the light of the full moon the myriads of semi-precious stones glow, taking on a special effulgence in the pearly blue of Sharad Purnima – the winter full moon – usually at the end of October.

This huge and intricately decorated building cost a vast amount of money, emptying the imperial treasury at a time when it could be ill afforded. Shahjahan left Agra for the traditional capital of Delhi before his masterpiece was complete (it took 22 years to complete the building). His rather more prosaic son, Aurangzeb, then had him imprisoned for his profligacy in the Red Fort in Agra, where he spent the last years of his life gazing at the tomb down the river. Legend has it that he saw it for the last time in a small mirror set in a marble pillar of his prison.

Detail of Mumtaz Mahal's cenotaph.

MUGHAL PIETRA DURA

Inlays of soft stone, mainly of marble designs carved and laid in a sandstone setting, had been known in India from the 15th century. As in art and architecture generally, a major development took place in the region of the Mughal emperor Jahangir in the first three decades of the 17th century. This was the use of semi-precious stones of varied colours on a marble background.

Semi-precious stone inlay as a craft is not identical to soft stone inlay, but the traditional Indian skill of gem-cutting was available to the wealthiest patrons of the day, the Mughal emperors. It was thus a logical development for them to take to the representation in pietra dura of the art motifs favoured by the reigning monarch. Jahangir was a passionate lover of flowers, and his artists responded nobly to their patron's taste. Their flower paintings have been acclaimed by naturalists as well as by art historians. Though Jahangir's palaces in Agra Fort were demolished by Shahjahan to make room for his own, his tomb near Lahore, built by his empress Nurjahan, contains lavish displays in pietra dura of the emperor's favourite motifs of goblets and flowers. The craft attained full flowering, however, under Shahjahan. The motifs the latter favoured remained largely Jahangiri, but the range and expertise then attained have never since been excelled. In Shahjahan's marble palaces in Agra Fort and the Taj Mahal, pietra dura is used both for decoration and to moderate the dazzle of the white marble expanse.

Pietra dura detail from Taj northern wall.

The taste for pietra dura spread to the Mughal nobility as well. They could hardly compete with their emperor, but some of them found a means of satisfying their taste when objects decorated with inlay became available in India from Italy. Tavernier, the French jeweller, records that he made a present to Nawab Jafar Khan, the emperor Aurangzeb's uncle, on 12 September 1665, of "a board, with nineteen pieces to make a cabinet, the whole of precious stones of diverse colours representing all kinds of flowers and birds. The work has been done in Florence and cost 2,150 livres". There had been a contemporary development of pietra dura in Florence under the Medicis, but in wealth and resources of skilled artisans these cannot be viewed as rivals of the Mughal emperor. The scale on which the craft was practised in Lahore and Agra rules out any possibility of derivation from the relatively small development in Florence. By the time the Indian craftsmen were lavishing displays of flowers and other designs on the screen enclosing Mumtaz Mahal's tomb in the 1640s, they had already attained a level of perfection unequalled in Medici Florence.

Shahjahan himself adopted a solution seemingly favoured by his nobles while he was building the Delhi fort a decade later, that of buying ready-made art objects from Italian vendors. The niche behind the *jarokha* throne is decorated with plaques in the Florentine style, including one of Orpheus. When it is remembered that about half a century earlier, Jahangir's artists were able to reproduce a religious picture presented to him by Sir Thomas Roe so accurately that he could not distinguish one from the other, one may expect that Shahjahan's craftsmen were capable of depicting in pietra dura a foreign motif which appealed to their emperor.

The art continues to be practiced in Agra, but to much lesser degree than under the Mughal emperors. However, it is still possible to see fine work produced in the city at the U.P. Government Emporium.

AGRA FORT

Breaking out of his ancestral home in Central Asia, Babur, the first of the great Mughal emperors, fought his way into India and seized Agra, then the capital of the Lodi kings. Here it was that he and the first four of his successors created the famous buildings which yearly attract thousands of visitors from all over the world. Interest is naturally focussed on the Taj Mahal, the most celebrated of them all. However, those interested in Mughal artistic expression, architectural styles and the use of materials may find that the most rewarding sequence starts with Akbar's fort and his temporary capital of Fatehpur Sikri. Akbar's tomb at Sikandara is an unusual digression from a development leading to a high point of Indo-Persian architecture represented by the Agra fort's marble palaces and culminating in the Taj.

Akbar, arguably the greatest of the Mughal emperors and one of the outstanding rulers of his time, started construction of the majestic red sandstone fort in Agra in 1565 when he was just 23 years old. His grandfather Babur had been too busy fighting off threats to his newly established regime, and his father Humayun too harassed by his misadventures to undertake anything so ambitious. Besides, there was a fort in Agra already, built by a medieval Rajput dynasty, and given the evocative name of Badalgarh. Its turrets may not have mingled with the clouds, as the name suggests, but it was occupied by the Lodi Sultans of Delhi in AD 1504 when they made Agra their capital.

Babur did not need to make major improvements in Badalgarh after he captured the city in 1526. The old fort became the setting for lavish court ceremonies in the Central Asian style. The miniatures of the *Babur Nama*, though painted fifty years later in Akbar's reign, depict richly bedecked awnings and terraces laid thick with colourful carpets from his homeland. Both Babur and his daughter Gulbadan Begum, in their memoirs, have left vivid descriptions of court scenes with visitors from Persia and Central Asia, and Mughal dignitaries being entertained by dance, music and other diversions.

Badalgarh adequately served its original purpose as fortress, stately court for the ruler and guardian of the royal treasures. But it was not enough for Akbar: according to his biographer Abul Fazl, he gave instructions in 1565 "for the building in Agra – which by its position is the centre of Hindustan – of a grand fortress such as might be worthy thereof, and correspond to the dignity of his dominions".

Three years earlier, when he was just 20, Akbar had launched on a whirlwind career of conquest which confirmed his supremacy over the whole of northern India. Young as he was, he realised that military might alone would not win him

Left, Agra Fort, once the nerve centre of the Mughal empire. Right, the splendid Delhi Gate, one of its entrances.

the hearts of his people. He therefore set himself the more difficult task of breaking with the long-established tradition of Muslim rule to create an atmosphere of reconciliation. Discriminatory taxes against Hindus were abolished, and he contracted marriage alliances with princesses of the leading Rajput royal houses, conferring military ranks on distinguished Rajput commanders. These measures paid off handsomely. Except for Mewar, most of the leading Rajput families became closely associated with Akbar's regime and served him with exemplary loyalty.

The fort itself and the varied buildings within its walls were the earliest embodiment of the syncretic spirit of Akbar's reign. To start with, the Hindu Raja of the neighbouring state of Karaoli was pressed into taking part in the foundation-laying ceremony, in deference to the prevailing belief that this would ensure the protection of the fort from erosion by the river. There has been no damage on this account in all these 450 years. The fort was Akbar's first great architectural venture in North India, and he went about it with characteristic vigour. Within eight years, three or four thousand labourers working day and night completed the massive walls and imposing gates, as well as most of the buildings inside – according to Abul Fazl, as many as 500 – made of sandstone "in the fine styles of Bengal and Gujarat". Akbar's Rajput queen of the house of Amber (Jaipur) was able to occupy her palace, Bengali Mahal, only four years after work started.

The fort's walls have survived precisely as Akbar built them, but since his successors demolished most of the buildings inside to make room for others of their own choice, it would be convenient to consider the two separately. The first impression of the towering walls is one of majesty. The precision with which the red sandstone slabs are laid bears out Abul Fazl's picturesque claim that they "were so joined together that the end of a hair

Water buffalo on the bed of the Yamuna.

could not find a place between them". Monserrat, a Jesuit priest who spent two years at Akbar's court, was no less enthusiastic: "The stones of these buildings are so cunningly fitted that the joints are scarcely visible, although no lime was used to fix them together. The colour of the stone, which is all red, also produces the same effect of uniform solidity." The walls are about 21 m (70 ft) high at the highest points, but the width at the base cannot be accurately determined because they are embedded in masonry and filling. The perimeter is about 2.4 km (1½ miles) long.

The layout of the fort was determined by the course of the river, which in those days flowed alongside. The main axis is parallel to the river and about 823 m (900 yards) long. The walls bulge out towards the city, suggesting to William Finch, who visited Agra during the reign of Akbar's son, Jahangir, that the entire complex "lyeth in manner of a half-moon, bellying to the landward". The prosaic traders in London, to whom the report was addressed, might have wondered whether their agent was becoming carried away.

When Finch was in Agra, the broad expanse of the river Yamuna had not been diminished by the canals which have since drained away its Himalayan waters for the development of the parched northern plain. Flowing alongside the eastern wall, it formed an integral defensive feature, also creating an environment of relaxation and enjoyment for the imperial court.

Controversy still surrounds the fate of the old Rajput fort of Badalgarh. An immense structure which had survived 400 years of buffeting by a stormy history and harsh weather could not have disappeared into the ground. Abul Fazl gives a revealing clue: "An inevitable mandate was issued that the old fort should be removed, and in that place should be founded an impregnable palace". In 1871, General Cunningham, who was Director General of the Archaeological Survey of India, came

Shahjahan's last view of the tomb from Agra fort.

to the conclusion that the old Pathan fort occupied exactly the same position as that of Akbar, with the the exception perhaps of some of the gateway out-works. The "Pathan fort" was of course Badalgarh, which the Pathan (Afghan) Lodis had taken over.

Akbar's fulsome biographer, Abul Fazl, tells us with characteristic hyperbole that the walls were "provided with four gates whereby the doors of the dominion were opened to the four quarters of the world". Of these only two remain open. The main entrance, now called **Amar Singh Gate**, originally was given the more appropriate name of Akbari Gate. **Hathi Pol** or Elephant Gate, to the northwest, led towards the city. It was here that the people of the realm gathered for business, for it was the seat of the Qazi (judge under the traditional law), and of the Vizier (revenue minister). According to Finch he sat there every morning for three hours, to deal with "all matters of rents, grants, lands, firmans, debts etc.".

The northern gate led to what might be called the store of ordinance, while the fourth gate, facing east, overlooked the river. This was called **Darshani Gate**, from which the emperor gave audience to the general public who did not have access to the court itself. The gate, says Finch, led "into a faire court extending alongst the river, in which the king looks forth every morning at sunrising which he salutes, and then his nobles resort to their *tessilam* (deep salaam)". This ritual became so formalised that many would neither eat nor wash before appearing in the ruler's presence.

The Darshani Gate had another purpose. Akbar used it to view elephant fights, and in his younger days he would dash out and mount the most ferocious beast. His son Jahangir surrendered to the pleasure of watching animal fights of all kinds. Once a week, Finch has it, "is a day of blood, both of fighting beasts and justiced men, the king judging and seeing execution".

Throne in Shahjahan's Hall of Public Audience.

Little is left of the architectural and decorative styles which evolved in this most formative and and culturally effervescent of periods. The buildings inside the walls underwent so many changes in the two succeeding reigns that it became a veritable display of all the styles of decoration developed under the Mughals. These spanned Akbar's synthesis of Hindu and Muslim traditions, the poetic interlude of Jahangir in which the emphasis shifted to the pictorial arts, and the eventual efflorescence of Indo-Persian forms and decorative arts favoured by Shahjahan.

Nothing remains of the 500 or so buildings completed under Akbar, except the Jahangiri Mahal facing the end of the ramp from the main gate. Only a few ruins tell the tale of Akbar's own palace, overlooking the river, and the **Bengali Mahal** embodies a pleasing synthesis of the Akbari period with a few marble touches added by his son. The interiors are believed to have been inspired by the Man Mandir palace in Gwalior, and probably also executed by artisans from there. Their chiselled sandstone work was excelled only in the pavilion facing Anup Talao at Fatehpur Sikri. Floral designs alternate with arabesques with a fluency found only in the finest wood carvings.

From Amar Singh Gate, a ramp leads straight to the **Chihl Satun**, a pavilion of forty beautifully proportioned pillars, with a satin finish of lime, eggshell and resin. This is the **Diwan-i-Am**, or hall of public audience, overlooked by the *jarokha*, or window throne, from which the emperor gave audience. Here the visitor gets a foretaste of the marble and semi-precious stone inlays lavished by Shahjahan on the space between the *jarokha* and battlements overlooking the river.

An explanation of Shahjahan's ambition to outdo his ancestors was given by Mulla Abdul Hamid Lahori in his *Badshah Nama*: "In this everlasting reign the demand for arts has a different

Below left, Pillar detail from the Diwan-i-Khas. **Below right,** water chute in private mosque.

market and the Divine care has adopted a new method of embellishing the world; at the place of the old have been built sky-touching mansions of marble". It was indeed a taste altogether different to Akbar's eclectic preference for prevailing Indian styles brought to perfection by local craftspeople.

A narrow staircase takes the visitor behind the *jarokha* to the courtyard of **Machi Bhawan**. Further southward is the beautiful double-pillared **Diwan-i-Khas**, or hall of private audience. An inscription on the southern wall opens with the lines:

"The erection of this delightful lofty palace
Has exalted Akbarabad to the Arsh [ninth heaven]",

a claim which few visitors are likely to question. The verse provides confirmation that after his death Agra was regarded as Akbar's city.

A series of marble palaces and pavilions were built by Shahjahan behind the Diwan-i-Khas, each one excelling the other; but the prize, if it can be awarded, must go to the **Daulatkhana-i-Khas**, or royal residence. Its **Tambi Khana** or parlour is the gem in this imperial diadem. Projecting beyond the wall is the **Jasmine Tower** from which Shahjahan gazed at his greatest creation of all, the Taj Mahal, floating in the distance. His daughter Jahanara occupied the **Khas Mahal** further on, with the recessed **Anguri Bagh** or Garden of Grapes providing colourful relief from the dazzling marble all around.

The **Hamam**, or royal baths, according to the contemporary historian Mulla Abdul Hamid Lahori, consisted of several buildings overlooking the river. This too was pillaged – by the British, who sent the most magnificent of the marble baths to the Prince Regent. The Hamam is now closed, but the visitor can visit the fairyland of the **Shish Mahal**, or palace of mirrors.

Two mosques should not be missed. Aurangzeb built the **Nagina Masjid** next to Machi Bhawan for the women of the palace. Discreetly hidden away in an elevated courtyard of its own is Shahjahan's **Moti Masjid** or Pearl Mosque. The name was conventionally given to a white marble place of prayer intended for the emperor, his family and chosen attendants. There are similar mosques in the forts at Delhi and Lahore, but the Moti Masjid in Agra excels them in scale and sheer purity of line. The women of the harem offered prayers in side rooms screened by marble lattices. The mosque took seven years to build; when it was completed in 1653, Shahjahan travelled from Delhi by boat to offer prayers in this, the last of his architectural creations in Agra.

Despite the elegance of Shahjahan's additions, the fort pre-eminently expresses Akbar's majestic sense of empire and the synthesis of the new nationhood he sought to create. For sheer presence, the great red fort of Akbarabad is one of India's greatest.

Left, cattle-powered lawn-mower in Agra Fort. **Right**, detail of marble relief.

THE LEFT BANK

The old Lodi capital of Agra provided the first of the Mughals with the immediate requirements of his royal condition, but no relief from the unbearable heat of mid-summer. He lost no time in seeking out a retreat and found it on the relatively open left bank across the cooling waters of the river Yamuna.

Babur's passion for gardens is a recurring theme in his inimitable memoirs. In his ancestral home of Fergana, water flowing from the surrounding hills was a central feature of the landscape. Exiled from its green valleys, he found North India a region "of few charms and lamented its lack of fine fruits, ice and cold water". There was no refuge except in taking to the bath – but the mind still needed invigoration and the spirit, revival.

It was with this intention that, a few days after distributing the defeated Sultan Ibrahim Lodi's captured treasure to his wilting followers, Babur crossed over from the fort. He was disgusted with the barrenness of the area, but in these unprepossessing surroundings Babur hastily laid two gardens, to which he gave the emotive names of Gul Afshan (flower scatterer) and Zar Afshan (gold scatterer). With his *begs* or nobles following suit, the whole area was covered with gardens. "The people of Hind", Babur wrote with pride, "who had never seen grounds planned so symmetrically and thus laid out, called the side of the Jun [the river Yamuna] where [our] residences were, Kabul".

These delectable retreats languished after Babur's early death in 1530, four years after his victorious arrival. His successors spread the empire far and wide, discovering other pastures further afield. "Kabul" in Agra had served its immediate purpose. It was rediscovered nearly 100 years later by the nobles of the fourth emperor, Jahangir, for gardens of their own. A number of these sprang up, doubling in the usual way as tombs.

Left, the empress Nurjahan's memorial for her father Itimad-ud-daula.

In recent years, an attempt has been made to retrieve these sites from further ruin. Some of which were architecturally and decoratively innovative.

Arambagh: One of the two gardens Babur laid on the north bank is now known as Arambagh (garden of leisure), a more prosaic name than the one given to it by Babur himself. There is no positive identification, but of the two it is probably Gul Afshan. Much of it had been buried by rubble and encroached upon on three sides by the spread of untidy urban sprawl, but an attempt has been made to restore it. (When Babur died in 1530, this is where his body was laid until his son Humayun, after his defeat by Sher Shah, carried it away to Kabul. In accordance with Babur's wishes, he was buried there in his favourite garden in a grave open to the sky. These last rites were enjoined on Humayun by filial duty and even more so because Babur, in a remarkable act of self-renunciation, carried away his son's illness by insistent prayer.)

The solution to the problem of water came from a bullock lift which filled a reservoir from where water flowed into the channels over ribbed stones to simulate the sparkle of a mountain stream. This became a characteristic feature of the numerous formal gardens created in India by some of Babur's pleasure-loving successors. Dependence on river water led to another garden feature – the open river front. Walls on the other three sides effectively excluded the outside world.

But one element was still lacking – the flowers and delicious fruits of Transoxiana. When a melon was brought to Babur from Balkh, "to cut and eat it affected [him] strangely: [he] was all tears". He had them grown in Agra and was able to enjoy there both the melons and grapes of his Central Asian home. "Then in that charmless

Hind were seen laid out with order and symmetry, with suitable borders and parterres in every corner, and in every border rose and narcissus in perfect arrangement".

The honeycombed corbels of the modest pavilions on a terrace overlooking the river contain paintings of unusual interest in the development of Mughal art in India. Murals of figures, birds and ducks fill the spaces. Some of the figures are winged, suggesting Persian inspiration, while two half-figures in the outer panels have distinctly Central Asian features. There is no obvious link with the art of painting later developed in his grandson Akbar's ateliers which assimilated Indian traditions with amazing sureness of touch.

Chini ka Rauza: Downstream from Arambagh is the Chini ka Rauza. The first part of the name refers to the brilliant display of glazed titles all over the outer surface of this small gem of a tomb set in a garden. Hidden from the main road by nursery gardens, the Rauza in recent years has been successfully retrieved from the desolation which had overtaken it. Large portions of tile decoration had already disappeared, but what has been saved gives some idea of its former beauty.

The Rauza is the river front tomb of Shukrulla, one of Shahjahan's finance ministers. As in many tombs of the period, both husband and wife were buried there. This unusual Rauza must have been a striking addition to the tomb architecture of Mughal Agra. The technique of firing tiles had already been perfected in Multan and Lahore, where several fine displays still exist. The stucco interior is covered with floral and conventional designs, while the soffit of the double-dome corbel, cut in seven concentric rings.

Itimad-ud-daula: Lower downstream, close to a river crossing, is the tomb of the empress Nurjahan's father, Mirza Ghiyas Beg. He arrived at the court of the emperor Jahangir a penniless

The exterior covered with geometric mosaic decoration.

immigrant from Persia – with, however, one prize asset: his very intelligent 34-year-old daughter. The emperor immediately succumbed to her charms and married her in 1611. This single event led to the subjugation of the Mughal court by the culture of Safavid Persia. Many Persian courtiers rose to important positions in the governing class. Ghiyas Beg was made prime minister, with the title of Itimad-ud-daula (Confidence of the State), and his son's, Asaf Khan's, daughter was married to the third son of Jahangir, Prince Khurram. (After a ruthless war of succession, Khurram was to seize the throne as Shahjahan, and Nurjahan's niece was to become the empress Mumtaz Mahal, whose tomb is the Taj Mahal.)

The riverside tomb which Nurjahan built for her father at the height of her ascendancy marked a transition from the rugged sandstone buildings of the earlier Mughals, with their distinctive Indian inspiration, to the jewelled marvels of his son. This *rauza* is a miniature casket, lacking some of the spatial harmonies of the Taj. But every inch of the marble surface is covered by coloured stone inlay with relieving touches of sinuous decoration. A notable feature is the use of stones such as marble and jasper of different colours, and the soothing tone of the ochre-coloured cenotaphs in the midst of this profusion. The mortuary chamber is at ground level, reproduced in the cenotaph chamber above.

While the Taj impresses with its stately elegance, Itimad-ud-daula's tomb captivates with its accessible brilliance. Thus the corner minarets, which seem disproportionately short, do not overshadow the low, square roof with its intricate lattice walls covering the cenotaph chamber below. Even at the height of the Persian ascendancy, the departure from indigenous features was never complete. Corner kiosks and bracket-supported eaves acknowledge the authority of Indian artistic styles as much as the compulsions of climate.

Entrance to the cenotaph chamber.

Drawn by W. Purser. Sketched by

FUTTYP

FISHER, SON

. Elliot, R.N. Engraved by W. Brandard.

E SICRI.

NDON. 1834.

Plan of the Palace at Fatehpur Sikri (Akbar's City of Victory)

60m

1 Diwan-i-Aam
2 Throne
3 Diwan-i-Khas
4 Pachisi Court
5 Garden for Male Residents
6 Anup-Talao
7 Emperor's Living Quarters
8 Main Harem ("Jodhbai's Quarters")
9 Residence of Senior Queen ("Birbal's House")
10 Residence of Senior Queen ("Maryam's House")
11 Workshops ("Stables")
12 Garden for Female Residents
13 Panch Mahal
14 Daftar Khana (Records Office)

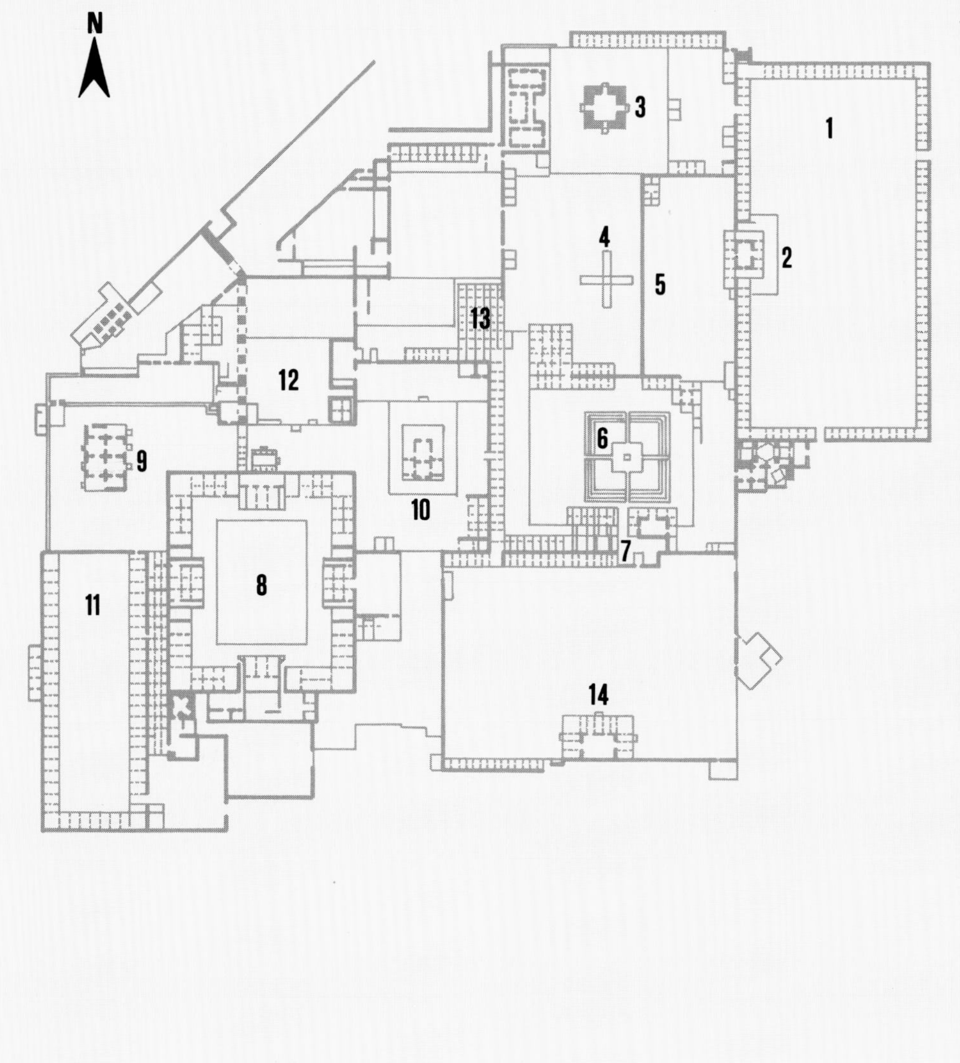

FATEHPUR SIKRI

Perched on top of a rocky ridge, 37 km (23 miles) west of Agra, a smattering of tiny black domes and red sandstone minarets pierces the sky. Fatehpur Sikri came into being just over 400 years ago, when the third Mughal emperor of India, Muhammad Jalaludin Akbar, took on for the first time in the history of Islamic-Indian architecture the task of planning an entire township. Akbar's city skilfully hugs the contours of its site. Its interlocking courts of red sandstone offer the visitor a steady stream of surprises. The juxtaposition of the palace buildings is such that it appears ad hoc, relaxed, and yet carefully composed at the same time.

The city poses some intriguing questions. Why was Fatehpur Sikri built in such an enormous hurry and deserted barely 15 years after its conception? Why do buildings of such disparate nature stand randomly strung together in one complex, and in what order were they erected? What makes its planning hint at some underlying order? What, then, makes Fatehpur Sikri unique?

Most cities are the work of many generations, each adding its own themes, with new areas frequently replacing the old. Many styles can be seen side by side or as overlays, depicting different stages of their growth. But behind Fatehpur Sikri is the vision of one man, in a single phase of his life, built with great energy while the impulse lasted, and completely abandoned soon after. It was a vigorous city, planned with inspiration and genius by a ruler who had not yet reached the age of 28.

Preceding pages, 19th-century British engraving of the Buland Darwaza, one of Fatehpur Sikri's nine gates.

The Chisti's Boon: By the time Akbar came to the throne in 1555, his father and grandfather before him had firmly implanted the roots of Mughal rule in Indian soil, establishing Agra as their capital. Brilliant, capable and farsighted, Akbar was from the beginning a man filled with an urgent need to implement his ideas for his empire. It was during his reign that the Mughal style acquired its unique identity, a synthesis which arose from a shrewd political design to unify the country. It was not an assertion of a royal Islamic set of values but, rather, a cultural amalgam of all that he had keenly observed around him. The 1560s were a period of comparative peace for Akbar, reflecting the security of his political and military triumphs, and it was the right moment for him to achieve ideological reforms and promote religious harmony. At this stage of his life he had ample funds, as well as the leisure to articulate a synthesis of the multiple, complex influences to which he had been exposed.

But in 1568, though Akbar was probably the most powerful, and one of the most influential, monarchs India would ever see, he had no son and heir to his vast empire. He anxiously visited several shrines and holy men offering prayers, seeking blessings for the birth of a successor to the throne, but in vain – till one day the spreading fame of a Sufi mystic, Shaikh Salim Chisti, brought him barefoot to the saint's door. The spell of the octagenarian saint's personality and his prophecy of three sons comforted Akbar 's mind; the impact was immediate. A few royal palaces were hurriedly constructed close to the saint's hermitage, and a queen who had just conceived moved in. The long-awaited boy was named Mohammad Salim after the Shaikh, and an overjoyed Akbar decided to move his court from Agra to Sikri in gratitude for the boon he ascribed to the saint's intervention.

City of Victory: Akbar's passion for building was insatiable, and despite the fact that he had already started work on the Lahore and Agra forts, he was eager to take on the building of his new city of victory – "Fatehpur". This new imperial residence was conceived as a joint capital with Agra. That it was intended to be a residential city for the court, and not just another Agra, is demonstrated by the insufficiency of its military defences as well as by its size. Even allowing for temporary constructions, Fatehpur Sikri was far too small to accommodate Akbar's entire court. But beyond its political intention, the city embodies a moment of victory and of joy, an affirmation of faith.

When Akbar chose to build his new imperial residence in Sikri, it was uninhabited, save for the meagre stone huts of the saint and some of his followers. At the time, the rocky outcrop was being quarried for stone for Akbar's Agra buildings, and the stone-cutters living in the area had erected a small mosque for the saint. This ridge, however, had many links with a pre-Akbar past, being a 12th century stronghold of the Sikarwar Rajputs (who gave Sikri its name), and later a strategic frontier station for subsequent Muslim rulers. In 1526, Babur, the founder of the Mughal empire, defeated the last of these Muslim Sultans and, setting up base in Agra, used the ridge of Sikri as a military gathering point. Being a lover of gardens, he ordered one to be laid on its slopes, and also began work on damming a river to create the lake beside which his grandson Akbar built his palace.)

The siting of the **Jama Masjid**, the first, the largest and highest building in Sikri, marked the actual beginnings of the city, which then came up around it.

Facing Mecca, and based traditionally on the ground plan of the Prophet Muhammad's house, the mosque is entered through a doorway in the east – the **Badshahi Darwaza**, or imperial gate. A series of monastic cells, where Chisti would teach his followers, were arranged around a vast red sandstone courtyard, below which an underground reservoir stored water for ritual ablutions.

The western portal of the mosque – its actual prayer chamber – is a splendid

The 45-m (150-ft) tall Buland Darwaza, "Mighty Portal", reached by a 14-m (46-ft) high flight of steps.

domed affair painted internally in blues, chocolate, gold and white. Akbar is noted to have once recited the Friday prayer here, otherwise performed only by the head Imam – possibly wishing to allude to himself as God, since the opening words of the Islamic call for prayer, "Allah-ho-Akbar", can be read as either as "God is great", or as "Akbar is God".

On one side of the court, the small jewel-like tomb of the saint glows with the translucence of its exquisite marble screens, carved in delicate geometric patterns. It is the only structure in Sikri built entirely of white marble. Bits of string, available at the door, are knotted into these screens by believers in the hope that the saint will grant them too the boon of a son. The brackets, so fine and elaborate as to transcend the obvious suggestion of a stylised snake, retain a graceful suppleness of form more akin to works of nature than of art. Within Chisti's tomb chamber, intricate inlay work in mother-of-pearl, topaz and lapis lazuli provides a brilliant contrast to the white marble.

A few years after the completion of the mosque, when Akbar returned to Fatehpur Sikri from a triumphant campaign in the Deccan, he decided to erect a victory arch. The southern doorway of the mosque was remodelled into a stupendous gateway fifteen stories high, the greatest monumental structure Akbar ever built. The **Buland Darwaza**, set atop a broad flight of steps 12 m (40 ft) high, overlooks the town below, and is visible for miles around, proclaiming Akbar's triumph in a spectacular display of red sandstone and marble inlay.

In most towns of the time, the acropolis containing royal residences was heavily guarded, separated from the general hubbub of the city by high walls and wide moats. Islamic architects often left the layout of the city to chance, allowing streets to develop organically as the settlement grew. Fatehpur Sikri was different: it was a

Below left, supplicants tie threads to the screen around the Chisti's tomb. Below right, chiselled sandstone detail.

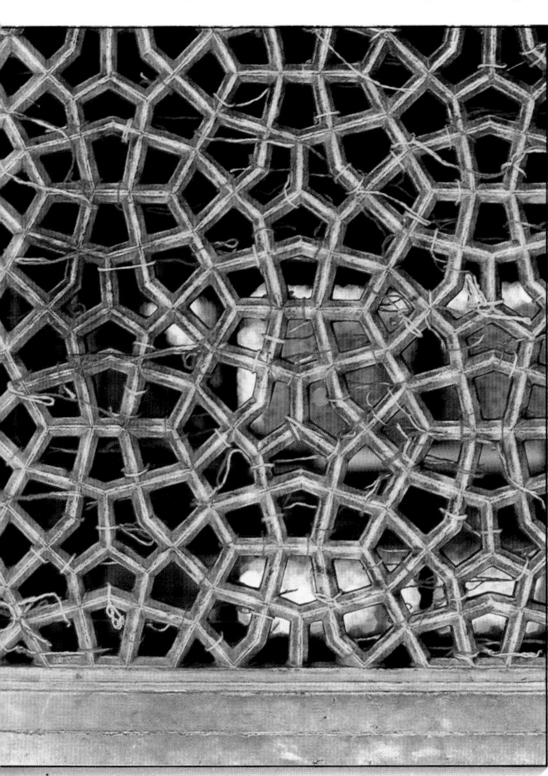

planned city, speaking in its entirety of a single innovative architectural mind at work.

In the attempt to control the unitary form of the town, a modular grid became a systematic design instrument on all scales. Recent research has shown that the whole city, the sweep of its walls, the placement of its main gates and the road network, all seem to be based on a definitive mathematical grid. Similar modules, of proportions sacred to Islam, were used in the analogous buildings of Akbar, Babur and Jahangir, but later abandoned by Shahjahan, who reverted to a more orthodox Persian tradition.

Moreover, Fatehpur Sikri was a dynamic, open city, with an unfortified citadel that was placed uninhibitedly upon the ridge top. With the massive Jama Masjid forming a spectacular western backdrop, Akbar's own palace was to be constructed on the high strip of rock overlooking the lake to the northwest, with the rest of the city spreading out below towards the south.

Tents in Stone: In the year 1571, when the architects of Fatehpur Sikri sat down to plan this imperial residence, what would their concept of a citadel have been? How should it have looked and felt? What sort of spaces would they have envisaged as palatial?

The Mughals, being constantly on the move, usually lived in large encampments comprising magnificent tents of varying sizes, erected from fine cloths in a matter of hours. The beautiful carpets and rich brocades within recalled the splendour of the palaces of Persia and Afghanistan, where their early ancestors had led less nomadic lives. But when the Mughals did settle down, in Delhi, Agra, Lahore and elsewhere, it was not those palaces which they imitated; their built structures, particularly of their secular architecture, seem more to resemble their temporary encampments.

On an average, Akbar spent more than four months a year travelling. On

The Buland Darwaza opens onto a vast courtyard fronting the Chisti's tomb and mosque.

most of these expeditions, he would be accompanied by state departments, the treasury, and noblemen and princesses with their retinues. Soldiers on horseback and road-building gangs would form a considerable part of this vast, moving army. Each halt was an elaborate exercise in town planning and construction. A noted Jesuit visitor to Akbar's India was struck by the organisational expertise which went into the making and unmaking of these huge "towns-in-tents" at every halt.

An ever enthusiastic and innovative organiser, Akbar had devised a flexible plan ordaining broad zoning concepts for these imperial encampments: a diagrammatic representation of the various spaces required, carefully determined for maximum convenience and order. This Mughal camp order, slightly modified each time to suit the topography of the new camp site, turned out to be a virtual design brief for Akbar's palace at Sikri, and for many Mughal cities to follow.

Depicted in this sketch of the camp layout are four central enclosures meant for royal use. In the first enclosure the king would meet his people, soldiers and commoners, while only privileged noblemen, high officials and intimate friends would find access to the second enclosure. A two-storey central tent was used in this enclosure to issue state orders and receive intelligence reports. The third enclosure housed the king's day palace and bed-chamber where he could rest or retire, and the fourth enclosure, strictly guarded, was for the royal women. The four enclosures were thus arranged axially in a series in order of increasing privacy and security. All the services, workshops and stores for the palace were placed around the central core, and were accessible from an outer road. Day and night guards formed an outer ring protecting the royal interior. Research has shown that this overall arrangement must have formed the basis for the planning of Akbar's new palace precinct.

Interior of Akbar's mosque at Sikri.

The site at Sikri comprised a narrow rocky ridge running diagonally northeastwards from the mosque, and the space available for the palace was small – smaller, perhaps, than any of the encampment sites. The linear camp layout had therefore to be adapted to suit the shape and topography of the site, and it is here especially that we observe the genius of the architects of Sikri.

The palace courts were laid out parallel to the Jama Masjid – which, being a mosque, was cardinally aligned – rather than follow the incidental disposition of the site. With the background knowledge of geometry as a major guiding force, the four enclosures of the camp order fitted perfectly like pieces of a jigsaw puzzle. This spatial setting, based on an interlocking axial system, creates an ordered composition inducing a relaxed mood and pleasure of movement. No one axis prevails, and everything is mathematically ordained – the sizes of the courts and buildings, the modules of the paving stones, the shift of the multiple axes.

The sequential order of these courts was further emphasised by changes in their levels, the hierarchy also being ingeniously integrated with the contours of the site. The most public enclosure was at the lowest level, while on the highest part was placed the most private of the palace zones, the royal harem. The slope of the ridge was used imaginatively to control the flow of water which would collect in a huge reservoir measuring 8 sq. m (90 sq. ft) and 9 m (30 ft) deep. Pavilions on the wide retaining walls caught the breeze and afforded a panoramic view over the lake.

For reasons of convenience, the service structures such as the mint, workshops, kitchen and baths were laid along the contours of the ridge, while all buildings for royal use were placed carefully parallel to the mosque, high on the ridge. Locating the "consumers"

Anup Talao.

directly above the "producers" resulted in an economy of movement which lent itself easily to Akbar's daily task of supervision. This combination of parallel and diagonal placement of buildings produced many unusual, irregular open areas around the palace. This open-plan and accessible design is very different to that of the Red Fort in Delhi, and a long way from the quiet symmetry of Humayun's tomb.

To facilitate the efficient and speedy construction of the palace, Akbar had devised a system of prefabrication whereby the sandstone blocks were fashioned into modular panels and columns down at the quarries, which were reassembled at the site.

A Walk Through the City: Today, much of the city is in ruins, and the usual point of entry is from the east through the **Agra Gate** (the other point of entry is via the present-day village and the Jami Masjid). The present road to the palace swings clear to the left, and below a triple-arched gateway, the **Naubat khana**. This point of entry would have led one straight to the first enclosure of the palace – a vast courtyard in which the emperor would give daily public audience to his people, listening to their grievances and dispensing justice. With its pillars and floors decorated with tapestries and carpets, this **Diwan-i-Am** also functioned as a large hall for formal receptions and celebrations (Jahangir's wedding took place here) and, on some occasions, even public prayers.

There is nothing grand or monumental about Akbar's Sikri architecture, but rather, a quiet elegance in its endlessly varied forms. Built almost entirely of red sandstone quarried on the spot, it has a restrained integrity in the use of this material, which is relieved only occasionally by trimmings of white marble and the odd blue-tiled roof. It is this subtlety and grace, coupled with the informal geometry of its planning and its fusion of Hindu and Islamic detailing, that sets

Birbal's House.

Fatehpur Sikri so distinctly apart from its ornate Mughal counterparts.

Corresponding to the second and third enclosures of the camp layout is the large quadrangle containing all major functions of the palace proper, which was solely a male domain. Every nobleman had to kiss its threshold before entering this enclosure, within which are perhaps the most celebrated buildings of Fatehpur Sikri.

At the northern end of this court stands the elegant **Diwan-i-Khas**. It is an astonishing chamber dominated by a massive, richly carved pillar, which supports fantastic capital: a circular arrangement of brackets, holding aloft a circular balcony to which narrow bridges run from each corner of the building. Yet the purpose of this extraordinarily inventive building remains ambiguous; it could have been the emperor's private audience chamber, a discussion chamber of sorts, or even a storehouse for the royal jewels. Akbar sat suspended in air, as it were, atop this great capital, looking onto his palace, the monarch of all he surveyed.

Imperial encampments on the march had a large open court separating the emperor's private living quarters from the treasury and offices, an enclosure "lit up by the moon" where the emperor would sit with selected noblemen and visitors. Here in Fatehpur Sikri, within the quadrangle forming the palace proper is an open stretch of sandstone; in its centre the paving is laid out to resemble the cruciform board on which the game of Pachisi is played. The popular myth has it that Akbar played the game with live pieces, and it may well be true. In Akbar's day this court, transformed by screens, brocade awnings and rows of tall lights, must have been used for entertaining high-ranking courtiers and foreign envoys.

Tucked into the southwest corner of this court stands a two-storey structure popularly but incorrectly called the **Girl's school**. The presence of a great

Akbar's intriguing Diwan-i-Khas.

many deep shelves and niches, and a reference in chronicles to its location, indicates that it was most probably used as a storehouse for the special fruit and Ganges water that Akbar favoured, and also as a pantry to reheat and serve food arriving from the kitchens located much further away.

Clustered about a square pool, at the southern end of the large quadrangle, are the emperor's private living quarters. Into the south wall of the court was built a once richly painted set of rooms, serving as Akbar's private library and as the scene of his intellectual activities. He sat cross-legged on a high, carpet-covered platform, receiving noblemen and scholars whom he would involve in discussions lasting well into the night. Even though Akbar was illiterate, a wide range of literature used to be read out to him daily, and he managed to initiate a glorious flowering of intellectual and cultural activities in his court. He was responsible for the founding of an eclectic, syncretic religion, Din-i-Illahi, which, though it had only 17 followers, was a revolutionary concept for its time. As Richard Lannoy wrote, even though Fatehpur Sikri was "a tragic political failure, its failure has nothing to do with its architecture, which remains the most perfect expression of the liberal society which [many] Indian rulers have vainly striven to realise". A window in this room looked out into the court of the records office or **Daftar khana** through which he would address his officers and administrators. Hot and cold water, depending on the season, flowed in channels cut into the floor, warming or cooling the space.

Above this "drawing room" and library was a small, beautifully painted chamber, popularly called the **Khwabgah** which literally means "palace of dreams". In this bedroom, profusely surfaced with gilt calligraphy and images from Persia and Turkey, his wives could easily visit him via a

The capital inside, rich in decoration.

screened passageway (now partially broken) coming from the main harem.

A central axis runs through the palace courtyard, piercing the Diwan-i-Khas, the Pachisi court, the Khwabgah and the offices of the Daftar Khana in a single imaginary line. Sitting up in his dream chamber overlooking the pool, Akbar could thus have a direct view of his Diwan-i-Khas to the north and his office to the south, with all of the red sandstone palace before him.

Contrasting with Fatehpur Sikri's red sandstone expanses, the green waters of the square pool are bridged by a cruciform causeway leading to a central platform where Akbar would sit in the evenings.

Looking onto the pool, in a corner of the court, is a tiny but exquisitely ornate pavilion, the **Turkish Sultana's residence**. Situated as it was, however, in a male part of the palace, it was more likely to have been the site of the emperor's private discussions. While other buildings in Sikri were elaborately ornamented with painted wall surfaces and tapestries, this miniature structure is rich and unified in its carved imagery and intricate sandstone embellishments. The carved motifs – date palms, pomegranates, fauna and curling clouds – speak of Persian, Turkish and even Chinese influence.

Leaving the male zone (the "palace proper") to the east, the visitor enters the women's quarters, comprising the main harem, the residences of the senior queens, and a private garden for the royal women. A small doorway off the pool court leads one to **Mariam's palace**, the home of Akbar's mother, though it is popularly ascribed to a Christian queen Mariam (of whom there is no mention in any chronicle of the time). Severe and sober, the exterior of this building belies the sumptuously painted walls within, which were, till even as late as the 19th century, richly glowing with gold. Gilded angels race through clouds, and a profusion of birds and animals once scampered through

Life continues in the ruins of Akbar's city.

fields of flowers. An inscription on its wall reads:

"The gardens painted on these walls are on level with the gardens of paradise".

Unfortunately, time and Sikri's harsh climate have taken their toll, leaving only faded reminders of this beauty.

Built at the highest level in the palace is the main harem, commonly called **Jodhbai's palace**. Solemn and massive, this imperial residence is probably the most important, and certainly the largest, of all the buildings in the palace. The staggered entrance assured its inmates privacy and safety, as did a force of eunuchs. Arranged around a great central court are a series of rooms forming the living quarters of Akbar's many wives, including a section supposedly converted into a temple for the Hindu princesses. Here we observe the most interesting fusion of stylistic detailing: local elements from Gujarat, Mandu and Gwalior are blended with traditional Islamic design to form the distinctive early Mughal features, including the elegant tulip pattern which was to characterise Sikri. The only splash of colour in all of Sikri is furnished by the bright blue tiled roofs of this building. A small screened wind-tower – the **Hawa Mahal** – attached to this palace permitted the emperor to spend hot summer evenings in a carved chamber with the cool northwesterly breeze wafting through. A screened viaduct emanating from the north wall of the harem gave the imperial women private access to the lakeside pavilions, and to the weekly bazaar spread out at the foot of the palace.

The third residence in the women's domain was the beautifully carved **palace** generally ascribed to **Birbal**, the legendary wit and most favoured of Akbar's courtiers. Birbal could most certainly not have lived here; nor could any other male, since it was an integral part of the harem. Travellers have called it the finest domestic building of Sikri,

The saint's tomb attracts many devotees.

and if the main harem is to be exempted, the richness, extent and intricacy of carving on all its surfaces, as well as the glorious view it commands of the lake, aptly justify the epithet. Every square inch of wall and ceiling is overrun by swirls of tiny flowers, interlocking octagons and lotus blossoms, so delicate and profuse that the interior gives the illusion of stone carpeting. The prominent style of decoration seems decidedly Hindu.

Relieving the starkness of the hot, red sandstone, we come upon a patch of green, overlooking and stepping down towards the lake – a formal Mughal garden laid out on the "Charbagh" principle, emulating the gardens of paradise. Once walled in for privacy, it was central to the three female establishments of the palace, complete with a small bathhouse, pavilions and a central fishpond. Water from the lake was fed to the garden through aqueducts, and running into the pond over a wall pierced with niches for oil lamps, it formed a glittering veil as it fell over the flickering lights.

In the heat and dust of Sikri, basements could have offered respite in hot summers, but were difficult to carve out of the rocky outcrop. As an alternative, breeze-catching wind towers were constructed, rising into the skyline in fairy-tale forms. Lending particular emphasis to the silhouette of Sikri is the famous **Panch Mahal**, an extraordinary structure, entirely columnar, consisting of five storeys of upwardly decreasing size. Its 176 columns, of which no two are exactly alike (except for pairs), offer a veritable museum of styles, many of Hindu inspiration. Set into a corner formed by the "male" and "female" zones of the palace, this pleasure pavilion was used by Akbar and his special consorts. Opening out towards the lake, it commanded a magnificent view of the imperial palace below.

While the "palace proper" occupied the upper strata of the ridge, the slopes

Soffit detail: red sandstone treated like wood.

accommodated the various service functions of the royal palace. Among these are still discernible the kitchens and baths to the south, workshops (the **Mint**) to the northeast, and elaborate water-works near the lake.

This northern aspect formed the second approach to the palace, possibly the major imperial entrance, with the royal entourage arriving on elephants and horses past the lake, up a long ramp, and through the monumental doorway called the **Hathi Pol** or Elephant Gate. Now ruined (possibly by the zeal of Aurangzeb), a pair of splendid rubble elephants, 3 m (10 ft) high, once welcomed arrivals to the palace. From here, the imperial women could enter the harem discreetly via the screened passage, and the emperor could approach his offices from doorways in the north.

The feel of the site, and the open vistas of the citadel, with its wide ramps and high gateways for elephant movement, contribute to the dramatic character of most of the palace approaches from the north. Unfortunately, it is no longer possible to approach the palace from this direction.

Beside the lake were dotted recreational spots – water pavilions, baths, and even a polo ground, a game of Inner Asian origin of which the emperor was particularly fond. Dominating the lakeside view from the palace, and rising 21 m (70 ft) into the air, is an amazing tower-like structure, studded with upward curving stone cylinders, like a collection of elephant tusks. Its popular name, **Hiran Minar**, meaning "deer tower" is of later origin, having nothing to do with its function, which remains ambiguous. Its positioning seems to imply a sort of marker – a tall milestone visible from afar, signifying the royal entrance to the palace.

The large man-made lake helped solve the city's water supply problem. A carefully detailed system transported water to a great well, lifted it up in stages over cattle-drawn wheels and supplied it via aqueducts to all parts of the palace.

The airy five-storeyed Panch Mahal overlooking the Diwan-i-Khas.

A covered drainage system was ingeniously incorporated in the level differences of the palace courtyards, and the water was cleverly run off, stored and recycled. The extensive and complex **Court Baths**, on the southern slope behind the **Records Office**, are somewhat reminiscent of the Roman baths of Caracalla, though on a more intimate scale.

Sikri Abandoned: This dream city, with its lofty mosque, pleasure pavilions, sunken gardens and multi-level courts, enjoyed but a brief moment of glory. Fifteen years after its foundations were dug, Akbar's entire court – 5,000 women, 1,000 doorkeepers and 1,200 horses – packed up and moved on, leaving behind only dead sandstone and a few descendants of Shaikh Salim. The reasons ascribed to this abandonment have been many: that Akbar was sorely disillusioned by his son Jahangir; that an acute water shortage rendered life difficult; and that he found it impractical to maintain two establishments (one at Agra and the other at Sikri) simultaneously. All these factors may have contributed to his decision to move, but the clinch was a pressing political reason: the emperor was urgently needed on the northwest frontier, to gain a stronghold and consolidate his empire further.

During his 50-year reign, Akbar never established a permanent capital, shifting whenever he felt necessary. There was always a correlation between the location of the capital and the empire's strategic interests. Also, the relatively minor share that building activity claimed in the imperial budget (the making of Fatehpur cost only one-fiftieth of its total net revenue) made its abandonment easy. For this nomadic existence, it seemed perfectly appropriate that when Akbar did settle down, his architecture too should have the impermanent quality of his lifestyle; the cities he built were merely stone actualisations of his temporary encampments. Fittingly, a passage concerned with the transient nature of all things is inscribed on the Buland Darwaza, a quotation from the *Hadith* which reads:

"Said Jesus (blessings be upon him):
'The world is a bridge;
cross it therefore,
But do not build upon it'".

Walking through Fatehpur Sikri's now desolate palaces, it is still possible to imagine how it must have looked 400 years ago, when the empty courts teemed with activity, transformed by rich brocade curtains, beautiful carpets and flowing water. With the dawning of each new day, the muezzin still calls for prayer, but the hot sandstone courts are now bare. The gilded frescoes have faded, the lake run dry and the rose bushes are long dead. What remains is the spirit of impulse and devotion, and the dynamic informality of its ever exciting architecture. Fatehpur Sikri stands as a unique monument to the ambition and organisational genius of Muhammad Jalaludin Akbar.

Left, Akbar supervising construction at Fatehpur Sikri. Right, the emperor receiving the *Akbarnama*.

SIKANDARA

Along the northern road, barely 5 km (3 miles) from Agra's Delhi Gate, is the small hamlet of Sikandara. This was the isolated site that Akbar chose for his final resting place. Even at first glance, the red sandstone open pyramidal tomb stands out. Akbar started it himself but made little headway. Astrologers had predicted that he would live to be 120 years old. He was in no hurry – or perhaps he was superstitious enough to fear that its completion would invite death before his time was up. He actually died in 1605, at the age of 63.

The deceased emperor's artistic and pleasure-loving son Jahangir took up the thread, though in desultory fashion. The process lingered on for several years, with the result that the monument has evident traces of conflict of design. This is particularly apparent in the finishing touches, such as the crowning pyramid of marble and the flamboyant gateway giving entry to the extensive grounds in which the tomb is placed. This gateway is one of the few surviving examples of Jahangir's architectural achievement in Agra. Most of the additions he made in Akbar's fort were arbitrarily demolished by his son Shahjahan. The stylistic transition and emerging preference for the use of marble thus marks out Sikandara as a bridge between the rugged sandstone favoured by Akbar, and the dazzling marble and pietra dura of his grandson.

There seems little doubt that Akbar's original conception of an open pyramid had some mystical significance. Affinities have been suggested with the five-storey Panch Mahal he built in Fatehpur Sikri. Jahangir's contribution is characteristic: touches of marble in the main structure, and the gateway already mentioned. The gateway's four minarets rising from the corners are particularly striking. The original cupolas were carried away by the Jats

Akbar's tomb, started by him in sandstone and completed by Jahangir in marble.

when they occupied Agra in 1764, but have been successfully restored.

The open fifth floor, which is the last step of the ascending pyramid, is girdled by a marble cloister enclosed by screens fretted in sophisticated geometric designs. There are indications, as Fergusson has suggested, that its central platform was meant to support a light dome. Finch, who visited Sikandara in 1611, was more emphatic. The tomb, he says, was intended "to be inarched over with the most curious white marble, and to be seeled all within with pure sheet-gold, richly inwrought". When he visited it again, Finch saw drawn over "a rich tent, with a semaine over the tombe". Marble rings at the corners of the cloisters were apparently used to hold the "rich tent" in place. Jahangir may have left it open intentionally in compliance with his father's wishes, with arrangements for it to be covered during the celebration of the Urs.

As may be expected, the sarcophagus is on the ground floor, covered with a plain slab of white marble. Midway between the staircases of the fourth storey is a small opening through which it is possible to crawl into a low-roof secret chamber containing a false tomb. The culmination of this unusual arrangement is a white marble cenotaph in the centre of the open cloister. It is inscribed with the 29 names of God, but there is no mention of the Prophet. This omission might be attributed to the curious system of belief Akbar propagated in his lifetime in which he came close to claiming divinity. Cloud motifs appear on the head and foot panels, which is also exceptional in Mughal tombs, though not necessarily attributable to Chinese workmen.

In retrospect it is unfortunate that Akbar did not complete his own mausoleum at Sikandara. Had he been able to do so, posterity might have had the good fortune of gaining further insights into the character of this most unusual monarch.

Mathura and Vrindavan

The road between Delhi and Agra once passed through a more ancient and venerated city than either – Mathura and neighbouring Vrindavan. Mathura was known to the Greeks as *Madoura ton theon* (Mathura of the Gods). It was the second capital of the Kushan empire (1st–3rd century AD). Pilgrims like Fa-hsein (5th century AD) and Hsuan Tsang (7th century AD), and travellers like Tavernier (1650) and Father Tieffenthaler (1754), amongst others, journeyed to this area and recorded its cultural and religious importance. Its prosperity and accessibility was an invitation to plunderers like Mahmud of Ghazni (AD 1017) and others. But today, the busy traveller flies over it by air and by-passes it on the road – which is a pity, because Mathura and Vrindavan are quintessential Indian towns, where the life of the people is as much on display as their monuments. In this respect they resemble other pilgrimage centres in India, like Varanasi in Uttar Pradesh or Pushkar in Rajasthan. However, they contain no extraordinary examples of architecture – though as an ensemble certain parts of the town, especially the river front, do achieve a certain grandeur.

Mathura and Vrindavan lie in the heart of a region known as Brajbhumi – the Land of Braj. Geographically, it is an area roughly 70 km (44 miles) long and 45 km (28 miles) wide, straddling the river Yamuna. Culturally, it is the holy land of Vaishnava Hinduism, whose followers propitiate Vishnu, the Protector in the Hindu trinity. This is the hallowed region where, incarnate as Krishna, he lived and played. Krishna, besides ridding the world of evil, revealed the *Bhagvadgita*, the preeminent Hindu scriptural text, during the epic battle of Kurukshetra narrated in the *Mahabharata*. His dalliances with the milkmaids of Vrindavan inspired some of the finest lyrical poetry, music and painting in the country. His worship in Mathura and Vrindavan is conducted by means of communal pilgrimages to all the sacred spots associated with his life, and by the chanting of the *mahamantra* – the great mantra:

Hare Krishna, Hare Krishna,
Krishna Krishna, Hare Hare,
Hare Rama, Hare Rama,
Rama, Rama, Hare Hare.

A visit to the land of Braj will not be memorable for visits to monuments but for experiencing its vibrant living culture. Mathura and Vrindavan are, therefore, different from better known sites of architectural importance or even Shaivite religious centres like Varanasi. Here the devotion of the people to the story of Krishna is palpable.

Most of contemporary Mathura is only a few centuries old, though tradition maintains that it is a very ancient site indeed. Although a Hindu centre, the earliest verifiable references to Mathura are of Buddhist or Jain origin. Gautama Buddha died in 477 BC and is known to have established institutions in Mathura during his lifetime, but Krishna is believed to have preceded him by several centuries. However, there is only inferential evidence to support this belief. The Vedas, Puranas and the epics, which were finally compiled around AD 400, possibly reflect the state of affairs existing in North India from about the 10th century BC, at the time when Krishna is associated with this region.

Historical evidence of Mathura is available from about 2,500 years ago, during the Buddhist hegemony over this region, and comes into focus at the time of the Kushans, Indo-Bactrian rulers who had converted to Buddhism and held sway over this area in the wake of Alexander's conquests. Their rule introduced Hellenistic aesthetics into Indian art. The Kushans who followed the Sakas made Mathura their winter capital and wholeheartedly patronised

Preceding pages, ras-lila performer in Brajbhumi. **Left**, devotees bathe in Goverdhan tank on the occasion of Gurupurnima.

Buddhism. This patronage was reflected in the flowering of the arts and emergence of which is known as the Mathura School. The most famous Kushan ruler, Kanishka, started an era in AD 78 known as the Saka era, which is used by the Government of India in its official calendar.

Being on the trade routes and with strong royal patronage, Mathura developed into an important commercial and cultural centre. The Mathura school of art was prolific in its output and is recognised by its products made of local red and buff-coloured sandstone. While the images of Buddha were influenced by the Graeco-Roman style introduced by the Kushan rulers through their empire, the work of this school strongly retained its indigenous characteristics. At present the Mathura Museum possesses the largest collection of sculptures and other artefacts produced in this style in India. Besides beautiful images of Buddha and Buddhist themes, the Chinese pilgrims mention seeing a vast complex of stupas and religious institutions, of which only fragmentary evidence now remains. The archaeological excavations at Sonkh near Mathura offer significant evidence of the existence of this culture.

Some time after this period, Mathura regained its Hindu antecedents, except for occasional periods of religious persecution. The epics which were compiled during this period naturally reflected the politics of their times, and it is conjectured that Krishna owes such of his present lustre to the gratitude of the Brahmans, who under his banner recovered their ancient influence. Today there is little doubt that the Vaishnava culture is deeply embedded in the consciousness of the people of Brajbhumi. Each village hill or pond is associated with the boyhood events of Krishna's life. The source of this belief is the *Bhagvat Purana*, traditionally ascribed to the grammarian Bopadeva who lived in the 12th or 13th century AD.

Barsana steps flanked by houses.

One cannot understand contemporary Mathura or Vrindavan without knowing this ancient story.

The Legend: Over 3,000 years ago, King Kansa usurped the throne of Mathura and began a tyrannical reign from which his subjects prayed for deliverance. A prophecy told Kansa that his nemesis would be the son of his sister Devaki and her husband Vasudev. He incarcerated the couple and slew every child born to them in prison; but on the night of Krishna's birth, Vasudev managed to smuggle him out through divine intervention, putting him under the care of the cowherd Nanda and his wife Jasoda in Gokul, across the river from Mathura.

Krishna grew up with his foster-parents and became known throughout the countryside for his supernatural feats, and also for his mischievous pranks like stealing butter and enchanting the milkmaids with the divine music he played on the flute. Radha was his favourite, and their various assignations at Vrindavan have added countless embellishments to the basic story.

Kansa heard of this extraordinary cowherd and recognised the fated avenger. He invited Krishna to a tournament in the hope of forestalling providence, but Krishna defeated all comers and finally slew Kansa. He dragged the tyrant's body to the banks of the Yamuna for creation and at last "rested" at a place still known as *Vishram Ghat* or the Resting Ghat. This is the holiest spot in Mathura.

After accomplishing this mission, Krishna spent his adulthood in Dwarka, in Western India, and took part in the great war described in the *Mahabharata*, but his association with Mathura had ended. In Mathura, Vrindavan and other places linked with his boyhood, however, people implicitly believe in his continued presence. It is this faith that mixes history and myth into the everyday life of Brajbhumi.

The Sacred Forest: Vrindavan means a forest of *vrinda* or *tulsi* (basil) plants. The forest cover consisted of the Kadamba tree. Both plants have a special significance for Vaishnavas and almost every Hindu grows a *tulsi* shrub at home which is ritually worshipped every day. Unlike other *tirthas* (pilgrimage destinations) of India, Vrindavan was in essence a forest, not a city. Ancient documents listing principal places of pilgrimage understandably did not mention it, though Mathura is identified as an important *tirtha*.

When Chaitanya (1486-1533) – the great Vaishnava saint from Bengal primarily associated with the emergence of the Krishna cult – visited Vrindavan, it was a forest. It is believed that he instructed his followers to establish temples here. Sanatana and Rupa, two of his disciples from Bengal, erected the first shine, of which no trace remains, and also became the first priests of the Govind Deva temple. (It

Temple in a Vrindavan verandah: Krishna subduing the horse-demon.

MATHURA MUSEUM

The Government Museum in Mathura is an important regional museum. It contains a definitive collection of the Mathura school which flourished in this region about 2,000 years ago and was seminal to the development of Indian art. Curiously, in an area steeped in Krishna *bhakti* (devotion), the pride of the collection is its examples of traditional art and sculptures with Jain or Buddhist themes.

There was little concrete evidence of these local cultures until 1837 when accidental discoveries made during excavations for new construction in the vicinity of Mathura alerted the nascent British colonial administration to its existence. Archaeology in India was in its pioneering phase at this time, and Sir Alexander Cunningham, the first Director General of the Archaeological Survey of India, and several others, made substantial discoveries.

In 1874, F.S. Growse, a sympathetic scholar as well as a colonial administrator, decided to stem the out-flow of Indian art treasures to museums in Britain by establishing a museum in Mathura. It was known as the Curzon Museum for Archaeology until 1973.

While the cultures of this region produced a variety of artefacts, the Museum collection is built around its terracotta and sandstone sculptures. The terracotta collection reveals more clearly the development of sculptural technique. There is a significant difference between the earlier mother-goddesses (4th century BC) whose anatomical features were created by pinching the clay and whose ornamentations were punch-marked, and the works of the Sunga period (2nd to 1st century BC) when the clay was skilfully molded as in the 1st century BC Kamadeva. These skills developed further, when sandstone became the preferred medium of expression, as can be seen in the beautiful 4th century Kartikeya.

Mathura is best known for its sandstone sculptures in the style identified as the Mathura school. The city was a well known cultural centre from the time of Buddha and, being on the trade routes, it became a melting-pot where local and external artistic traditions mingled and were synthesised into a distinct regional style, particularly during the Kushan period (1st to 3rd century BC).

The Kushans had an empire stretching from Afghanistan to Bihar. Mathura was their winter capital and provided generous patronage to the arts in this region. The Kushan art of Mathura was, however, totally different from the Kushan art of Gandhara where the Hellenic influence was noticeably strong. The Mathura school was a continuation of the indigenous traditions of Bharhut and Sanchi. The Yakshis in the museum display indigenous aesthetic traditions – notice the triple flexion or *tribangha* peculiar to Indian art. The representations of Buddha evolved from these traditions had round faces, full lips and monastic robes and were very different from the "Apollonian" Buddha of the Gandhara region of northwestern South Asia.

The Mathura school is recognised for two major innovations. Firstly, it fused the traditional arts of the local people with the parallel court traditions based on the Iranian and Indo-Bactrian traditions of the ruling elite. This created new iconographic formulae for both Buddhist and Hindu iconic art which were followed in later Indian statuary. Secondly, it replaced the symbolic worship of Buddha by his image in human form, and this revolutionised the development of art in India.

These developments reached their climax during the Gupta period between AD 325 and 600. Thereafter, the sculptures from this school display greater formality, heavier ornamentation and more complex groupings, as seen in the 10th century seated Vishnu and standing Surya. With the rise of Brahmanism, the themes naturally changed to reflect religious beliefs.

With the emergence of Krishna as the titular deity of Mathura, however, one wonders why this tradition of expression ceased and why the artists of this region moved to other media when there was such a wealth of sculptural skill.

fell into disuse after the image of the deity was removed to Jaipur to escape Aurangzeb in the 17th century, and only recently has another image been installed.) Gopal Bhatt from South India established the Radha Raman temple, and his descendants have served the deity ever since. The image of Krishna in this temple is notable for having remained in Vrindavan for the longest continuous period of time. It escaped the notice of the iconoclast Aurangzeb because it is only 30 cm (12 inches) tall.

The other impetus to the development of the town was provided by the emperor Akbar. It is said that Akbar wanted to meet the saint Hari Das, who had been the guru of his court musician, Tansen, and invited him to Agra. Hari Das sent a message back to the effect that he preferred to attend the court of his Lord. Thus, it was Akbar who made the pilgrimage in 1573, and in honour of that event four temples were duly erected – Govind Deva, Gopinath, Jugal Kishore and Madan Mohan.

Vrindavan has a population of about 40,000, but several times that number visit the town as tourists and pilgrims. It is also a place where Vaishnavites in their old age take refuge, especially widows. To die in Vrindavan, it is believed, is to be guaranteed *moksha*, release from the cycle of rebirth. The town, therefore, has several *dharamsalas* or pilgrim rest houses and widow-houses, donated and maintained by rich merchants from around the country as an act of piety.

Vrindavan was once a river-oriented town and had several *ghats* or steps leading to the river edge. The river gradually receded, leaving dry many of the 38 *ghats* along the 2.5-km (1½-mile) river front. In fact only five *ghats* are actually on the water. The town has a tightly knit fabric and is on slightly undulating land with well paved roads which drain the surface wastes to the river. Like most other traditional towns, open sewers run on the sides of these

Left, sandstone Buddha of the Mathura school. Below, Mathura temple: communal devotional singing.

streets, polluting the diminishing waters in the river.

The Kesi and Pandawala Ghats located at the extreme northeast are important pilgrimage points. The buildings along these Ghats are imposing, with exquisite workmanship in the traditional style, loosely referred to as the Jat style of architecture.

Important amongst the several temples of the town are the Govind Deva and Radha Balabh, built in the 16th and 17th centuries, and the Rangji and Shahji, built during the latter half of the 19th century.

Mathura: The modern town of Mathura has a population of around 250,000. With the location of a large oil refinery and other industries nearby, the profile of the population is becoming heterogenous, but it is still a city that has a strong sense of its traditions, with the lives of its people revolving around the cycle of festivals and religious rituals. There are 36 major festivals that fill the town with activity throughout the year.

In spite of its antiquity, Mathura is a relatively new town. After Mahmud of Ghazni in 1017, the town was sacked again by Nadir Shah in 1739 and Ahmad Shah in 1757. It was the Marathas and the Jat rulers of Bharatpur who began rebuilding the Mathura we see today. The town has a delightfully organic character with a strongly defined edge along the river. Unlike the deserted *ghats* of Vrindavan, those of Mathura are alive with activity. There are steps leading to the water, temples, residences, shops, *dharamsalas* and sacred trees. Pilgrims and locals mingle with sacred cows, monkeys and turtles. The most used stretch is between Vishram Ghat and the Sati Burj built in 1527 by the Raja of Jaipur to commemorate the self-immolation of his mother. Others claim that it was built to commemorate the *sati* of the wife of a local citizen, Behari Mal. In any case, it is an unusual monument with an incongruous dome on top. At Vishram Ghat the corpses are "rested" before being

Vrindavan Ghats under Yamuna monsoon spate.

carried through the bazaar to the cremation grounds south of the bridge.

Dwarkadhish, built in 1914 in the heart of the city, is its most important temple. The Jama Masjid, also in the heart of the city, was built over the ruins of the Keshav Deo temple in 1661. This temple had been built fifty years earlier to mark the site of Kansa's prison where Krishna was born. Tavernier, who visited it in 1650, considered it "one of the most sumptuous edifices in all India".

However, a visit to Mathura is not about a search for great works of architecture. One has to look beyond the typically anarchic traffic and bustle of activity, to witness the numerous festivals which fill the ritual calendar of Mathura.

Festivals: Pilgrims come to Mathura and Vrindavan throughout the year and undertake the ritual *parikrama* or circumambulation as an act of piety. The *parikrama* can encompass a few important shrines or the entire Brajbhumi, which takes several days to complete. They usually start with a ritual bath at the Vishram Ghat and end there too. Interestingly, even though a ritual bath at the end of the pilgrimage would be a welcome necessity, most pilgrims avoid it because they believe that it may wash away the merit acquired during the *parikrama*.

There are many special days like the *Purnima* (full moon) and *Ekadasi* (11th day of the moon's cycle) which are considered auspicious and draw crowds. Other prominent festivals include Holi (February–March) and Janmashtami (August–September), the birthday of Krishna. During Holi, the festival of colour, people intoxicate themselves with *bhang* and sing and dance in celebration. It is the Indian saturnalia. At Barsana, Radha's hometown, an amusing spectacle is enacted: a fight between the men from the neighbouring village of Nandgaon and the women of Barsana during which the men are beated with wooden poles, accompanied by ribald rhymes.

On Janmashtami, *parikramas* are undertaken and the *ras-lila* is celebrated. *Ras-lilas* are religious dance-dramas which represent the most popular incidents in the life of Krishna. The complete cycle extends over a month and each scene is enacted on the very spot with which the original episode is traditionally connected, known as *ras-mandals*. The troupe is lead by a guru who teaches the players. The parts of Krishna and the gopis are taken by young Brahman boys who, for the devotees in the audiences, become the living embodiments of the deity.

If one were to list all the festivals that are celebrated, it would appear that there is time for little else; life here appears to be one long series of rituals and devotion. Unlike in other *tirthas*, people come here not to facilitate their journey to the other world, but to be caught in the tide of ecstasy of faith, and thereby find tranquility in this life. To an outsider, it is one of the enigmas of Brajbhumi.

Below, ritual bath and prayer at Mathura Ghat. Following page, Amber temple doors donated by the wife of Maharaja Man Singh in 1939. It was in gratitude for his injury-free escape from a plane crash.

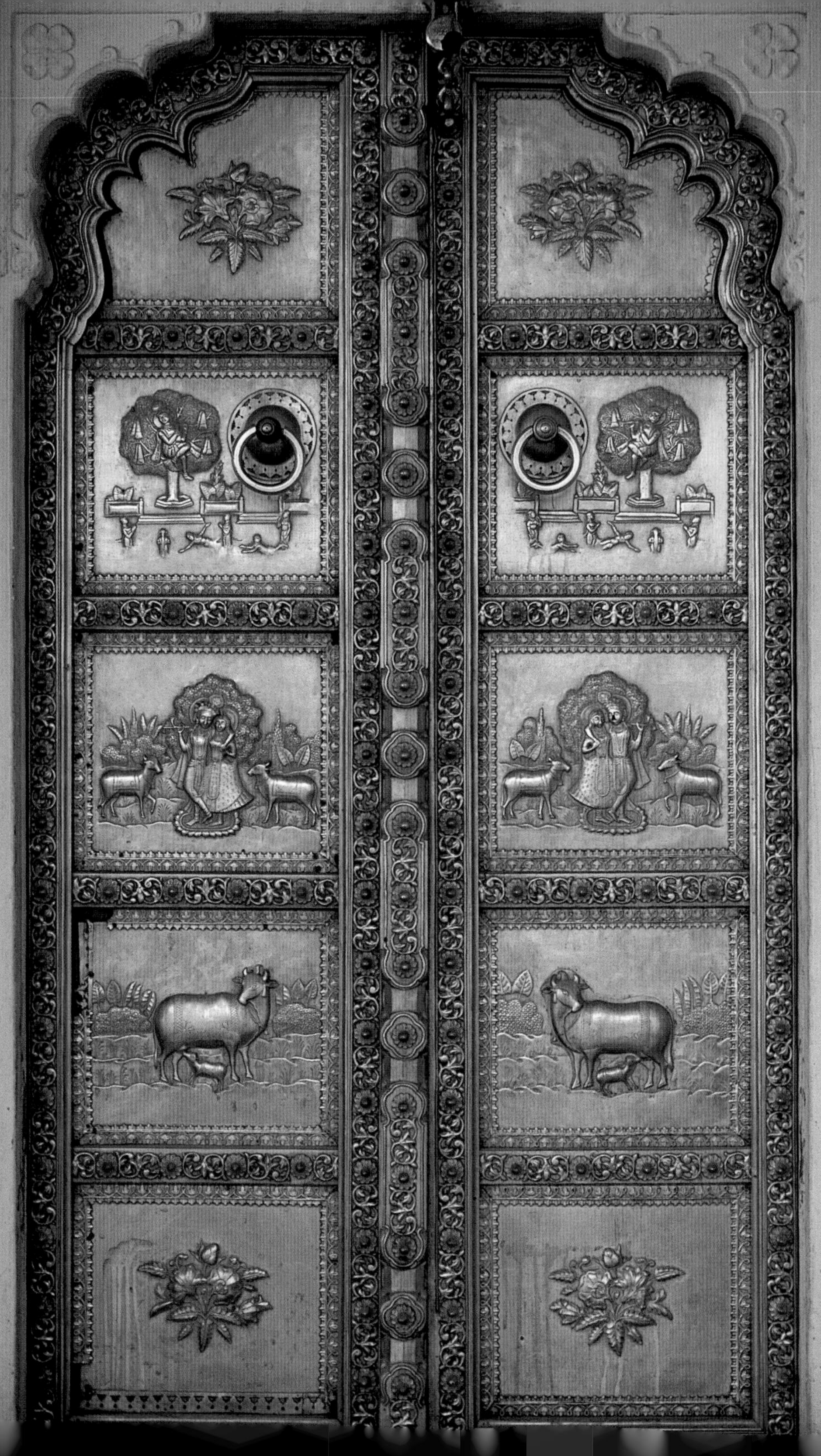

INSIGHT GUIDES

TRAVEL TIPS

TIMBUKTU KALAMAZOO

Global connection with the AT&T Network

AT&T direct service

www.att.com/traveler

AT&T Direct® Service

The easy way to call home from anywhere.

AT&T Access Numbers

Argentina .0800-555-4288	**Czech Rep.▲.00-42-000-101**
Australia...1-800-881-011	**Denmark........8001-0010**
Austria●....0800-200-288	**Egypt●(Cairo) ...510-0200**
Bahamas..1-800-USA-ATT1	**France.....0800-99-00-11**
Belgium● ..0-800-100-10	**Germany..0800-2255-288**
Bermuda✚ 1-800-USA-ATT1	**Greece● 00-800-1311**
Brazil 000-8010	**Guam 1-800-2255-288**
Canada...1 800 CALL ATT	Guyana○ 165
Chile 800-225-288	**Hong Kong ..800-96-1111**
China, PRC▲ 10811	**India▲ 000-117**
Costa Rica .0-800-0-114-114	**Ireland 1-800-550-000**

AT&T Direct® Service

The easy way to call home from anywhere.

AT&T Access Numbers

Argentina .0800-555-4288	**Czech Rep.▲.00-42-000-101**
Australia...1-800-881-011	**Denmark........8001-0010**
Austria●....0800-200-288	**Egypt●(Cairo) ...510-0200**
Bahamas..1-800-USA-ATT1	**France.....0800-99-00-11**
Belgium● ..0-800-100-10	**Germany..0800-2255-288**
Bermuda✚ 1-800-USA-ATT1	**Greece● 00-800-1311**
Brazil 000-8010	**Guam 1-800-2255-288**
Canada...1 800 CALL ATT	Guyana○ 165
Chile 800-225-288	**Hong Kong ..800-96-1111**
China, PRC▲ 10811	**India▲ 000-117**
Costa Rica .0-800-0-114-114	**Ireland 1-800-550-000**

Israel	**1-800-94-94-949**	**Portugal▲**	**800-800-128**
Italy●	**172-1011**	**Saudi Arabia▲**	**1-800-10**
Jamaica●	1-800-USA-ATT1	Singapore	800-0111-111
Japan●▲	**005-39-111**	**South Africa**	**0800-99-0123**
Korea, Republic●	**0072-911**	**Spain**	**900-99-00-11**
Mexico▽●	**01-800-288-2872**	**Sweden**	**020-799-111**
Netherlands●	**0800-022-9111**	**Switzerland●**	**0800-89-0011**
Neth. Ant.▲⊗	**001-800-USA-ATT1**	**Taiwan**	**0080-10288-0**
New Zealand●	**000-911**	Thailand❮	001-999-111-11
Norway	**800-190-11**	**Turkey●**	**00-800-12277**
Panama	00-800-001-0109	U.A. Emirates●	800-121
Philippines●	**105-11**	**U.K.**	**0800-89-0011**
Poland●▲	**00-800-111-1111**	**Venezuela**	**800-11-120**

FOR EASY CALLING WORLDWIDE

1. Just dial the AT&T Access Number for the country you are calling from. *2.* Dial the phone number you're calling. *3.* Dial your card number*

For access numbers not listed ask any operator for **AT&T Direct**® Service. In the U.S. call 1-800-222-0300 for **AT&T Direct** Service information. Visit our Web site at: **www.att.com/traveler**

Bold-faced countries permit country-to-country calling outside the U.S.

- ● Public phones require coin or card deposit to place call.
- ✚ Public phones and select hotels.
- ▲ May not be available from every phone/payphone.
- ○ Collect calling only.
- ▽ Includes "Ladatel" public phones; if call does not complete, use 001-800-462-4240.
- ⊗ From St. Maarten or phones at Bobby's Marina, use 1-800-USA-ATT1.
- ❮ When calling from public phones, use phones marked Lenso.
- * AT&T Calling Card, AT&T Corporate, AT&T Universal, MasterCard®, Diners Club®, American Express®, or Discover® cards accepted.

When placing an international call ***from*** the U.S., dial 1-800-CALL ATT.

WW ©6/00 AT&T

CONTENTS

Getting Acquainted

The Place 266
The Land 266
When to Go 266
Etiquette 266
The Government 267
The Economy 267

Planning the Trip

What to Bring 268
Entry Regulations 268
Customs 268
Maps 269
Health 269
Getting There 270
Money Matters 270
Special Facilities 271
Embassies & Consulates 271
Tourist Offices 272
Airline Office 272
Cyber Cafés 273

Practical Tips

Emergencies 273
Business Hours 273
Tipping 273
Women Travelling Alone 274
Postal Services 274
Telecommunications 274
Media 274
On Arrival 275
On Departure 275
Repairs and Tailors 275
Entrance Fees 275

Getting Around

Travel by Air 276
Travel by Bus 276
Rickshaws 276
Driving in India 276
Taxis 277
Car & Taxi Rental 277
Travel by Rail 277
Useful Trains 278

Where to Stay

Agra 279
Delhi 280
Jaipur 282

Where to Eat

Agra 284
Delhi 284
Jaipur 286

Shopping

What to Buy 287
Shopping in Agra 287
Shopping in Delhi 287
Shopping in Jaipur 288

Wildlife

Wildlife & Bird Parks 289

Language

Traveller's Hindi 289

Further Reading

History 291
Society, Culture & Religion 291
Fiction 292
Travel 293
Food, Language & Images 293

Getting Acquainted

The Place

Area India covers an area of 3,287,590 sq. km (1,269,346 sq. miles).
Capital New Delhi.
Largest City Mumbai (with more than 15 million inhabitants).
Highest point Kanchenjunga, in Sikkim (8,586 metres/28,170 ft).
Population All-India 1 billion; Delhi 12 million; Jaipur 1.5 million; Agra 956,000. There are 929 women for every 1,000 men, a difference which has steadily increased since the beginning of the 20th century.
Major Languages Hindi (mother tongue for more than 360 million speakers), Telugu, Bengali, Marathi and Tamil.
Major Religions Hindu (80 percent); Muslim (11 percent); Christian (2 percent); Sikh (2 percent), Jain, Buddhist.
Time Zones India is 5½ hours ahead of Greenwich Mean Time.
Currency The decimal system with 100 paise to the rupee.
Weights & Measures The metric system is uniformly used all over India. Precious metals, especially gold, are often sold by the traditional *tola*, which is equivalent to 11.5 grams (0.4 ounces). Gems are weighed in carats (0.2 grams/0.01 ounces).

Financial outlays and population are usually expressed in *lakhs* (100 thousand) and *crores* (100 *lakhs* or 10 million).
Electricity The voltage system in India is 220V AC, 50 cycles. DC supplies also exist, so check first. Sockets are of the two round-pin variety normally, but do vary. Take a universal adaptor for British, Irish and Australasian plugs. American and Canadian appliances will need a transformer.
Dialling Codes To call India from abroad, dial the international access code, followed by 91 for India, the local code less the initial zero, then the number.

The Land

India lies between latitude 8° north and 36° north, and longitude 68° east and 97° east. It is surrounded by the Arabian Sea on the west, the Bay of Bengal on the east and the Indian Ocean to the south. It shares borders with Pakistan, China, Nepal, Bhutan, Burma (Myanmar) and Bangladesh, and is divided into seven major regions: Himalayas, Indo-Gangetic Plain, Central Highlands, Deccan Plateau, Western Ghats, Eastern Ghats and the bordering seas and islands.

Delhi and Agra lie on the Jamuna river, which flows east across the Indo-Gangetic plain, joining the Ganga at Allahabad. Jaipur is situated 240 km (149 miles) to the west of Agra in the Aravalli hills of Rajasthan.

When to Go

In general, the best time to visit India is after the southwest monsoon, when the land is refreshed and green, and temperatures are not too high.

October to March is the cool season following the rains. On the whole, the weather is beautifully predictable in winter, with blue skies and bright sunshine during the day. At night, during December and January, temperatures can fall quite low (down to 1–2° C/33–35° F in Delhi) making early morning starts very chilly.

Summer, from April to June, is very hot and dry. This can be a difficult time to travel, with temperatures in Delhi, Agra and Jaipur pushing 50 degrees centigrade (122° F) on the hottest days. There may be dust storms in the plains, and as the humidity builds just before the onset of the monsoon, spectacular dry thunderstorms.

The southwest monsoon begins to set in along the western coast towards the end of May, bringing welcome respite from the heat and varying amounts of rain. It moves across the country during June and July, and withdraws by late September.

Etiquette

- Removing one's shoes before entering a temple, mosque or *gurdwara* (sikh temple) is essential. Overshoes are provided in some places at a nominal cost and stockinged feet are usually permissible.

Average Monthly Temperatures & Rainfall

		Jan	Feb	Mar	Apr	May	June	July	Aug	Sep	Oct	Nov	Dec
Agra	Max/Min °C	22/7	26/10	32/16	38/22	42/27	41/29	35/27	33/26	33/25	33/19	29/12	24/8
	Rainfall mm	16	9	11	5	10	60	210	263	151	23	2	4
Delhi	Max/Min °C	21/7	24/10	30/15	36/21	41/27	40/29	35/27	34/26	34/25	35/19	29/12	23/8
	Rainfall mm	25	22	17	7	8	65	211	173	150	31	1	5
Jaipur	Max/Min °C	22/8	25/11	31/15	37/21	41/26	39/27	34/26	32/24	33/23	33/18	29/12	24/9
	Rainfall mm	14	8	9	4	10	54	193	239	90	19	3	4

- Avoid taking leather goods of any kind into temples as these can often cause offence.
- Photography is prohibited inside the inner sanctum of many places of worship. Do obtain permission before using a camera. Visitors are usually welcome to look around at their leisure and can sometimes stay during religious rituals. For visits to places of worship, modest clothing is essential. In Sikh temples, your head should be covered. In mosques, women should cover their head and arms and wear long skirts. A small contribution to the donation box is customary.
- In private, visitors are received as honoured guests and your unfamiliarity with Indian ways will be accepted and understood. When eating with your fingers, remember to use only the right hand.
- Avoid pointing the soles of your feet towards anyone as this is considered a sign of disrespect. Don't point with your index finger: use either your extended hand or your chin.

The Government

The Indian Union is a federation comprising 25 states (soon to be 28 with the new states of Uttarkhand, Chattisgarh and Jharkand) and six union territories. Each state, and some union territories, has its own legislative assembly and government, headed by a chief minister. The central (federal) government is headed by a prime minister and council of ministers (cabinet) responsible to the two houses of parliament: the Lok Sabha (Council of the People) and the Rajya Sabha (Council of State). The Lok Sabha is composed of 543 members directly elected by the people on the basis of adult franchise (530 seats for the states and 13 for the union territories), plus two nominated members.

The Rajya Sabha is an indirectly elected body of 232 members renewed every two years, which functions somewhat like the British House of Lords. The president is elected for a five-year term by an electoral college consisting of members of parliament and members of the state legislatures. Since 1997 the president has been Kocheril Raman Narayanan. Each state has its own legislature and is responsible for a number of administrative functions such as health, education, forests and surface transport (except railways).

Elections are normally held every five years but can, in certain situations, be called earlier. There are six national parties, 37 state parties and 301 registered parties. The recognised national parties are: Bharatiya Janata (BJP); The Communist Party of India (Marxist) (CPI[M]); The Communist Party of India (CPI); Indian National Congress; Janata Party (JP); and Janata Dal.

The Economy

With a well-developed, democratic political and administrative structure, a large, skilled labour force and an adequate communications system, the country has changed considerably since Independence. Neverthless, the national debt had reached US$70 billion by the 1990s and inflation 10 percent, partly due to the disastrous effects of the Gulf War, political instability and to the security problems facing the country.

Of the labour force, 70 percent is employed in agriculture, 13 percent in industry and 17 percent in services. The rural population represents about 75 percent of the total with 12 cities having more than one million people. Greater Mumbai is the largest with 15 million inhabitants.

Despite the agrarian bias of its economy, industry has grown enormously, placing India among the 15 top industrial nations of the world. Her relatively low level of exports is partly due to a large volume of domestic consumption. The per capita national income, although meagre in comparison with the rest of the world, is a considerable improvement over 1947. In the matter of production of foodgrains in particular – once a chronically deficit area – the advance has been spectacular, India now exports foodgrains. However, 37 percent of the population remains below the poverty line.

Sixty-four percent of villages now have electricity. The literacy rate from seven years and above is 52 percent, 64 percent for men and 39 percent for women – a large improvement from 18 percent just after Independence.

Greetings

The *namaste*, the greeting with folded hands, is the Indian form of salutation and its use will be appreciated, though men, especially in the cities, will not hesitate to shake hands with you if you are a man. A handshake would even be appreciated as a gesture of special friendliness.

Most Indian women would be taken aback at the informality of interaction between the sexes common in the West and physical contact between men and women is to be avoided. Men should not shake hands with a woman (unless she first offers to).

Planning the Trip

What to Bring

Clothing

Travel light; during summer it is best to wear cotton. During the winter, sweaters and jackets are required – it can get very chilly in Agra and Delhi. Cotton shirts, blouses and skirts are inexpensive and easily available. Remember to bring underwear (especially bras) and swimwear. Comfortable footwear, trainers for winter and sandals for summer, make walking on uneven surfaces easier.

For their own convenience, women should not wear sleeveless blouses, mini skirts and short, revealing dresses. Cover up – it's a good idea in the Indian sun anyway – locally available *shalwar kamiz*, a long tunic top worn over loose trousers, are ideal.

Film

Colour print film, developing and printing facilities are available in all big cities. Colour slide film can only be found in major cities and it may be safer to bring your own.

There are few places where prompt and reliable camera servicing can be done, so photographic equipment should be checked before the trip. Protect your camera and film from excessive exposure to heat, dust and humidity. Do not leave them in direct sun or in a locked car (which can get incredibly hot) as heat affects film.

Carry film by hand in a plastic bag which can be given to airport security officers for inspection rather than being put through X-ray machines. There are strict restrictions on photography of railways, military installations, bridges and dams, airports, border areas and Adivasi/restricted areas.

Other Essentials

If travelling away from the major cities or big hotels, take a sheet, sleeping bag, pillowcases, medical kit, padlock, sewing kit and ear-plugs among other items. Sun cream, sun and insect repellent are not readily available so they should be brought with you, along with cosmetics and tampons. A hat is a sensible item. A basin/bath plug is also useful in smaller hotels, which often do not have them.

Public Holidays

There are many festivals in India, but only a few of these are full public holidays:

- **26 January**: Republic Day.
- **15 August**: Independence Day.
- **2 October**: Mahatma Gandhi's Birthday.
- **25 December**: Christmas Day.

Entry Regulations

Tourist visas for all nationalities are issued either for one month from the date of entry, with that entry having to be within a month of issue (this visa is not available by post), or for six months from the date of issue (not entry). It is safer and preferable to take a multiple-entry visa, in order to have the option of visiting a neighbouring country.

The best place to obtain a visa is from the embassy or high commission in your country of residence, rather than risk the complications and delays involved in applying for one in neighbouring countries.

Tourist visas can no longer be extended, you must leave the country and re-enter on a new one. It may be difficult to apply for a new visa from neighbouring countries. Five-year visas are also issued to businesspeople and students. Check with the embassy for current details.

If you stay for more than 180 days, before leaving the country you must have a tax clearance certificate. These can be obtained from the foreigner's section of the income tax department in every city. Tax clearance certificates are free, but take bank receipts to demonstrate that you have changed money legally.

Customs

Customs procedures have recently been simplified. Visitors fill in declaration forms on the plane, and then proceed to the relevant red or green channels. Tourists seldom have any trouble. Occasionally, customs officials ask to see one suitcase at random and make a quick check.

Prohibited articles

These include certain drugs, live plants, gold and silver bullion, and coins not in current use. Firearms require possession licences (valid for six months) issued by Indian embassies or consulates abroad or, on arrival in India, by a district magistrate. For further details, check with the issuing authority.

All checked luggage arriving at Delhi airport is X-rayed before reaching the baggage collection area in the arrival hall.

Duty-free imports

These include 200 cigarettes (or 50 cigars), 0.95 litres (2 pints) of alcohol, a camera with five rolls of film and a reasonable amount of personal effects, including binoculars, laptop computer, sound recording equipment, etc.

Professional equipment and high-value articles must be declared or listed on arrival with a written undertaking to re-export them. Both the list and the articles must be produced on departure.

As this formality can be a lengthy process, allow extra time, both on arrival and at departure. For unaccompanied baggage or baggage misplaced by the airline, make sure you get a landing certificate from customs on arrival.

Exports

To avoid last-minute departure problems, remember that the export of antiques (over 100 years old), all animal products, and jewellery valued at over Rs2,000 (in the case of gold) and Rs10,000 (in the case of articles not made of gold) are banned. When in doubt about the age of semi-antiques, contact the office of the Archaeological Survey of India in Delhi or Mumbai.

Currency declaration

At present, forms for amounts of cash in excess of US$10,000 must be completed at customs on arrival.

Health

No inoculations are legally required to enter India, but it is strongly advised that you get inoculations against typhoid (Typhim Vi gives protection for 3 years), hepatitis A (Havrix gives immunity for 1 year, up to 10 years if a 6-month booster is given), polio (a booster is needed every 5 years) and tetanus (booster injection every 10 years). Other diseases against which vaccinations might be considered, particularly for longer trips, include meningitis, rabies and Japanese B encephalitis.

Malaria prophylaxis is essential. The usual anti-malarial protection consists of a combination of daily proguanil (Paludrine) and weekly chloroquine (Avoclar, Nivaquin). These are now bought across the counter in the UK, but consult your doctor for the correct dosages. An alternative drug is mefloquine (Larium), taken weekly. However, its strong side effects mean it is rarely prescribed and then only for short periods. The best, and only certain, protection against malaria is not to get bitten. Sleep under a mosquito net whenever possible, cover up in the evenings and use an effective insect repellent such as DEET (diethyltoluamide). Burning mosquito coils, easily obtainable in India, is a good idea.

Bring along a personal medical kit to take care of minor ailments. This should include anti-diarrhoea medication, a broad spectrum antibiotic, aspirin, clean needles and something for throat infections and allergies would be a good idea. Take your regular medications, tampons and panty-liners, contraceptives and condoms, as these may be difficult to find.

Also include plasters, antiseptic cream and water purification tablets. All cuts, however minor, should be cleaned and sterilised immediately to prevent infection. Locally available oral rehydration powders (such as Vijay Electrolyte) containing salts and dextrose are an ideal additive to water, especially when travelling in the summer months or when suffering from diarrhoea. If oral rehydration salts are not available then one teaspoon each of salt and sugar in 500 ml of water is a useful substitute.

Prickly heat is a common complaint caused by excessive perspiration. Try to keep the skin dry by using talcum powder and wearing loose-fitting cotton clothes. Fungal infections are also common and can be treated by exposure to the sun and/or by the application of Caneston cream.

- **Traveller's diarrhoea** is usually caused by low-level food poisoning and can be avoided with a little care. When you arrive, rest on your first day and only eat simple food; well-cooked vegetarian dishes, a South Indian *thali* and peeled fruits are perhaps best. An upset stomach is often caused by eating too many rich Indian meat dishes (often cooked with vast amounts of oil and spices) and failing to rest and let your body acclimatise.

Drink plenty of fluids but never drink unboiled or unfiltered water. When in doubt, stick to soda, mineral water, or aerated drinks of standard brands. Avoid ice as this is often made with unboiled water. All food should be cooked and eaten hot. Don't eat salads and always peel fruit.

With all cases of diarrhoea, including dysentery and giardia described below, it is not a good idea to use imobilising drugs such as loperamide (Imodium) and atropine (Lomotil) as they prevent the body ridding itself of infection. These should only be used if you have to travel. The most important thing to do in cases of diarrhoea and/or vomiting is to rehydrate, preferably using oral rehydration salts.

- **Dysentery and giardia** are more serious forms of stomach infection and should be suspected and treated if the diarrhoea lasts for more than 2 days.

Dysentery is characterised by diarrhoea accompanied by the presence of mucus and blood in faeces. Other symptoms include severe stomach cramps and vomiting. Bacillic dysentery comes on quickly and is usually accompanied by fever. It may clear up by itself but its usual treatment is with 500mg of ciprofloxacin or tetracycline twice daily for 5 days. Amoebic dysentery has a slower

Maps

Obtaining good maps of India can be difficult; the government forbids the sale of detailed maps in border areas, which includes the entire coastline, for security reasons, and those which can be bought may not be exported.

Some good maps to bring along are: Bartholomew's 1:4,000,000 map of South Asia; Lascelles map of the same scale and Nelles Verlag maps. Tourist offices can supply larger scale city maps. State and city maps are also published by the TT company, 328 G.S.T. Road, Chromepet, Chennai, Tamil Nadu 600 044, or the Survey of India, Janpath Barracks A, New Delhi 110 001.

Other highly recommended maps are the Eicher series of detailed city maps, along with their guidebook to Delhi, available from local bookstores.

onset and will not clear up on its own. If you suspect you have amoebic dysentery you should seek medical help as it can damage the gut. If this is not available then self-treat with 400mg of metronidazole (Flagyl) three times daily with food for 7 days. You must not drink alchohol when taking metronidazole.

Giardia is a similar infection caused by a parasite. Like amoebic dysentery it comes on slowly and its symptoms include very loose and foul-smelling diarrhoea, feeling bloated and nauseous, and stomach cramps. Giardia will not clear up on its own and will recur; its treatment is the same as for amoebic dysentery.

- **Heat exhaustion** is common, and indicated by shallow breathing, a rapid pulse, or pallor, and is often accompanied by leg cramps, headache or nausea.

The body temperature remains normal. Lying down in a cool place and sipping water mixed with rehydration salts or plain table salt will prevent loss of consciousness.

- **Heatstroke** is more serious, and more likely to occur when it is both hot and humid. Babies and elderly people are especially susceptible. The body temperature soars suddenly and the skin feels dry. The victim may feel confused, then pass out.

Take them quickly to a cool room, remove their clothes and cover them with a wet sheet or towels soaked in cold water. Call for medical help and fan them constantly until their body temperature drops to 38°C (100°F).

HOSPITALS

Agra

District, M.G. Road
Tel: 363 043
SN, Hospital Road
Tel: 361 314

Delhi

All India Institute of Medical Sciences, Ansari Nagar
Tel: 686 4851
Kripalani Hospital, Panchkuin Road
Tel: 336 3788
Safdarjang General Hospital, Sri Aurobindo Marg
Tel: 616 5060

Jaipur

Santokba Durlabhji, Bhawani Singh Road
Tel: 566 251
SMS, Sawai Ram Marg
Tel: 560 291

Getting There

By Air

The majority of visitors now arrive in India by air. Delhi is the obvious entry point for anyone planning a trip of the Delhi–Agra–Jaipur triangle. However, good flights are also available into Mumbai (Bombay), and rail and air links between there and Delhi are fast and frequent (less so between Mumbai, Agra and Jaipur).

Agra has an airport with limited international air access and customs and immigration facilities, but is not international airport in the real sense of the term. Agra also serves charter flights from the UK.

Discounts are often available during the off-peak season, so it is worth making enquiries. Many long-haul flights unfortunately arrive between midnight and 6am, apparently to suit the night landing regulations of European and Far Eastern cities but, in reality, often because of weight restrictions for a full plane taking off in the thin air of an Indian summer.

Once you have bought a ticket, check with the airline to confirm your booking then note down the ticket and flight numbers and computer reference code, and keep them separate from the ticket so, in case of loss or theft, you can obtain a replacement.

India's major airports are constantly improving and all have left-luggage facilities. Porters and licensed taxis are available. Delhi and Mumbai have duty-free shops in both the arrival and departure halls. Airport banks are open 24 hours for currency change.

Money Matters

All encashments of traveller's cheques and exchange of foreign currency used to have to be recorded on a currency declaration form, or receipts kept as proof of legal conversion. The laws have eased, but some businesses and hotels may still insist. Visitors staying more than 180 days will have to produce proof of encashment of traveller's cheques or exchange of currency for income tax exemption and show they have been self-supporting.

Indian currency is based on the decimal system, with 100 paise to the rupee. Coins are in denominations of 5, 10, 20, 25 and 50 paise. Also in use are 1, 2 and 5 rupee coins. Notes are in 1, 2, 5, 10, 20, 50, 100 and 500 rupee denominations. Indian rupees may not be brought in nor taken out of the country. Exchange rates fluctuate against other currencies.

Traveller's cheques should be well-known brands such as Thomas Cook, American Express and Visa. A slightly better exchange rate is offered by banks, but not all banks will accept traveller's cheques.

Credit cards are increasingly accepted by hotels, restaurants, large shops, tourist emporia and airlines. Again, it is preferable to have a well-known card such as American Express, Access/MasterCard or Visa. A number of banks will now issue rupees against a Visa card and Amex issues rupees or traveller's cheques to cardholders against a cheque at their offices. ATMs that will issue cash against a Visa card are now found in many cities.

Changing money on the black market is illegal and not worth the premium.

By Rail

There is a train from Lahore in Pakistan to Amritsar in India which crosses the Wagah-Attari border. It stops for a couple of hours for customs and immigration at the border.

By Road

The border crossing from Pakistan to India is from Wagah to Attari. You used to have to travel to Wagah by public transport, cross the border on foot and take another bus or taxi to the nearest town, but there is now a direct bus from Lahore to Delhi. However, if the political situation worsens the service may be shelved, so check before you travel. The border with Nepal is only open for non-Indian or Nepalese nationals at Birganj/Raxhal, Bairwa and Kakarbitta/Naxalbari.

The old overland route through Turkey, Iran, Afghanistan and Pakistan is little-used by tourists now, but when peace returns to this fascinating area, it might again become popular with the more adventurous traveller. Some companies in the UK and Germany, do still operate a few departures. In London, Trailfinders (42–48 Earls Court Road, London W8 6EJ, tel: 020 7937 5400) can advise.

Special Facilities

Travelling with Children

Indians love children and are very tolerant and indulgent with them. The problem is that children can be more easily affected by the heat, unsafe drinking water and unfamiliar food seasoned with chillies and spices. In case of diarrhoea, rehydration salts are vital.

Keep the child away from stray animals, especially dogs and monkeys. To avoid the risk of rabies, it may be safer to take an anti-rabies vaccine.

For infants, it is difficult to find nappies and places to change them. Consider bringing a supply of disposables, or changing to washables. A changing mat is essential, as is powdered milk of a brand that your child is familiar with. For touring, walking and hiking, a child-carrier backpack is worth the weight.

Disabled Travellers

Although disability is common in India, there are very few provisions for wheelchairs and special toilets. The roads are full of potholes and kerbs are often high and without ramps. If you have difficulty walking, it may be hard to negotiate street obstacles, beggars or steep staircases.

On the other hand, Indians will always be willing to help you in and out of buses or cars, or up stairs. Taxis and rickshaws are cheap and the driver, with a little *bakshish*, will probably help.

You could employ a guide who will be prepared to help with obstacles. Another option is to go with a paid companion.

In the UK, the **Holiday Care Service**, 2 Old Bank Chambers, Station Road, Horley, Surrey RH6 9HW (tel: 01293 774535), could put you in touch with someone.

Some package holiday operators cater for travellers with disabilities, but first ensure that your needs have been understood before making a booking. Contact an organisation for the disabled for further information.

Gay & Lesbian Travellers

Homosexuality is still a taboo subject for many Indians. Sexual relations between men are punishable with long prison sentences and cruising in public could come under public disorder laws. There is no similar law against lesbians.

While general attitudes are discriminatory, things are changing slowly, and at least the issue of gay and lesbian rights is starting to be discussed, due in no small part to Deepa Mehta's 1998 film *Fire*, which depicted an affair between two married women. Attacks on cinemas by the religious right brought counter demonstations onto the streets of major cities.

However, gay and lesbian travellers should be discreet and avoid any public displays of affection (as should heterosexual couples). On the plus side, hotels will think nothing of two men or women sharing a room.

Embassies & Consulates

Delhi

Australian High Commission
Australian Compound, 1-50G Shantipath, Chanakyapuri, New Delhi 110 021 (PO Box 5210)
Tel: 688 8223/687 2035/688 5637

British High Commission
Shantipath, Chanakyapuri, New Delhi 110 021
Tel: 687 2161 (24 hrs)
Fax: 687 0065

Canadian High Commission
7–8 Shantipath, Chanakyapuri, New Delhi 110 021 (PO Box 5207, Chanakyapuri, New Delhi 110 021)
Tel: 687 6500
E-mail: delhi@delhi01.x400.gc.ca

Irish Embassy
13 Jor Bagh, New Delhi
Tel: 462 6714

New Zealand High Commission
50N Nyaya Marg, Chanyakapuri, New Delhi
Tel: 688 3170

US Embassy
Shantipath, Chanakyapuri, New Delhi
Tel: 419 8000
Fax: 419 0017

Indian Embassies

Australia
High Commission of India, 3–5 Moonah Place, Yarralumla, Canberra ACT-2600
Tel: (06) 273 3774/273 3999
Fax: (06) 273 3328/273 1308

Canada
High Commission of India, 10 Springfield Road, Ottawa, Ontario KLM 1C9
Tel: (613) 744 3751–3
Fax: (613) 744 0913

UK
High Commission of India, India House, Aldwych, London WC2B 4NA
Tel: (0891) 880 800 (24-hours recorded visa information);

Insurance

It is always advisable to obtain good travel insurance to cover the worst possible scenario. Take a copy of your policy and keep it separately as a safeguard.

(020) 7836 0990 (specific visa enquiries); (020) 7836-8484 (general)
US
Embassy of India, 2107 Massachusetts Avenue NW, Washington DC 20008
Tel: (202) 939 7000
Fax: (202) 939 7027

Tourist Offices

Agra

Government of India Tourist Office
191 The Mall
Tel: 363 959/363 377
Uttar Pradesh Tourist Office
64 Taj Road
Tel: 360 517
Railway Station
Tel: 368 598

Delhi

Government of India Tourist Office
88 Janpath
Tel: 332 0008
Fax: 332 0342
Domestic airport information counter
Tel: 329 5296
International airport information counter
Tel: 329 1171

Indian Tourist Offices Abroad

Australia
Level 2 Piccadilly, 210 Pitt Street, Sydney, New South Wales 2000
Tel: (02) 9264 4855
Fax: (02) 9264 4860
Canada
60 Bloor Street West, Suite 1003, Toronto, Ontario M4N 3N6
Tel: (416) 962 3787–8
Fax: (416) 962 6279
France
13 Boulevard Haussmann, F-75009 Paris
Tel: (01) 45 23 30 45
Fax: (01) 45 23 33 45
Germany
Baseler Street, 48, D-60329, Frankfurt Am-Main 1
Tel: (069) 242 9490
Fax: (069) 242 9497
Great Britain
7 Cork Street, London W1X 2AB
Tel: (020) 8812 0929 (24-hour tourist information); (020) 7437 3677 (general)
Fax: (020) 7494 1048
Italy
Via Albricci 9, 21022 Milano
Tel: (02) 804 952/805 3506
Spain
Avenida Pio XII 30, 28016 Madrid
Tel: (91) 345 7339
US
1270 Avenue of America, Suite 1808, New York 10020
Tel: (212) 586 4901–3
Fax: (212) 582 3274

Jaipur

Government of India Tourist Office
State Hotel Khasa Kothi
Tel/fax: 372 200
Rajasthan Tourist Office
Paryatan Bhavan, M.I. Road
Tel: 365 526
Fax: 376 362
Railway Station
Tel: 315 714

Airline Offices

Agra

Indian Airlines
Tel: 360 948
Fax: 263 116
Flight info: 301 180

Delhi

Aeroflot
1 B.M.C. House, Connaught Place
Tel: 331 0411
Air India
Jeevan Bharti, 124 Janpath
Tel: 373 6446
Fax: 373 9796
E-mail: ddr@del2.vsnl.net.in
British Airways
DLF Plaza Tower, DLF Qutb Enclave, Phase 1, Gurgaon 122002, Haryana
Tel: 359 911
Fax: 359 926
Airport:
Tel: 565 2078
Gulf Air
G12 Connaught Place
Tel: 332 4293
Fax: 372 1756
Indian Airlines
Malhotra Building, F Block, Connaught Place (open 10am–5pm)
Tel: 371 9168/331 0517
Main Booking Office, Safdarjang Airport (open 24 hours)
Tel: 462 4332
Reservations tel: 462 0566/463 1337
Flight arr/dep tel: 301 4433
Jet Airways
Jetair House, 13 Community Centre, Yusuf Sarani
Tel: 652 3345/685 3700
Fax: 651 4996
Airport
Tel: 566 3404
Lufthansa
56, Janpath
Tel: 332 3310
Fax: 332 4524
Pakistan International Airlines
102 Kailash Building, 26 Kasturba Gandhi Marg
Tel: 373 7791
Fax: 373 7796
Sahara India Airlines
7th Floor, Ambadeep Building, 14 Kasturba Gandhi Marg
Tel: 332 6851
Fax: 566 5362/566 2312
Sri Lankan Airlines
1, Hotel Janpath, Janpath
Tel: 336 8843
Fax: 336 8274
Swiss Air
DLF Centre, 1st Floor, Parliament Street
Tel: 332 5511
Fax: 332 6999

Jaipur

Air India
M.I. Road
Tel: 368 569
British Airways
Nijhawan Travel Service Pvt. Ltd., G2 Usha Plaza, M.I. Road
Tel: 370 374/361 065
Indian Airlines
Tel: 743 324
Fax: 743 407
Flight info: 743 500
Jet Airways
Tel: 360 763/370 594

Airport
Tel: 551 733
Sahara Indian Airlines
203 Shalimar Complex, M.I. Road
Tel: 377 637/365 741/373 748
Fax: 367 808
Airport
Tel: 553 525

Cyber Cafés

Agra

Internet Café
Basement, Neelam Nursing Home, Balu Ganj
Open 11am–9pm, Rs100 per hour

Delhi

CyberHut
H35-3 Connaught Place
Open 9am–11pm, Rs100 per hour
DishnetDSL
1st Floor, B45 Inner Circle, Above Volga Restaurant, Connaught Place
Open 9am–11pm, Rs60 per hour
Steven's Cafe
1587 Main Bazaar, Paharganj
Open 10am–8pm, Rs180 per hour
X29
Hauz Khas
Open 10am–9pm, Rs60 per hour

Jaipur

Jaipur Communicator
G4–5, Jaipur Towers, M.I. Road
Open 8am–11pm, Rs60 per hour
Mewar Internet Café
Hotel Mewar, Sindhi Camp, Station Road
Open 6am–11.30pm, Rs150 per hour
Royal's Business Centre
Opposite AIR, M.I. Road
Open 8.30am–9.30pm, Rs60 per hour
Tirupathi Communications
Sansar Chandra Road
Rs70 per hour

Practical Tips

Emergencies

Generally speaking, India is a safe place to travel, but a tourist is a natural target for thieves and pick-pockets, so take the usual precautions and keep money, credit cards, valuables and passport in a money belt or pouch well secured with a cord around your neck. A protective hand over this in a crowded place could save you a lot of heartache and hassle.

Do not leave belongings unattended. Invest in good strong locks for all stages of travel. Chaining luggage to the berth on a train, or to your seat on a bus, is another precaution that travelling Indians often take. Watch your luggage carefully, especially during loading and unloading.

Credit card frauds do exist so make sure that shops and restaurants process your card in front of you.

Another sensible precaution is to keep a photocopy of your passport and visa, traveller's cheque numbers and receipts, ticket details, insurance policy number and telephone claims number, and some emergency money in a bag or case separate from your other cash and documents. If you are robbed, report the incident immediately to a police station (be patient, this can take hours).

Business Hours

Government offices

Officially 9.30am–6pm Monday to Friday, but most business is done between 10am and 5pm with a long lunch break.

Post Offices

Open from 10am–4.30pm Monday to Friday, and until 12 noon on Saturday. However, in most of the larger cities, the Central Post Office is open until 6.30pm on weekdays, 4.30pm on Saturday. On Sunday some open until noon. Major telegraph offices are open 24 hours.

Shops

Open from 10am–7pm. Some shops close for lunch. Although Sunday is an official holiday, different localities in major cities have staggered days off so that there are always some shopping areas open.

Restaurants

Usually open until 11pm. Some nightclubs and discoteques close very much later. Hotel coffee shops are often open around the clock.

Banks

Open from 10am–2pm weekdays, 10am–noon Saturday for most foreign banks and nationalised Indian banks (of which the State Bank is the largest). Some banks

Tipping

There is no harm expressing your appreciation with a small tip. Depending on services rendered and the type of establishment, this could range from Rs2–Rs10.

In restaurants, the tip is customarily 10–15 percent of the bill. Leading hotels add a 10 percent service surcharge and tipping in such places is optional.

Although tipping taxis and three-wheelers is not essential, it is appreciated. Again, 10 percent of the fare or leaving the change, if substantial, would be adequate. Porters at railway stations would expect around Rs2 a bag. At airports, one rupee per bag in addition to the fee charged by the airport authority would be welcome.

Women Travelling Alone

Take the normal precautions such as avoiding local public transport, which can become crowded very quickly (crowds are a haven for gropers). "Eve-teasing" is the Indian euphemism for sexual harassment. Do not wear clothes that expose legs, arms and cleavage – *shalwar kamiz* are ideal, and a shawl is handy to use as a cover-all when required.

More serious sexual assaults on tourists are rare but do tend to occur in popular tourist areas such as Delhi, Agra and Jaipur. In case something should happen, call for help from passers-by.

On the up-side, there are "ladies-only" queues at train and bus stations, and "ladies-only" waiting rooms at stations and compartments on trains.

operate evening branches, while others remain open on Sunday and close on another day of the week, and some open 9am–1pm. ANZ Grindlays has two branches open 24 hours; one in Connaught Place, New Delhi, the other at Breach Candy, Mumbai. All banks are closed on national holidays, on 30 June and 31 December. Most businesses close on public holidays.

Postal Services

The internal mail service is efficient in most areas. It is advisable to personally affix stamps to letters or postcards and hand them over to the post office counter for immediate franking rather than to post them in a letterbox.

Sending a registered parcel overseas is a complicated and time-consuming process. Most parcels should be stitched into cheap cotton cloth and then sealed (there are people outside major post offices offering this service). Two customs forms need to be completed. Once the parcel has been weighed and stamps affixed, make sure it is franked and a receipt of registration is issued. Important or valuable material should be registered.

Many shops offer to dispatch goods, but not all of them are reliable. It is usually only safe when handled by a government-run emporium.

Airfreighting purchases is possible but can be equally time-consuming. You will need to produce the bill and receipt, encashment certificate, your passport and onward airline ticket. There are many airfreight agents throughout India and most travel agents can provide assistance.

Telecommunications

India's telephone system is steadily improving and international calls can now be dialled direct to most parts of the world or booked through the operator. Calling from hotels can be extremely expensive, with surcharges of up to 300 percent, so check rates first. Mobile telephones have also made an appearance in India and may be rented for the duration of your stay.

Privately run telephone services with international direct-dialling facilities are very widespread. Advertising themselves with the acronyms STD/ISD (standard trunk dialling/international subscriber dialling), they are quick and easy to use. Some stay open 24 hours a day. Both national and international calls are dialled direct. To call abroad, dial the international access code (00), the code for the country you want (44 for the UK, 1 for the US or Canada), the appropriate area code (without any initial zeros), and the number you want. Some booths have an electronic screen that keeps time and calculates cost during the call. Prices are similar to those at official telecommunications centres.

Home country direct services are now available from any telephone to the UK, US, Canada, Australia, New Zealand and a number of other countries. These allow you to make a reverse-charges or telephone credit card call to that country via the operator there. If you cannot find a telephone with home country direct buttons, you can use any phone toll-free by dialling 000, your country code and 17 (except Canada, which is 000-167).

Many privately run telephone services have fax machines and most large hotels have a fax.

E-mail and the internet are now very popular and widely available. All large cities, and many smaller places, have internet cafés or similar places where you can surf the net or send e-mails. Charges are usually by the minute or hour, and are usually around Rs60 per hour.

Media

Newspapers & Magazines

With a large number of English-language dailies and hundreds of newspapers in Indian languages, the press in India provides a wide and critical coverage of national and international events.

Among the better-known national English language dailies are the *Times of India*, *The Indian Express*, *The Hindu* and *The Hindustan Times* (all available on-line). There are also two Sunday papers, *The Sunday Observer* and *The Sunday Mail*. The main newspapers in Delhi are the *Asian Age* and *Pioneer*.

The top news magazines include *India Today*, *Outlook* and *Frontline* (also on-line). There are also excellent general-interest magazines such as *Sanctuary* (specialising in South Asian natural

Poste Restante

Generally this works well, but make sure your name is clearly written. Most towns have only one main post office but there is often confusion between Delhi and New Delhi. New Delhi's main post office is near Connaught Circus while Delhi's main post office is between the Red Fort and Kashmir Gate in Old Delhi.

history) and *The India Magazine*. Travel magazines like *Travel Links* and city magazines such as *Delhi Diary* and *The Delhi City* give current information on internal travel and local cultural events.

International newspapers are available in Mumbai and Delhi within 24 hours and some international magazines are also available.

There are several glossy magazines in English, including *Society*, *Bombay* and *First City*, and women's magazines such as *Femina*. Indian editions of *Cosmopolitan* and *Elle* magazines are for sale.

Television & Radio Stations

Doordarshan is the government television company and broadcasts programmes in English, Hindi and regional languages. Local timings vary, but generally the news in English can be heard daily at 7.50am and 9.30pm.

Satellite television is available almost everywhere, including Star TV's five-channel network incorporating the BBC World Service and MTV. Other stations include VTV (local youth-orientated music channel) and Zee TV (Hindi). There are channels showing sport, American soaps and sitcoms and English-language movies. Up to 30 channels can be picked up, given the right equipment.

All India Radio (AIR) broadcasts on the short-wave, medium-wave and in Delhi and Mumbai on FM (VHF). The frequencies vary, so check with your hotel.

Courier Services

Most of the major international courier networks have agency agreements with Indian companies. DHL, Skypak and IML all work under their own brand names while Federal Express operates as Blue Dart. These companies have offices in the major towns and operate both international and extensive domestic networks.

Note: The government's Speedpost service delivers quickly at a similar price.

On Arrival

Once through customs the visitor is often besieged by porters, taxi drivers and others. Choose one porter and stick to him. There is a system of paying porters a fixed amount per piece of baggage before leaving the terminal: a tip of Rs5, once the bags are aboard the taxi or bus, is sufficient. If a travel agent or a friend is meeting you, he or she may be waiting outside the building.

Some major hotels operate courtesy buses, and a public service known as EATS (Ex-Serviceman's Transport Service) operates an airport bus service in Delhi and Mumbai with stops at hotels and major points en route to the city centre.

On Departure

It is essential to reconfirm your reservations for all outward-bound flights 72 hours before departure, especially in the peak season, when most of the flights are overbooked.

Security procedures can be intensive and time-consuming, so allow at least two hours for check-in.

An airport tax is charged on departure and must be paid prior to check-in (check the cost with your airline at the time of booking). Do ensure that the name of your outward-bound carrier is endorsed on the tax receipt.

For visitors with entry permits, exit endorsements are necessary from the office where they were registered.

Should a stay exceed 180 days, an income tax exemption certificate must be obtained from the Foreign Section of the Income Tax Department in Delhi or Mumbai.

Repairs and Tailors

Traditionally, India's use of resources is very efficient, reflected in the way almost everything can be recycled and/or repaired. Since travelling around India can be hard on your shoes, baggage and clothes, this is very useful.

Chappal-wallahs, shoe repairers, can be found everywhere, usually sitting by the side of the road with their tools in a wooden box. For an embarassingly small charge, they will be able to glue, nail or stitch almost any pair of shoes or sandals back into shape. (A somewhat more inconvenient service is offered by the shoeshine boys around Connaught Place in New Delhi. They can throw a dollop of shit onto your shoe without you noticing, and will then offer to clean it off for an exorbitant fee.)

Indian tailors are very skillful and can run up a set of clothes quickly. Although they can do fair copies of Western fashions, they are, obviously, much better at stitching *sari* blouses or *shalwar kamiz*. The process of buying fabric is one of the great pleasures of visiting India, and if you want it made up, most shops will be able to recommend a good tailor.

Tailors will also be able to repair your existing clothes, even badly torn ones, and – just as useful – can stitch up rucksacks which are on the point of collapse.

Departure Tax

Remember before you leave that there is a departure tax of Rs600 (Rs150 for neighbouring SAARC countries) for all international departures. This should be included in your ticket, but do check with your airline or ticket agent.

Entrance Fees

The Archaeological Survey of India has recently announced its intention of raising the entrance fee for foreign tourists to its sites. The proposals are to raise the usual fee of around Rs10 (this varies from place to place) to the fee currently charged for the Taj, Rs500/$US10 (rumoured to be rising further to Rs2,385/$US53), with further charges for photography and video cameras. The fee for Indian nationals is to go up from Rs5 to Rs10.

Getting Around

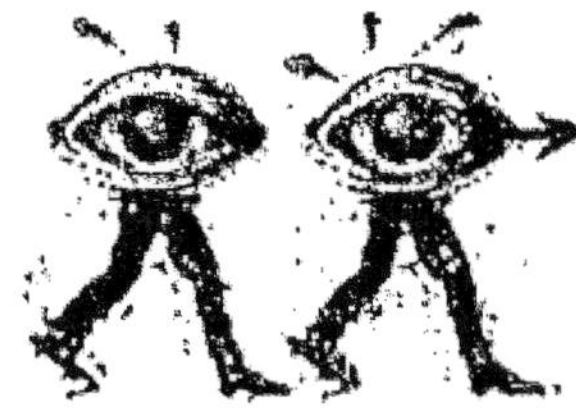

Travel by Air

Indian Airlines (not to be confused with the international carrier, Air India), has one of the world's largest domestic networks. The reservations system has been improved by the introduction of computers. For travel during the peak season (September–March), try and make reservations in advance as flights are usually heavily booked.

With time-consuming check-in and security procedures, you must be at the airport an hour before departure time. Coach services from some city terminals are available. In-flight service is adequate. Alcohol is only available on international flights.

Indian Airlines has a good safety record. Its fares are often lower than those charged for comparable distances elsewhere. The baggage allowance per adult is 20kg in economy and 30kg in business class.

Cancellation charges on tickets purchased locally are extremely high, but none are applicable for domestic sectors issued on international tickets.

The Discover India fare valid for 21 days of travel all over the country and the Tour India Scheme valid for 14 days and limited to six flight coupons are both particulary attractive. These tickets must be purchased abroad, or paid for in India using foreign currency. For details, contact your travel agent or an Air India office abroad, or write to: Traffic Manager, Indian Airlines House, Parliament Street, New Delhi.

Air India carries domestic passengers on its linking flights between Mumbai and Delhi. These flights leave from the international terminal.

The privately operated airlines Jet Airways and Sahara Indian Airlines fly certain domestic routes.

Timetables

Airline timetables are published in *Divan* and *Excel* magazines and are shown on teletext. They are also available at travel agents and information counters at all major airports. A local travel magazine, *Travel Links*, also publishes air and rail timetables.

Travel by Bus

Almost every part of the country is connected by an extensive and well-developed bus system with the railway stations being the natural hubs for both local and regional services. Some of the more rural routes are serviced by noisy dilapidated vehicles, but an increasing number of deluxe and air-conditioned expresses ply the trunk routes.

Many of the trunk routes are now operated by video coaches – if you have never been to an Indian cinema, a night bus journey is an introduction to the popular variety of Hindi or regional film.

There are many parts of the country where the bus service is the only means of public transport, and at times may be more convenient than the train – particularly between Agra and Jaipur.

On many routes, even local ones, reservations can be made. Most baggage is carried on the bus roof, so all bags should be locked, and checked at intermediate stops. Most cities have a bus service; Mumbai's bus service is excellent whereas Delhi's is inadequate and crowded.

In cities it is preferable to use taxis or the three-wheeled "auto-rickshaws".

Rickshaws

The most convenient way of getting around town is by rickshaw. These come in two types, a cycle rickshaw (a tricycle with a seat for two people on the back), and an "auto" (a motorised three-wheeler).

Autos are, like taxis, supposed to use a meter. You should insist on this and get out if they refuse. Meter rates are subject to periodic changes, and extras for late-night journeys etc., which the driver should show you on a card. In popular tourist spots, during rush hour and bad weather, you may find it impossible to persuade the drivers to use the meter. A tactic that might work is to offer "meter plus five" (the cost plus Rs5). If not, you'll have to negotiate the fare. After a short while in the country you will get a feel for what is acceptable, given that as a relatively well-off foreign tourist you are expected, quite reasonably, to pay a little more.

Cycle rickshaws are more convenient in some places, like the very congested streets of Old Delhi. With these you should negotiate the fare before you set off.

Driving in India

The best advice to anyone who is thinking about driving in India is don't. Roads can be very congested and dangerous and there are many unwritten rules followed by other drivers. It is far better, and cheaper, to hire a car and driver.

However, if you do have to drive you will need your domestic licence, liability insurance, an international driver's permit and your vehicle's registration papers. Information regarding road conditions can be obtained from national and state automobile associations which periodically issue regional motoring maps, general information regarding roads and detailed route charts.

Contact: the **Automobile Association of Upper India** Lilaram Building, 14-F Connaught Circus, New Delhi 110001, tel: 331 4071,

Taxis

When taking a taxi or bus into town from the airport, it is advisable to change money in the arrival hall. In Delhi and Mumbai, a system of prepayment for taxis into the city is operated by the traffic police. This saves considerable anguish when the occasional unscrupulous driver takes a long route or tries to overcharge. Elsewhere, enquire at the information desk for the going rate for a journey to your destination before getting into the taxi; and make sure the meter is "down" before you embark. It is alright to share a taxi even if the destination may not be the same (although in the same area). In some cities, taxis have fare charts which, when applied to the amount on the meter, give the correct fare. There is often a night surcharge of 10 percent between 11pm and 6am and a rate of Rs1 to Rs2 per piece of baggage.

331 2323–5; **Western India Automobile Association** Lalji Narainji Memorial Building, 76 Veer Nariman Road, Mumbai 400 020, tel: 291 085/291 192; and the **UP Automobile Association** 32-A Mahatma Gandhi Marg, Allahabad, tel: 2445.

Car & Taxi Rental

Chauffeur-driven cars, costing about US$20 a day, can be arranged through tourist offices, hotels, local car rental firms, or branches of Hertz, Budget or Europcar.

The big international chains are best for self-drive car rental. They charge 30 percent less than for chauffeur-driven cars with about a Rs1,000 deposit against damage if paid in India, more if paid in country of residence. In some places motorbikes or mopeds are available for hire.

Taxis are both air-conditioned and non-air-conditioned. Charges vary, ranging from Rs325 for eight hours and 80 km (50 miles) to Rs450 for an air-conditioned car. For out-of-town travel, there is a per km charge, usually between Rs2.30–Rs3 per km, with an overnight charge of Rs100. Package tours, sold by travel agencies and hotels, include assistance, guides and hotel accommodation, in addition to taxi charges.

The local yellow-top black taxis are metered, but with constant hikes in fuel prices, charges may often be higher than indicated on the meter. If so, this will be prominently stated in the taxi and the driver will have a card showing the excess over the meter reading that can be legitimately charged.

The fare for three-wheelers is about half that of taxis. Do not forget to ensure that the meter in the three-wheeler is flagged down to the minimum fare.

Travel by Rail

Rail travel is safe, comfortable and by far the best way to get around the country.

Indian Railways has a number of different classes, of varying degrees of comfort. In descending order of price, they are:

- First class AC, very comfortable with lockable cabins of four berths each.
- AC II tier, partitions arranged in groups of 6 berths with curtains that pull across to provide privacy.
- AC III tier, partitions with groups of 9 berths, the middle berths fold down for sleeping.
- AC chair car.
- First class, non-AC but with ceiling fans. Has lockable cabins of four berths each. There is one cabin of two berths halfway down each carriage.
- Sleeper class, partitions of 9 berths with ceiling fans.
- Second class, unreserved with no berths and hard seats.

Reservations are required for all classes other than second class. In the summer months it is best to go AC. When the weather is cooler then first class can be an excellent option as it is possible to see the passing countryside without staring through the darkened windows of AC.

All carriages have both Western and Indian-style toilets. If you are up to squatting on a moving train, always use the Indian toilet as they are invariably cleaner and better maintained.

Advance reservation is strongly recommended. Over 400 stations now have very efficient computerised booking counters from where you can book any ticket for any route. Reservations may be made up to 60 days in advance and cancellations (for which you will need to fill in the same form as for a reservation) can be made with varying degrees of penalty depending on the class and how close the cancellation is made to the time of departure. In the larger cities, the major stations have tourist sections with English-speaking staff to reduce the queues for foreigners and non-resident Indians buying tickets; payment is in pounds sterling or US dollars (traveller's cheques or cash). If reservations are not available then certain trains have a tourist quota that may be available. Other options are to take a waitlisted ticket or the more assured reservation against cancellation (RAC); the booking clerk should be able to advise you on how likely you are to get a reservation. It is also possible to make bookings from abroad through Indian Railways representatives. They will accept bookings up to six months ahead, with a minimum of one month for first class, three months for second.

Trains are slow compared to those in the West, so if you are in a hurry, stick to the expresses. Fares are generally low. The Indrail Pass, available to foreign nationals and Indians resident abroad and paid for in foreign currency, can cut down on time getting reservations and be good value if you plan on travelling

Reservation Forms

To buy your ticket you must first fill out a Reservation Requisition Form, which will be available from one of the windows in the booking office. The form is in the local language on one side and English on the reverse. In addition to the obvious information such as where you wish to leave from and go to and when, to fill in the form you also need to know:

- The train number and name. You can get this from a timetable, or, if the train departs from the station you are booking from, it is usually displayed on a board in the booking office.
- The class you wish to travel and whether you require a berth (for overnight journeys, or any journey between 9pm and 6am), or only a seat.
- Whether you require a lower, middle or upper berth. An upper berth is a good idea as it can be used throughout the day, whereas the other two may only be used for sleeping 9pm–6am.

Foreign travellers should also fill in their passport numbers in the column that asks for your Concession Travel Authority Number, which is needed if the ticket is issued under the foreign tourist quota.

nearly every day (it is not valid for the Palace on Wheels, Royal Orient and Fairy Queen). In the UK the pass can be obtained through S.D. Enterprises, 103 Wembley Park Drive, Wembley, Middlesex HA9 8HG, tel: (020) 8903 3411; fax: (020) 8903 0392. They can also book single-journey tickets in advance for you. The Indrail pass can be bought in India at Railway Central Reservations Offices in Mumbai Central (tel: 292 122/222126/292 042/291 952); Mumbai CST (tel: 415 0079); and New Delhi (tel: 344 877/345 080/345 181).

Tourist Guide Offices at railway reservation centres are helpful in planning itineraries and obtaining reservations. Tourist Guides are available at New Delhi, tel: 352 164, and Mumbai, Churchgate, tel: 298 016 4577. Railway timetables available at Indian Tourist Offices abroad also contain much useful information.

Each regional railway prints its full timetable in Hindi, English and the regional language. There is also the monthly *Indian Bradshaw*, which lists all services across the country, or the concise but comprehensive *Trains At A Glance*, probably the most useful timetable for foreign tourists. These publications should be available from railway stations but they are updated and reprinted regularly so are periodically unavailable.

Remember to check which station your train departs from and do allow at least an hour to find your seat/berth. Lists of passengers with the compartment and seat/berth numbers allotted to them are displayed on platforms and on each carriage an hour before departure. The station superintendent and the conductor attached to the train are usually available for assistance.

Food can usually be ordered through the coach attendant and, on Shatabdi and Rajdhani trains, the fare covers food, drinks and snacks as well. Bedding consisting of two sheets, a pillow and a blanket is provided in first class AC, AC II tier and III tier, and is also available from the attendant for Rs20 in first class. In theory, if they want bedding, first class passengers should contact the Station Manager before travelling, but extra bedding is often available. If travelling sleeper class then it is a good idea to take a sheet sleeping bag (any Indian tailor will run one up for you).

Retiring rooms (for short-term occupation only) are available at over 1,100 stations on a first-come first-served basis, but these are usually full. All first class waiting rooms have couches for passengers using their own bedding. At New Delhi, a Rail Yatri Niwas has been built for transit passengers. Rooms can be booked in advance.

Cloakrooms are available at most stations where travellers can leave their luggage, but bags must be locked, and don't lose the reclaim ticket. Check opening times of the cloakroom for collection.

Pre-paid taxi and/or auto-rickshaw services are available at some stations, including Agra Cantt.

Useful Trains

The selective list below gives each train's starting and destination stations, the train's number and name, arrival and departure times, and the days it leaves on.

From Agra

Agra Cantt.–Alwar–Jaipur: 4853/4863 Marudhar Express, dept. 07.15, arr. Alwar 11.15, Jaipur 14.05, Mon, Wed and Sat/Tue, Thur, Fri and Sun

Agra Cantt.–New Delhi: 2001 Shatabdi, dept. 20.18, arr. 22.40, Daily

Agra Cantt.–Nizamuddin: 2179 Taj Express, dept. 18.35, arr. 21.45, Daily

Agra Cantt.–Nizamuddin: 4003 Intercity Express, dept. 06.00, arr. 09.23, Daily

From Delhi

Delhi–Alwar–Jaipur: 2916 Ashram Express, dept. 15.05, arr. Alwar 17.55, Jaipur 20.35, Daily

Delhi–Alwar–Jaipur: 2461 Mandore Express, dept. 21.00, arr. Alwar 23.52, Jaipur 22.35, Daily

Delhi–Alwar–Jaipur: 4859 Delhi Jodhpur Express, dept. 16.55, arr. Alwar 19.50, Jaipur 22.35, Daily

New Delhi–Agra Cantt.: 2002 Shatabdi, dept. 06.00, arr. Agra Cantt. 07.55, Daily

New Delhi–Jaipur: 2015 Shatabdi, dept. 06.15, arr. 10.30, Mon–Sat

New Delhi–Jaipur: 2958 Swarnajayanti Rajdhani, dept. 14.40, arr. 19.35, Tue, Thur, Sat

Nizamuddin–Agra Cantt.: 2180 Taj Express, dept. 07.15, arr. 09.47, Daily

Nizamuddin–Agra Cantt.: 4004 Intercity Express, dept. 19.35, arr. 23.05, Daily

From Jaipur

Jaipur–Alwar–Agra Cantt.: 4854/4864 Marudhar Express, dept. 15.20, arr. Alwar 17.55, Agra Cantt. 21.55, Mon, Thur and Sat/Tue, Wed, Fri and Sun
Jaipur–Alwar–Delhi: 4860 Jodhpur Delhi Express, dept. 06.00, arr. Alwar 08.30, Delhi 11.25, Daily
Jaipur–Delhi: 2414 Express, dept. 16.30, arr. 21.50, Daily
Jaipur–New Delhi: 2016 Shatabdi, dept. 17.55, arr. 22.15, Mon–Sat

Railway Tours

Indian Railways run three "Royal Trains", using luxury carriages with on-board catering. Book well in advance for these popular tours.

The Royal Orient Using the famous picturesque carriages of the Palace on Wheels, this is a luxury, refurbished, air-conditioned, metre-gauge train. Accommodation is mainly in coupés, with each carriage having a mini-bar, kitchenette and Western toilets. It departs from Delhi Cantonment Station on Wednesdays at 2.30pm and travels through Chittaurgarh, Udaipur, Junagarh, Veraval, Sasan Gir, Delwada, Palitana, Sarkhej, Ahmedabad and Jaipur over the next six days, arriving back in Delhi at 6am the following Wednesday. The train runs between September and April; a two-berth cabin costs from $150 to $200 per day. Bookings can be made through travel agents abroad. In India contact:

Tourism Corporation of Gujarat Limited
Nigam Bhavan, Sector 16, Gandhinagar, 382 016
Tel: (02712) 22645/22528
Fax: (02712) 22029
12-4 First Floor, East Patel Nagar, New Delhi 110 008
Tel: 572 0379

The Palace on Wheels Many of the tracks in Rajasthan have now been converted to broad gauge and the original Royal Train, the Palace on Wheels, now has new rolling stock. The 14 carriages leave Delhi every Wednesday between September and April, and stop at Jaipur, Bharatpur, Chittaurgarh, Udaipur, Sawai Modhopur, Jaisalmer, Jodhpur and Agra, returning to Delhi on the 8th day. A double cabin costs between $295 and $350. Contact a travel agent abroad. In India contact:

Senior Manager, Palace on Wheels, Rajasthan Tourist Reception Centre, Bikaner House, Pandara Road, New Delhi 110 011
Tel: 381 884
Fax: 382 823
Rajasthan Tourism Development Corporation, Hotel Swagatam Campus, Jaipur 302 006
E-mail: jaipur@palaceonwheels.net

The Fairy Queen Named after the engine which pulls the train (the oldest working broad-gauge steam engine in the world), this tour leaves one Saturday every month between November and February. It runs to Alwar, from where passengers are taken to the tiger reserve at Sariska. The next day they return to Alwar to see the fort and museum and return to Delhi in the evening. The cost is $235 per person. Contact travel agents for booking details.

Where to Stay

Agra (0562)

££££££

Hotel Clarks Shiraz
54 Taj Road, Cantonment, Agra 282 001
Tel: 361 421–7
Fax: 361 428
E-mail: clarkraz@nde.vsnl.net.in
Comfortable hotel on a large estate with facilities for croquet, tennis and swimming. Good shops, restaurants (especially the rooftop one), bar, travel services and banks.

Taj View Hotel
Fatehbad Road, Agra 282 001
Tel: 331 841–59
Fax: 331 860/332 705
E-mail: tjagra@nde.vsnl.net.in
Rooms with a view, twin pools and exquisite shops within a functional exterior. All five-star amenities.

The Trident Agra
Tajnagri Scheme, Fatehbad Road, Agra 282 001
Tel: 331 818
Fax: 331 827
E-mail: ttag@tridentag.com
New, modern, luxury hotel with very comfortable rooms. Good pool and restaurant.

Welcomgroup Mughal Sheraton
Fatehbad Road, Agra 282 001
Tel: 331 701–28
Fax: 331 730/330 701

Hotel Price Categories

The rates below are for a double room (AC where available) in high season, including taxes.

£££££	Rs4,000 and above
££££	Rs2,000–4,000
£££	Rs1,000–2,000
££	Rs400–1,000
£	Up to Rs400

E-mail: gm.mughal@welcomemail.wiprobt.ems.vsnl.net.in
Luxury hotel, built and furnished in Moghul style with good, but expensive, restaurants. Gardens, bar and pool. Some rooms have a view of the Taj Mahal.

££££

ITDC Hotel Agra Ashok
6B The Mall, Agra 282 001
Tel: 361 223–32
Fax: 361 620
A good-value government hotel, 3 km (2 miles) from the Taj Mahal. Spacious rooms, restaurants, gardens and pool.

£££

Hotel Amar
Tourist Complex, Fatehbad Road, Agra 282 001
Tel: 331 885–9
Fax: 330 299
Impersonal, modern hotel with restaurant, bar, health club and pool.

Grand Hotel
237 Station Road, Cantonment, Agra 282 001
Tel: 364 014/364 320
Fax: 364 271
E-mail: grand@nde.vsnl.net.in
Popular but faded hotel in large grounds with facilities for camping, tennis and badminton. Nice garden, restaurant and bar.

Lauries Hotel
M.G. Road, Agra 282 001
Tel: 364 536
Fax: 268 045
E-mail: laurieshotel@hotmail.com
A well-known, decrepit but popular hotel with facilities for camping. Pleasant grounds, restaurant and bar.

££

Mayur Tourist Complex
Tourist Complex, Fatehbad Road, Agra 282 001
Tel: 332 302/332 31o
Fax: 332 2907
Cottages around peaceful and well-maintained gardens with pool and fountains. Will only accept AMEX or cash.

£

Tourist Rest House
Kachahari Road, Baluganj
Tel: 363 3691
E-mail: trh@vsnl.com
The best low-cost place to stay in Agra. Clean rooms with attached bath around a courtyard. Friendly owners and good vegetarian food. Recommended.

Alwar (0144)

££

Hotel Alwar
26 Manu Marg, Alwar 301 001
Tel: 335 754
Fax: 332 250
E-mail: ukrustagi@hotmail.com
Good rooms with attached bath. Restaurant and pleasant garden.

Bharatpur (05644)

££££

Bharatpur Forest Lodge
Keoladeo Ghana National Park
Tel: 22722
Fax: 22864
Situated inside the park, this hotel offers luxury rooms with balconies, an excellent buffet restaurant and a bar. Book in advance.

Laxmi Vilas Palace
Kakaji ki Kothi
Tel: 23523
Fax: 25259
This former palace on the outskirts of the city dates from 1899. It has some luxury suites and comfortable rooms. The food is recommended and the service is excellent.

£££

Chandra Mahal Haveli
Peharsar
Tel: (05643) 3238
The turn-off for this lovely 1850s *haveli*, set in the middle of a small village, is 22 km (14 miles) out of town down the Jaipur–Agra road. There are suites overlooking the garden, and a good restaurant.

££

Forest Rest House
Tel: 22777
Situated in the forest, popular rooms with bath, restaurant and gardens. Book in advance.

£

Spoonbill
Fatehpur Sikri Road
Tel: 23571
Decent rooms and dormitory beds with very good food and friendly service. Close to the national park.

Delhi (011)

£££££

Ashok Hotel
50-B Chanakyapuri, New Delhi 110 021
Tel: 611 0101
Fax: 687 3216/687 6060
E-mail: ashoknd@ndb.vsnl.net.in
Huge, mock-Mughal luxury hotel, flagship of the Ashok group. Amenities include 6 restaurants, pool and beauty parlour.

The Ambassador Hotel
Sujan Singh Marg, Subramaniam Bandi Marg, New Delhi 110 003
Tel: 463 2600
Fax: 463 2252/463 8219/469 7232
E-mail: ambassadorhotel@vsnl.com
Old-fashioned hotel near Khan Market with spacious rooms and good South Indian restaurant.

Claridges
12 Aurangzeb Road, New Delhi 110 011
Tel: 301 0211
Fax: 301 0625
E-mail: claridge@del2.vsnl.net.in
Elegant, old-fashioned hotel with great restaurants, good pool and beauty parlour.

Hotel Diplomat
9 Sardar Patel Marg, Diplomatic Enclave, New Delhi 110 021
Tel: 301 0204
Fax: 301 8605
E-mail: diplomat@nda.vsnl.net in
Quiet and popular hotel with pleasant garden. Advance booking advisable.

Hotel Inter-Continental
Barakhamba Avenue, Connaught Place, New Delhi 110 001
Tel: 332 0101/370 9000
Fax: 332 5335/370 9123
E-mail: newdelhi@interconti.com
A top-class modern, luxury hotel located near Connaught Place. Good restaurants, bar, pool and disco.

Hyatt Regency
Bhikaji Cama Place, Ring Road, New Delhi 110 066
Tel: 679 1234
Fax: 679 1024

E-mail: hyatt@del2.vsnl.net.in
Luxury hotel in South Delhi. Pleasant environment, excellent restaurants, very good pastry shop, airy bar with live jazz, good pool. Disco is free for women every Wednesday.

Hotel Imperial
Janpath, New Delhi 110 001
Tel: 334 1234/334 5678
Fax: 334 2255/334 8149
E-mail: gminp@giasdl.01.vsnl.net.in
Colonial-style hotel, centrally located, with a popular open-air restaurant, large bar, nice pool and shopping arcade.

Le Meridien
Windsor Place, Janpath, New Delhi 110 001
Tel: 371 0101
Fax: 371 4545
E-mail: info@lemeridien-newdelhi.com
Five-star, ultra-modern hotel south of India Gate. Restaurants, bars, swimming pool and disco.

Welcomgroup Maurya Sheraton Hotel and Towers
Diplomatic Enclave, Sardar Patel Marg, New Delhi 110 021
Tel: 611 2233
Fax: 611 3333
E-mail: maurya@welcomgroup.com
Luxury hotel, great restaurants and the best lap-swimming pool. Small disco (Ghungroo), popular with young Delhiites.

Oberoi
Dr Zakir Hussain Marg, New Delhi 110 003
Tel: 436 3030
Fax: 436 0484/430 4084
E-mail: oberoi2@giasde101.vsnl.net.in
Centrally located, elegant, exclusive and very expensive. Restaurants and good bakery, bars, bookshop (the Ritka Book House), pool, beauty parlour and health club.

The Oberoi Maidens
7 Sham Nath Marg, Delhi 110 054
Tel: 397 5464/291 4841/252 5464
Fax: 398 0771
E-mail: bsparmar@tomdel.com
Colonial-style hotel in Old Delhi. Large rooms, attentive service, pleasant gardens, pool and restaurant. Recommended.

Hotel Price Categories

The rates below are for a double room (AC where available) in high season, including taxes.

£££££	Rs4,000 and above
££££	Rs2,000–4,000
£££	Rs1,000–2,000
££	Rs400–1,000
£	Up to Rs400

Radisson Hotel
National Highway 8, New Delhi 110 037
Tel: 612 9191
Fax: 612 9090
E-mail: raddel@del2.vsnl.net.in
Well maintained luxury hotel near the airport. Non-smoking rooms available. Amenities include pool and squash court. Good kebab café.

The Suriya
New Friends Colony, New Delhi 110 065
Tel: 683 5070
Fax: 683 7758
E-mail: suryahot@ndf.vsnl.net.in
Modern hotel in South Delhi. Comfortable rooms, trendy restaurants, pool and health club.

Taj Mahal
1 Man Singh Road, New Delhi 110 011
Tel: 302 6162
Fax: 302 6070
E-mail: tajmahal@giasdel01.vsnl.net.in
The flagship of the Taj Group. Luxurious and comfortable with good restaurants, coffee shop, pool and beauty parlour.

Taj Palace
Sardar Patel Marg, Diplomatic Enclave, New Delhi 110 021
Tel: 611 0202
Fax: 611 0808
E-mail: bctpd@tajgroup.sprintrpg.ems.vsnl.net.in
Another luxury Taj Group hotel. Large and comfortable, all five-star facilities, disco (My Kind of Place). Convenient for the airport.

££££

Janpath Hotel
Janpath, New Delhi 110 001
Tel: 334 0070
Fax: 334 7083/335 8618
E-mail: janpath@ndf.vsnl.net.in
Large, clean rooms and good restaurants. Reports of poor service.

Jukaso Inn Downtown
L-1, Connaught Place, New Delhi 110 001
Tel: 332 4451–3
Fax: 332 4448
Good value, central hotel close to Nirula's. Modern and clean AC rooms.

Hotel Marina
G-59 Connaught Place, New Delhi 110 001
Tel: 332 4658
Fax: 332 8609
E-mail: marina@nde.vsnl.net.in
Well-established, renovated hotel with comfortable rooms, restaurant and good travel service.

Nirula's Hotel
L-Block, Connaught Place, New Delhi 110 001
Tel: 332 2419
Fax: 335 3957
E-mail: delhihotel@nirula.com
Well-established little hotel with AC single and double rooms. Two restaurants and a very popular ice-cream parlour. Book in advance.

£££

Hotel Broadway
4–15A Asaf Ali Road, Delhi 110 002
Tel: 327 3821
Fax: 326 9966
E-mail: owhpl@nda.vsnl.net.in
A lovely hotel close to Old Delhi. Clean rooms, good service and an excellent restaurant.

Hotel Fifty Five
H-55 Connaught Place, New Delhi 110 001
Tel: 332 1244/332 1278
Fax: 332 0769
E-mail: hotelfiftyfive@hotmail.com
Centrally located with AC rooms, attached baths and 24-hour room service.

YMCA Tourist Hostel
Jai Singh Road
Tel: 374 6031
Fax: 374 6032
Over-priced but wide range of rooms, some AC. Restaurant, pool and gardens, breakfast included in price.

Heritage Hotels

Some of India's most atmospheric and romantic hotels are in Rajasthan, many of them in converted palaces, forts or *havelis* (merchants' houses).

When the civil list of the Indian aristocracy was abolished by Indira Gandhi in the 1970s, some of the ex-rulers of the princely states, particularly in Rajasthan, turned to tourism to fund the upkeep of their properties by turning them into luxury hotels. These proved popular, and profitable, and soon many owners of run-down old buildings were busy renovating them and taking in guests.

The facilities can be luxurious – and expensive – with marble swimming pools, beautifully decorated suites and well-maintained grounds. Food is usually available to guests, most commonly an Indian buffet of about seven different dishes.

YWCA International Guest House
10 Sansad Marg
Tel: 336 1561
Fax: 334 1763
Clean AC rooms with attached bath. Convenient location and reasonable restaurant.

££

Hotel Indraprastha (formerly the ITDC Ashok Yatri Niwas)
19 Ashok Road, New Delhi 110 001
Tel: 334 4511
Fax: 336 8153
Mixed reports but generally good-value large rooms. Two restaurants, one self-service and the **Coconut Grove** serving vegetarian and non-vegetarian South Indian dishes.

Hotel Palace Heights
D-Block, Connaught Place, New Delhi
Tel: 332 1419/332 1377/ 332 1369
Very central hotel with large but dark, depressing and run-down rooms, some with AC. No hot water.

Metropolis
1634 Main Bazaar, Paharganj
Tel: 753 5766
Fax: 752 5600
The best hotel in Paharganj. Clean and comfortable rooms, hot water and a good restaurant.

Naari
B1–7 Vishal Bhawan, 95 Nehru Place, New Delhi 19
Tel: 646 5711/618 7401
Fax: 647 2549/623 4621
A women-only guesthouse in South Delhi. Comfortable rooms, pleasant garden and meals. Tours arranged. Safe and hassle-free for women travelling on their own. Recommended.

£

Ajay Guest House
5084A Main Bazaar, Paharganj
Tel: 777 7617
Clean but small rooms with attached bath. Good bakery.

Anoop
1566 Main Bazaar, Paharganj
Tel: 352 9366
Similar rooms to the Ajay. Pleasant rooftop restaurant.

Hotel New City Palace
725 Jama Masjid, Delhi 110 006
Tel: 327 9548/325 520
Fax: 328 9923
Just behind the mosque in Old Delhi, in the same building as the post office. Clean, light, air-cooled rooms with attached bath. Rooms at front have great view. Recommended.

Major's Den
2314 Lakshmi Narain Street, Paharganj, New Delhi 110 055
Tel: 262 9599/355 6665/351 4163/353 9010
A cheap, well-run hotel with clean, air-cooled rooms and attached bath.

Rail Yatri Niwas
Ajmeri Gate, New Delhi Railway Station
Tel: 332 3484
Good-value rooms dormitories and self-service restaurant for travellers holding onward railway tickets (maxmimum 3 days). Book in advance at New Delhi Station.

Youth Hostel
5 Naya Marg, Chanakyapuri
Tel: 611 9841
Inconvenient location but modern and very good value. YHA members only (membership fee Rs250).

Jaipur (0141)

£££££

Rajvilas
Goner Road, Jaipur 302 016
Tel: 640 101
Fax: 640 202
E-mail: reservations@rajvilas.com
This is as good as it gets: an ultra-luxurious and ultra-expensive 13-hectare (32-acre) complex, 12km (7.5 miles) outside the city. Elegant rooms and suites in beautiful gardens with every conceivable amenity. Excellent food and an adventurous menu.

Rambagh Palace Hotel
Bhawani Singh Road, Jaipur 302 005
Tel: 381 919
Fax: 381 098
E-mail: rambagh@jp1.dot.net.in
The ultimate art deco palace for film-star fantasies. Posh interiors, health club, squash court and indoor pool. Folklore programmes nightly on fountained lawns.

Jai Mahal Palace Hotel
Jacob Road, Civil Lines, Jaipur 302 006
Tel: 371 616
Fax: 365 237
A top-class Taj-group hotel. Lovely gardens and an excellent restaurant.

Welcomgroup Rajputana Palace Sheraton
Palace Road, Jaipur 302 006
Tel: 360 011
Fax: 367 848
E-mail: rajputana@welcomgroup.com
Modern and luxurious five-star hotel. All amenities, including good pool and restaurants.

Raj Mahal Palace Hotel
Sardar Patel Marg, C Scheme, Jaipur 302 001
Tel: 381 757381 676/381 625
Fax: 381 887
Old British Residency converted into a tasteful lodging.

££££

Bissau Palace
Chandpole Gate, Jaipur 302 016
Tel: 304 371/304 391
Fax: 304 628
E-mail: sanjai@jpl.dot.net.in
Grand building with Rajput warrior decor. Gardens, pool and tennis

court. Some rooms lack AC, but with lofty ceilings stay cool.

Narain Niwas Palace
Kanota Bagh, Narain Singh Road, Jaipur 302 004
Tel: 561 291/563 448
Fax: 561 045
Roomy and regal, with 19th-century royal relics of the Kanota ruler's family. Vegetarian restaurant and pool. Rooms completed in September 2000 now overlook the very attractive garden.

Samode Haveli
Gangapole, Jaipur 302 002
Tel: 632 370/632 407/631 068
Fax: 631 397
E-mail: reservations@samode.com
An excellent place to stay. This 150-year-old converted *haveli* has 20 spacious rooms and two wonderfully decorated suites (no. 115, covered in wall-paintings, and no. 116 with mirror-work overlooking the garden). Recommended.

£££

LMB
Johari Bazaar, Jaipur 302 003
Tel: 565 844/565 856–7
Fax: 562 176
E-mail: info@lmbsweets.com
Vegetarian hotel in walled city.

Madhuban Guest House
D237 Behari Marg, Banipark, Jaipur 302 016
Tel: 200 033/205 427
Fax: 202 344
20 rooms, some AC (standard rooms better, de luxe rooms a little dark), in very friendly, family-run hotel which was renovated in 2000. Quiet and secluded with nice garden.

Nana ki Haveli
Moti Dungra Road, Fatehtibba, Jaipur 302 004
Tel/fax: 605 481
An intimate, central hotel in a family home. Comfortable and close to the Central Museum. Excellent cooking. Recommended.

££

Diggi Palace
Diggi House, Shivaji Marg, Hospital Road
Tel: 373 091
Fax: 370 359
Good deal for budget travellers. Beautiful old palace with lawns and good terrace restaurant.

Hotel Arya Niwas
Behind Amber Tower, Sansar Chandra Road, Jaipur 302 001
Tel: 372 456/371 773/368 524/371 776
Fax: 361 871
E-mail: aryahotl@jp1.dot.net.in
The best budget hotel in Jaipur. Very clean and comfortable, AC and non-AC rooms. Also bizarre, but cheap and spotless, self-service restaurant, which will appeal to those who like being institutionalised. Pleasant terrace overlooking the front lawn. Recommended.

£

Jaipur Inn
17 Shiv Marg, Bani Park
Tel: 316 821
Clean rooms and dormitory. Food and camping facilities. Popular so book ahead.

Hotel Price Categories

The rates below are for a double room (AC where available) in high season, including taxes.

£££££	Rs4,000 and above
££££	Rs2,000–4,000
£££	Rs1,000–2,000
££	Rs400–1,000
£	Up to Rs400

Mathura (0565)

££££

Best Western Radha Ashok
Masani By-Pass Road, Mathura 281 001
Tel: 405 557
Fax: 409 557
E-mail: radhaanila@hotmail.com
Attractive, modern hotel with comfortable rooms, pool and good restaurant.

£££

Hotel Madhuvan
Krishna Nagar, Mathura 281 004
Tel: 420 064/420 058
Fax: 420 684
E-mail: bhul@nde.vsnl.net.in
AC rooms with attached bath, pool and restaurant.

Hotel Mansarovar Palace
Mansarovar Crossing, Mathura 281 001
Tel: 408 686/409 966/406 525
Fax: 401 611
AC and non-AC rooms and restaurant.

Ranthambore (07462)

£££££

Sawai Madhopur Lodge
Ranthambore Road, Sawai Madhopur 322 001
Tel: 20541
Fax: 20718
E-mail: sawai.madhopur@tajhotels.com
Taj group palace hotel. Comfortable accommodation with all the usual luxuries. Well managed and close to the park.

£££

Castle Jhoomar Baori
8 km from the station
Tel: 20495
A hill-top hunting lodge. A little run-down but the great views are some compensation.

££

Ankur Resorts
Ranthambore Road, Sawai Madhopur 322 001
Tel: 20792
Fax: 20697
A good option. Clean, comfortable rooms, some individual cottages, and good restaurant.

Samode

££££

Samode Bagh
3 km (2 miles) from Samode village
Run by the owners of Samode Palace *(below)*, accomodation is in luxury "tents", with attached bathrooms, set in beautiful gardens with a lovely pool. Book through the palace or **Samode Haveli** in Jaipur.

Samode Palace Hotel
The palace, which has 20 rooms, is the main attraction of this small village. It contains an excellent *Shish Mahal* (hall of mirrors). The rooms are luxurious and beautifully furnished, and it has a great pool. Bookings can be made through **Samode Haveli** in Jaipur. Recommended.

Sariska (01465)

££££
Hotel Sariska Palace
Alwar District 301 022
Tel: 24247
The most elegant option close to the park. A converted, French-designed 1892 palace with the usual Heritage Hotel facilities.

Siliserh (0144)

£££
Lake Castle Hotel
Tel: 86322
Palace hotel in fabulous position overlooking the lake. Some AC rooms and restaurant.

Hotel Price Categories

The rates below are for a double room (AC where available) in high season, including taxes.

£££££	Rs4,000 and above
££££	Rs2,000–4,000
£££	Rs1,000–2,000
££	Rs400–1,000
£	Up to Rs400

Where to Eat

Agra (0562)

NB: avoid the travellers' eating places in and around Taj Ganj. The Agra police have reported a nasty scam whereby unsuspecting travellers are given food poisoning and then taken to a fake doctor, who keeps them ill for as long as possible, all the while claiming outrageous expenses on their health insurance. As well as the excellent restaurants in the five-star hotels, the restaurants below are all reputable and safe.

Chinese Banzara (**Chung Wah**)
Gopi Chand Shivhare Road, Sardar Bazaar
Tasty and authentic Chinese food in a small and friendly place tucked away from the road. Generous portions.
Dasaprakash
Meher Theatre Complex, 1 Gwalior Road, Cantoment, Agra 282 001
Tel: 260 269
Very good South Indian food, especially the *dosas*, and wicked desserts. Very clean and well run. Open 12.30–3.30pm, 6–11pm.
Pizza Hut
8 Nawdi Craft Nagar, Fatehbad Road, Agra 282 001
Tel: 333 051–3
The usual array of pizza, pasta and salad, some with an Indian twist. Spotless and reassuring for weary travellers. Open 11am–11pm.
Zorba the Buddha
E13 Shopping Arcade, Gopi Chand Shivhare Road, Sadar Bazaar
Very clean and popular vegetarian restaurant serving tasty and imaginative dishes. Run by followers of Osho. Open 12–3pm, 6–9pm, closed in the summer. Recommended.

Delhi (011)

Annapoorna
81 Janpath
Take-away run by women's cooperative, on the corner before the Tibetan market. Great pies, pasties, pastries and cakes.
Basil & Thyme
Santushi Shopping Complex, Chanakyapuri
Tel: 467 4933
A place to be seen, with good and reasonably priced Western food. Open 10.30am–5.30pm.
Café 100
20-B Connaught Place, New Delhi 110 001
Tel: 335 0051
Burgers, pizzas and ice creams to eat in or take away. Very popular. Open 10.30am–11.30pm.
Chor Bizarre
Hotel Broadway, 4/15A Asaf Ali Road, New Delhi 110 002
Tel: 327 3821–5
Excellent Kashmiri and *tanduri* food, served in bizarre surroundings – including a buffet from an old car. Open 12–3.30pm, 7–11.30pm.
Dilli Haat
Off Aurobindo Marg, between Kidwai Nagar West and Lakshmibai Nagar
The place to head for to sample foods from all over the country. Pick and choose from the very clean stalls. Entry Rs5, open 10am–10pm.
Gaylord Restaurant
16 Regal Building, Connaught Circus, New Delhi 110 001
Tel: 373 4755/373 4677
Expensive Indian and Continental food from a posh, long-established restaurant. Open 11am–11.30pm.
Karim's
Gali Kababiyan, Matia Mahal, near Jama Masjid, Delhi 110 006
Tel: 326 9880/326 4981
The best Muslim food in the city. Mouthwatering non-vegetarian tanduri dishes and excellent breads. There is a more expensive, and less good, branch in Nizamuddin, South Delhi.
Kwality
7 Regal Building, Sansad Marg, New Delhi 110 001
Dependable and clean non-

vegetarian restaurant serving Indian and Continental dishes. Open 12–11pm.

Nirula's Pot Pourri and Chinese Room
L-Block, Connaught Place, New Delhi 110 001
Tel: 332 2419
The popular Pot Pourri (open 7.30am–11pm) has tasty Continental and Indian food, including a salad bar, and is a good place for breakfast. The more expensive Chinese Room upstairs (open 12.30pm–4.00pm, 7.00pm–11.00pm) serves standard Chinese dishes. Nirula's also has branches elsewhere in the city.

Parikrama
UB-34 Antriksh Bhavan, 22 K.G. Marg, New Delhi 110 001
Tel: 372 1616/372 1617
Revolving restaurant with excellent views and surprisingly good North Indian, Chinese and Continental food. Open 12.30pm–11pm.

Park Balluchi Restaurant
Inside Deer Park, Hauz Khas Village, New Delhi 110 016
Tel: 685 9369/696 9829
Award-winning restaurant serving Mughlai and Afghan dishes. In a lovely setting on the edge of the park. Open 12pm–3pm, 7pm–11pm.

Pizza Express
D-10, Inner Circle, Connaught Place, New Delhi 110 001; 2–3, Block C, Ansal Plaza, Khel Gaon Marg
Tel: 373 9306/373 6391
Branches of the British chain, with the same menu. Great pizza, wine and desserts; a welcome relief from Indian food. Open 11am–11pm.

Rodeo
12-A Connaught Place, New Delhi 110 001
Tel: 371 3780–1
Good Tex-Mex food and cocktails served by waiters in cowboy outfits. A pleasant place for a drink, must be with food after 7pm. Open 12–11pm.

Sagar
18 Defence Colony Market
Tel: 469 8374
Very popular South Indian restaurant. Good *thalis*, *dosas* and coffee.

Siri Fort Village Restaurant Complex
Asian Games Village, Khel Gaon Marg, New Delhi 110 049
Tel: 649 2348/649 3628/ 649 3945
Four good restaurants, comprising the **Angeethi** (Indian *tanduri*, open

Delhi's Hotel Restaurants

Some of the best food in India can be found in Delhi, and many of the top restaurants are found in its five-star hotels (for locations and telephone numbers see *Where to Stay* above). All of them are expensive (count on at least Rs1,200 for two people) and reservations are recommended.

Ashok

Tokyo Elegant Japanese restaurant with an emphasis on seafood.

Hyatt Regency

La Piazza Excellent Italian food, including pizzas cooked in a wood-fired oven.

The Oberoi

Baan Thai One of the best Thai restaurants in Delhi.
La Rochelle Expensive and formal French restaurant.

Le Meridien

Golden Phoenix Great Cantonese and Schezwan food.
Le Belvedere Continental and Indian dishes.
Pakwan Top tandoori restaurant.
Pierre Very fine French cuisine.

Maurya Sheraton

Bukhara Beautifully prepared food from NWFP.
Dum Phukt Delicious Avadhi dishes prepared by lengthy steaming in a sealed pot.
West View Pick your own ingredients from a wide choice of meats, seafood and vegetables.

Inter-Continental

Baluchi Dishes from the *tandur* and NWFP.
Grill Room Good steak and seafood.
Silk Orchid Popular Thai restaurant.

Taj Mahal

Captain's Cabin Great seafood.
Haveli North Indian dishes accompanied by live music.
House of Ming Exceptional Chinese food, possibly the best in Delhi.
Longchamp Widely considered to be the best French restaurant in Delhi.

Taj Palace

Orient Express Excellent Continental food served in a recreated railway carriage.
Tea House of the August Moon Superb Chinese restaurant, with lotus pond, pagoda and goldfish.

Park Hotel

La Meninas Delhi's first Spanish restaurant serving great *tapas*.

Oberoi Maidens

The Curzon Room Food from the British Raj in period surroundings.

The Claridges

Corbett's Garden *tanduri* restaurant with a jungle theme.
Dhaba A recreation of a Punjabi wayside *dhaba*, complete with lorry.
Jade Garden Good Chinese food in an evocative setting.

The Ambassador

Dasaprakash The place to head for if you are craving top-notch South Indian vegetarian food.

The Imperial

Garden Party Open-air restaurant, good for a breakfast splurge.
Spice Route High-quality Thai dishes, very popular.

7.30–11.30pm), **Ankur** (Mughlai and Avadhi, open 12.30–3pm, 7.30–11.30pm), **Ankur Coffee Shop** ("ACS", Tex-Mex and Continental, open 11.30am–11.30pm), and the excellent **Chopsticks** (Chinese and Thai, open 12.30–3pm, 7.30–11.30pm).

The Buck Stops Here
CG-01 Ansal Plaza, Khel Gaon Marg, New Delhi 110 017
Tel: 625 7696–7
Inventive new café and restaurant serving Mediterranean-inspired food. Displays of designer cutlery and crockery, paintings and the furniture are all for sale. Soon to acquire an *espresso* machine.
Open 11am–11pm.

The Village Bistro Restaurant Complex
12 Hauz Khas Village, Near Deer Park, New Delhi 110 016
Tel: 685 2227/685 3857/656 3905/656 3970/652 2227
A group of six restaurants serving Indian (**Village Mohalla**, **Khas Bagh**, **Top of the Village**, open 12.30–3.30pm, 7.30–11.30pm), Chinese (**The Village Kowloon**, open 12.30–3.30pm, 7.30–11.30pm), and Continental food (**Le Cafe**, a coffee shop open open 11am–Midnight). The **Village Durbar** (open 12.30–3.30pm, 7.30–11.30pm) is multi-cuisine. The rooftop Top of the Village looks out over the ruined *madarsa* and tomb of Firoz Shah Tughlaq, and stages a daily traditional dance show, 7pm–7.45pm.

Wenger's
A-16 Connaught Place, New Delhi 110 001
Tasty and cheap take-away pastries, bread and cakes.

Wimpy
N-6 Janpath, New Delhi 110 001
Tel: 331 3910
Western fast food place, popular with travellers, serving lamb-burgers and fries. Open 10am–11pm.

Zen
B-25 Connaught Place, New Delhi 110 001
Tel: 335 7444/335 7455
A Chinese restaurant, very popular with Delhi's middle class, which also serves good Japanese dishes. A great place for people watching. Open 10.30am–11pm.

Jaipur (0141)

NB: food poisoning scams have been reported in restaurants in the Walled City *(see Agra above)*. In addition to the, often very good, restaurants in the listed hotels, the restaurants below are all safe.

Chanakya Restaurant
M.I. Road, Jaipur 302 001
Tel: 376 161/378 461
Very well-presented food in posh surroundings. Has a reputation for the best traditional Rajasthani food in Jaipur. However, this may be a shock to the unwary – lots of *ghi* is used in the cooking, which may not sit well on a weak stomach. Open 12–11pm.

Copper Chimney Restaurant
Maya Mansions, M.I. Road, Jaipur 302 001
Tel: 372 275/364 839
Smart, AC restaurant serving good western and excellent non-vegetarian Indian dishes. Open 11.30am–3.30pm, 6–11pm.

Lassiwala
M.I. Road
Series of streetside stalls serving snacks and renowned clay cups of *lassi* to long queues of customers. Early morning–late evening.

Neel Mahal and **Polo Bar**
Rambagh Palace Hotel, Bhawani Singh Road
Tel: 381 919
The restaurant and bar of the famous five-star hotel. You can wallow in luxury here even if you can't afford a room. The bar is great and even has a marble fountain. Ask to take your drinks out on to the terrace, which looks out over the beautiful gardens.

Niros
M.I. Road, Jaipur 302 001
Tel: 371 746/374 493/371 874
Cool, AC restaurant, very clean and central. Tasty food and prompt service from an extensive menu of Indian, Chinese and Continental dishes. A little more expensive than other places in town.

LMB
Johari Bazaar, Jaipur 302 003
Tel: 565 844/565 846–7
Below the hotel with the same initials. Jaipur's most famous sweet shop. The restaurant serves traditional high-caste Rajasthani vegetarian food (cooked in lots of *ghi* with no onions or garlic). Open 8am–11pm.

Mediterraneo
9 Khandela House, behind Amber Tower, S.C. Road
Rooftop Italian restaurant just along from the Arya Niwas hotel. Great fresh pasta, and pizzas cooked in a wood-fired oven.

Pizza Hut
109 Ganapati Plaza, M.I. Road, Jaipur 302 001
Tel: 362 055
Familiar pizza and pasta in a spotless environment – good if you are home-sick. Free hotel delivery. Open 11am–11pm.

Shopping

What to Buy

The assortment of goods is staggering, so look around first and check out the differing quality and prices before you buy anything.

Places selling handicrafts (of all kinds) are a good first stop. Carpets are available in different sizes and knot-counts. Unless you know a lot about carpets, shop at a Government Emporium. Less expensive are rugs and *dhurries* from all over the country. There is a huge assortment of precious and semi-precious gem-stones, jewellery set in both gold and silver, traditional as well as modern, often much cheaper than in Europe.

India is famous for its textiles which come in a bewildering array of natural and man-made fibres, textures, weaves, prints, designs and colours.

Carved sandalwood figures and elaborately worked wooden panels come from the South. There are also many objects in brass, copper and gun metal, inlaid, enamelled, worked or beaten.

Marble inlay work and papier mâché items with intricate designs, reproductions of miniature paintings on paper or cloth, and leather wallets, shoes and bags are all good buys. Hand-painted pottery, and cane goods ranging from table mats to furniture, are popular, and so are ready-made clothes.

Antiques and semi-antiques are governed buy strict laws limiting their export, also beware of fakes. Export of skins, furs and ivory is either banned or strictly regulated. You must get a certificate of legitimate sale and permission to export for these items.

Shopping in Agra

Agra is famous for its carpets and inlaid marble. As elsewhere, be careful about what you buy and look around before making any purchase. Many items passed off as marble are soapstone or chalk. The test is to check if the stone is translucent (will light up from the other side) and whether it leaves a mark when rubbed on a rough surface; marble will light up and will not leave a mark. Silk carpets change colour and sheen when viewed from different directions.

A very good place to start looking for carpets is the **Harish Carpet Company** on Vibhav Nagar Road (tel: 331 213). The carpets are made by some 12,000 weavers across town, but you can see a demonstration downstairs of the weaving, washing and trimming of the carpets. Even better, you can inspect the raw yarns that they are made from: either wool, wool/silk mix or pure silk yarns, all with natural dyes (the yarns are sourced from Kashmir). They use a minimum of 440 knots per square inch (2.5 square cm) and most of the designs are traditional Indo-Persian patterns. You should expect to pay, fixed prices, from Rs550 per square foot (30 square cm) for wool, Rs650 for wool/silk mix, and Rs1,000 for pure silk.

For marble inlay work, the best place in town is the government **U.P. Handicrafts Development Centre** (Handicraft Nagar, Fatehbad Road, tel: 331 200/331 666). They have their own factory employing some 500 people. Some of the work is exquisite and a large piece can take up to a year-and-a-half to complete. A small box costs from around Rs600. They also sell fabrics by the metre, *saris*, shawls and ready-mades, all at fixed prices.

Shopping in Delhi

Central Delhi

Connaught Place was built as the commercial centre of Lutyen's new city. Nowadays it is full of restaurants, Western sports shops and places trying to lure in tourists. It is probably best to avoid shopping here as the prices are over-inflated, although the bookshops are worth having a browse through. Also avoid the tourist traps in the underground Palika Bazaar. Connaught Place does have a useful 24-hour branch of **ANZ Grindlays** with an ATM (10 E-Block).

The **Tibetan market** at the top of Janpath has stalls selling Tibetan curios. Opposite, at Jawahar Vyapur Bhavan, Janpath, is the huge government-run **Central Cottage Industries Emporium** (tel: 332 1909/332 1157, 10am–7pm Mon–Sat). The fixed prices and wide variety of goods, spread over 6 floors, make it a good place to start looking. It is a particularly good place to buy fabrics. Also on Janpath is the **Survey of India Map Sales Office** (2A Janpath Barracks), where you can pick up large-scale maps (**NB.** any maps over 1:250,000 may not be exported. However, they may be used while you are in the country). Another good place for maps is **International Publications** (40 Hanuman Lane, Connaught Place, tel: 336 6113).

Baba Kharak Singh Marg, near Connaught Place, is where all State Emporia are found (and the very popular government **Coffee Home**). A major refurbishment is planned which will include pedestrianisation.

Old Delhi

Between **Chandni Chowk** and **Chawri Bazaar** are the bazaars of Old Delhi. **Ghantewale** on Chandni Chowk is one of the oldest and best sweet shops in Delhi. Running south off Chandni Chowk, just past the Jain Mandir, is Dariba Kalan, the jeweller's street, famous for its gold but now mostly selling silver. **Katra Neel**, west of the town hall on Chandni Chowk, is a warren of small shops selling fabrics, particularly silk, by the metre. Check the purity of the silk by burning a strand or two. If the fibres burn away to ash that just crumbles in your fingers then it is pure silk, if there is a residue then the fabric is wholly or partly synthetic.

Nai Sarak, which runs between Chandni Chowk and Chawri Bazaar has bookshops, mostly of educational publications. By the Jama Masjid is the extraordinary spare car-parts bazaar.

South Delhi

The latest shopping sensation in South Delhi is the swish, air-conditioned **Ansal Plaza**, on Khel Gaon Marg. A good place to visit to see how the other 5 percent live, it has the Shoppers Stop department store, a branch of Music World with a great range of CDs and a branch of Archies, the Indian gift-shop chain.

The **Hauz Khas Village Complex** has numerous designer boutiques selling *shalwar* and *lehengas*. Try the shop of **Nasreen Qureshi** (26 Hauz Khas Village, tel: 696 1210), a Pakistani designer from Lahore, now living in Delhi. **Neelam Jolly's** (12 Hauz Khas Village, tel: 651 0958) has elegant and understated clothes. **Expressionist Designs** (1A Hauz Khas Village, tel: 651 8913) stock the clothes of Delhi designer Jaspreet, and are soon to expand into interior design. For a large stock, fast turnover (due to a sale or return policy) ensuring clothes are up-to-date, and the work of several Delhi designers go to **Marwari's** (15 Hauz Khas Village, tel: 656 6556). Next to Marwari's at no. 14 is **The Village Gallery** (tel: 685 3860) which showcases Indian artists working in a variety of media. Exhibitions change every month and back-stock may be viewed on the first floor.

Near the zoo, **Sunder Nagar Market** has several art and antique stores.

Diplomatic Area

Near this area there is a chic shopping complex called **Santushti**, run by the Airforce Wives Association. There are branches of the Jaipur-based designers' shop **Anokhi**, and of **Padakkam**, which sells fabrics and accessories from South India, mostly Keralan. Although very popular, the prime minister's office want the complex closed down as it is said to endanger security. South of this and next to Chanakya Cinema, **Yashwant Singh Place** has several shops selling leather and fur items. **Sarojini Nagar Market**, nearby, is another "colony" market selling many goods including vegetables, household items, export surplus clothes and shoes. **Khan Market** has good bookshops – try the **Times Book Gallery** – and is a good place to pick up groceries. It also has a branch of **Anokhi**, an outlet for the Biotique range of *ayurvedic* skin-care products, and **Padakkam**, with a pleasant balcony where you can drink coffee.

Other "colony" markets worth visiting are **South Extension**, **Defence Colony**, **Greater Kailash** (N and M Block Market), and **Lajput Nagar Central Market**.

Shopping in Jaipur

Traditional tie-dyed textiles made by knotting the material and dipping it in dye to form delicate *bandhani* patterns are worth looking out for. The block prints of Sanganer, many with *khari* (over-printing with gold); *ajrah* prints from Barmer; *jajam* prints from Chittaurgarh; and the floral prints from Bagru can be found in the bazaars in the old city. The **Rajasthali Government Emporium** (just of M.I. Road) is the **only** government-run shop. It sells fabric by the yard, or made up into garments and wall hangings, gemstones and other jewellery. Another good place for fabrics and clothing is the **Gramya** khadi handicraft emporium (Panch Batti, M.I. Road, tel: 373 821). Jaipur is also the home of **Anokhi** (2 Tilak Marg, C Scheme, tel: 381 247). They sell elegant *shalwar* (in colours that will appeal to Western tastes), T-shirts, skirts, bed linen, throws etc., all in good-quality fabrics that are reasonably priced and ethically sourced.

Jaipur is famous as a centre for semi-precious gemstones. If you do want to buy these, check what you are buying very carefully. Rajasthali, above, is recommended, as is **The Gem Palace** on M.I. Road (tel: 374 175/363 061). This long-established jewellers has beautiful, and expensive, work. If you are buying gems from elsewhere, ask to take them to the government's **Gem Testing Laboratory** (Chamber 1, 3rd Floor, M.I. Road). The tests take about two hours and the charge is Rs200 per stone.

Jaipur and Sanganer are famous for their "blue pottery". These hand-painted vessels are decorated with floral motifs and geometric patterns in combinations of blue, white and occasionally other colours.

Leather workers using camel and other hides produce a variety of traditional footwear, including *jhutis* with their turned-up toes. In Jaipur the cobblers also make *mojadis*, soft slippers embroidered with bright colours.

Carpets and *dhurries* are made both for local and export markets. Jewellery can be found in the **Johari Bazaar**. Although it is well-known for its silver, the gold-work is finer. Make sure you bargain hard. Jaipur has the best selection of *pichwais* or cloth paintings. Try the **Friends of the Museum Master Craftsmen and Artists** display room inside the main courtyard of the City Palace, where you can watch the artists at work. Engraved brassware, and exquisite enamel work and inlay is also available; the best enamel work is done by **Kudrat Singh** (1565 Rasta Jarion, Chaura Rasta, tel: 561 135/572 284).

The HTDC bank on Ashok Marg has one of the only **ATMs** that will issue cash against a Visa card

Ethical Shopping

Some goods in India are produced using children as a cheap labour force. They are paid, if at all, barely subsistence wages, and work in cramped and dangerous conditions. There are many Indian organisations campaigning against the exploitation of workers, including children, and travellers should – if at all possible – try to buy items that are ethically sourced.

Wildlife

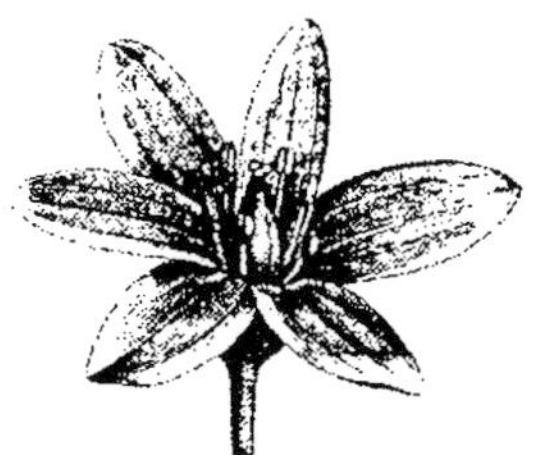

Wildlife & Bird Parks

Keoladeo Ghana (Rajasthan)

One of the world's greatest heronries is situated here. Famous for waterbirds including crane and migratory fowl. Mammals include sambar, blackbuck, chital, nilgai, fishing cat, jungle cat, otter and mongoose.

Best time: breeding, August–October; migrants, October–February

Contact: Chief Wildlife Warden, Keoladeo National Park, Bharatpur, Rajasthan

Ranthambore

An impressive range of animal species including sambar, chital, nilgai, chinkara, monkey, wild boar, sloth bear, hyena, jackal, leopard and tiger. Excellent birdlife including crested serpent eagle.

Best time: October–April

Contact: The Field Director, Ranthambore National Park, Sawai Madhopur, Rajasthan

Sariska National Park, Tiger Reserve and Sanctuary

Originally the shooting area of the Alwar ruling family, Sariska became a sanctuary in 1958. Most of Sariska is hilly with a wide valley from the gate to Thana Gazi. It has a good network of roads. Animals seen include leopard, wild dog (first sighted in 1986), nilgai, chital, chousingha, chinkara, ratel and tiger.

Best time to visit: November–June. Very dry summers make June good for game-viewing, although it is hot.

Contact: The Field Director, Sariska Tiger Reserve, Alwar district

Language

Hindi – the predominant langauge spoken in Delhi, Agra and Jaipur – is phonetically regular, based on syllables rather than an alphabet. Important differences are made between long and short vowels, and reteroflex, palatal and labial consonants – listen hard to get a feel for the vocabulary below. There are various systems of transliteration and you may see many of the words below spelt different ways in English. Where a consonant is followed by "h" this is an aspirated sound, "c" is usually pronounced "ch" ('c' followed by "h", is pronounced "chh").

Traveller's Hindi

Basics

Hello/goodbye *Namaste*
Yes *Ji ha*
No *Ji nehi*
Perhaps *Shayad*
Thank you *Dhanyavad/shukriya*
How are you? *Ap kaise hai?/Ap thik hai?*
I am well *Me thik hu/thik hai*
What is your name? *Apka nam kya hai?*
My name is (John/Jane) *Mera nam (John/Jane) hai*
Where do you come from? *Ap kahan se aye?*
From (England) *(England) se*
How much (money)? *Kitna (paise) hai?*
That is expensive *Bahut mahenga hai*
Cheap *Sasta*
I like (tea) *Mujhe (chai) pasand hai*
Is it possible? *Kya ye sambhav hai?*
I don't understand *Mujhe samajh nehi*
I don't know *Mujhe malum nehi*
Money *Paisa*
Newspaper *Akhbar*

Numbers

1	*ek*
2	*do*
3	*tin*
4	*char*
5	*panch*
6	*che*
7	*sat*
8	*arth*
9	*nau*
10	*das*
20	*bis*
30	*tis*
40	*chalis*
50	*pachas*
60	*sath*
70	*setur*
80	*assi*
90	*nabbe*
100	*sau*
1,000	*hazar*
100,000	*lakh*
10,000,000	*kror*

Sheet *Chadar*
Blanket *Kambal*
Bed *Kot/palang*
Bucket *Balti*
Room *Kamra*
Please clean my room *Mera kamra saf kijie*
Clothes *Kapre*
Cloth *Kapra*
Market *Bajar*

Pronouns

I am *Mai hun*
You are *Ap hain*
He/she/it is *Voh hai*
They are *Ve hain*

Verbs

To drink *Pina*
To eat *Khanna*
To do/make *Karna*
To buy *Kharidna*
To sleep *Sona*
To see *Dekhna*
To hear/listen to *Sunna*
To wash (clothes) *Dona*
To wash (yourself) *Nahana*
To get *Milna*

Prepositions, adverbs and adjectives

Now *Ab*
Right now *Abhi*

Quickly *Jaldi*
Slowly *Dirhe se*
A bit *Bahut*
A little *Tora*
Here *Yaha/idhar*
There *Vaha/udhar*
Open *Khola*
Closed *Bund*
Finished *Khatm hai*
Big/older *Bara*
Small/younger *Chota*
Beautiful *Sundar*
Old *Purana*
New *Naya*

Questions

What is? *Kya hai?*
Where is? *Kahan hai?*
Why? *Kyun?*
Who is? *Kaun hai?*
When is? *Kab hai?*
How? *Kaisa?*
How much? *Kitne?*

Most sentences in Hindi can be turned into a question by putting *"kya"* on the front and raising the pitch of the voice at the end, e.g. *"Dhobi hai"*, "There is a washerman", *"Kya dhobi hai?"*, "Is there a washerman?"

Days of the week

Monday *Somvar*
Tuesday *Mangalvar*
Wednesday *Budhvar*
Thursday *Guruvar*
Friday *Shukravar*
Saturday *Shanivar*
Sunday *Itvar*
Today *Aj*
Yesterday/tomorrow *Kal*
Week *Hafta*

Months

January *Janvari*
February *Farvari*
March *March*
April *Aprail*
May *Mai*
June *Jun*
July *Julai*
August *Agast*
September *Sitambar*
October *Aktubar*
November *Navambar*
December *Disambar*
Month *Mahina*
Year *Sal*

Travel

Where is (Delhi)? *(Dilli) kahan hai?*
Bus station *Bus adda*
Railway station *Tren stashan /railgari*
Airport *Hawai adda*
Car *Gari*
How far is it? *Kitna dur hai?*
In front of/opposite (the Taj Mahal) *(Taj Mahal) ke samne*
Near *Ke nazdik/ke pas*
Far *Dur*
Ticket *Tikat*
Stop *Rukh jaiye*
Let's go *Chele jao*
I have to go *Mujhe jana hai*
Come *Ayie*
Go *Jayie*

Health

Doctor *Daktar*
Hospital *Aspatal*
Dentist *Dentist*
Pain *Dard*
I am ill *Main bimar hun*
I have been vomiting *Ulti ho rahi thi*
I have a temperature *Mujhe bukhar hai*
I have a headache *Mere sir men dard hai*
I have a stomach ache *Mere pat men dard hai*
I have diarrhoea *Mujhe dast ar raha hai*

The English word "motions" is a common expression for diarrhoea.

Relatives

Mother *Mata-ji*
Father *Pita-ji*
Sister *Behen*
Brother *Bhai*
Husband *Pati*
Wife *Patni*
Maternal grandmother *Nani*
Maternal grandfather *Nana*
Paternal grandmother *Dadi*
Paternal grandfather *Dada*
Elder sister (term of respect) *Didi*
Daughter *Beti*
Son *Beta*
Girl *Larki*
Boy *Larka*
Are you married? *Kya ap shadishuda hai?*
Are you alone (male/female)? *Kya ap akela/akeli?*
How many children have you got? *Apke kitne bache hai?*
How many brothers and sisters have you got? *Apke kitne bhai behen hai?*

Food

I want (a thali) *Mujhe (thali) chahiye*
Without chilli *Mirch ke bina*
Little chilli *Kam mirch*
Hot *Garam*
Cold *Tanda*
Ripe/cooked *Pukka*
Unripe/raw *Kucha*

Basics

Mirch **Chilli**
Namak **Salt**
Ghi **Clarified butter**
Dahi **Yoghurt**
Raita **Yoghurt with cucumber**
Chaval **Rice**
Panir **Cheese**
Pani **Water**
Dudh **Milk**
Lassi **Yoghurt drink**
Nimbu pani **Lime water**
Tandur **Oven**
Pilao **Rice cooked with *ghi* and spices**
Biryani **Rice cooked with vegetables or meat**
Mithai **Sweets**

Breads *(Roti)*

Puri **Deep-fried and puffed-up wheat bread**
Chapati **Flat, unleavened bread**
Nan **Leavened flat bread**
Tanduri roti **Similar to *nan***
Paratha **Chapati cooked with *ghi***

Vegetables *(Sabzi)*

Palak **Spinach**
Allu **Potato**
Gobi **Cauliflower**
Bindi **Okra**
Pyaz **Onion**
Sarsun **Mustard greens**
Mattar **Peas**
Tamata **Tomato**
Baingain/brinjal **Aubergine**
Dal **Dried pulses**

Meat

Ghost **Lamb**
Murg **Chicken**
Machli **Fish**

Fruit

Kela **Banana**
Santra **Orange**
Aum **Mango**
Amrud **Guava**

Further Reading

History

Amritsar: Mrs Gandhi's Last Battle, by Mark Tully and Satish Jacob (Jonathan Cape, 1985). Account of Operation Blue Star, the storming of the Sikhs' Golden Temple, and the aftermath which scarred a nation following Indira Gandhi's assassination.
An Autobiography, or My Experiments with Truth, by M.K. Gandhi (Penguin, 1982). A translation from the original Gujarati which shows the complex and at times flawed nature of one of India's greatest popular leaders.
A Concise History of India, by Francis Watson (Thames and Hudson, 1979). Compact and thorough history in readable format, with illustrations and photographs.
The Discovery of India, by Jawaharlal Nehru (Asia Publishing House, 1966). Revealing history by India's first Prime Minister, which tells as much about the author as its subject.
Freedom at Midnight, by Larry Collins and Dominique Lapierre (Tarang, 1975). Gripping popular history of the birth of the Indian nation.
The Great Moghuls, by Bamber Gascoigne (Cape, 1971). Well-researched book which describes the dynasty that for two centuries ruled India, in turn both enlightened and decadent, austere and brutal. Sumptuous photographs complement highly readable text.
A History of India, Volume I, by Romilar Thapar (Pelican, 1980). Highly acclaimed history. Volume 1 traces the history of South Asia from ancient times through to the Delhi sultanate; Volume II, by Perceval Spear, continues from the Mughals to the assassination of M.K. Gandhi.
An Introduction to India, by Stanley Wolpert (Viking 1992). Informative account of India's complexities by an American academic.
India, by Barbara Crosette (University of Indiana Press, 1993). Contemporary Indian politics and international relations recounted by *New York Times* correspondent who was on the scene at Rajiv Gandhi's assassination.
India a History, by John Keay (HarperCollins, 2000), A new one-volume history by a well-respected writer. Also by Keay, **India Discovered** (Collins, 1998) documents the unearthing of India's past by British scholars and adventurers.
Liberty or Death: India's Journey to Independence and Division, by Patrick French (HarperCollins, 1997). Readable and well-researched account of the freedom struggle and Partition.
No Full Stops in India, by Mark Tully (Viking, 1991). Essays on modern political India by the BBC's ex-South Asia correspondent.
This Fissured Land, by Madhav Gadgil and Ramachandra Guha (Oxford University Press, 1993). Searching and thought-provoking ecological history of South Asia.
The Wonder that Was India, by A.L. Basham (Rupa, 1967). Learned historical classic in idiosyncratic, rapturous prose.

Society, Culture & Religion

A Book of India, by B.N. Pandey (Rupa, Delhi, 1982). A real *masala* mix of philosophies, traveller's notes, poetry and literary trivia, revealing a quixotic India. Recommended.
Changing Village, Changing Life, by Prafulla Mohanti (Viking, 1990). Wry account of village life in Orissa.
Conversations in Bloomsbury, by Mulk Raj Anand (Oxford University Press, 1986). In turns, amusing, scathing and enlightening account of an Indian author's meetings with 20th century luminaries of the British literary scene.
Everybody Loves A Good Drought, by P. Sainath (Penguin, 1996). Stories from India's poorest district, by an award-winning investigative reporter who looks at the human face of poverty.
Freedom in Exile, by Tenzin Gyatso (Rupa, 1992; Hodder and Stoughton, London, 1990). Eloquent autobiography of the Tibetan holy man, the 14th Dalai Lama.
Gods, Demons and Others, by R.K. Narayan (Heineman, 1986). Retellings of some of India's most popular religious myths by one of the country's greatest writers. Also worth looking out for are his retellings of **The Ramayana** (Penguin, 1977), based on the Tamil Kamban version, and **The Mahabharata** (Heineman, 1986).
The Idea of India, by Sunil Khilnani (Hamish Hamilton, 1997). Intellectual *tour de force* examines concepts about an ancient civilisation and its status as a relatively new nation.
India: A Literary Companion, by Bruce Palling (John Murray, 1992). Another compilation of impressions taken from literature, letters and unpublished diaries, skillfully presented.
India File, by Trevor Fishlock (John Murray, 1987). Witty observations of a resident British correspondent.
In Exile from the Land of the Snows, by John Avedon (Michael Joseph, 1984). Moving portrayal of Tibetan struggle and life of exile in India.
Intimate Relations: Exploring Indian Sexuality, Sudhir Kakar (University of Chicago Press, 1990). This study throws light on many aspects of Indian marital and family relations.
I Phoolan Devi, by Phoolan Devi with Marie Therese Cuny and Paul Rambi (Little Brown, 1996). The autobiography of an illiterate low-caste woman who fought convention, led a gang of bandits, and surrendered to the Indian government after years on the run. When freed from prison, she went on to win a parliamentary seat. A controversial insight into caste politics.
An Introduction to Hinduism, by Gavin Flood (Cambridge University Press, 1996). Perhaps the best general introduction to the

complexities of this diverse religion. Recommended.

Leaves from the Jungle: Life in a Gond Village, by Verrier Elwin (Oxford University Press, 1992). Very entertaining account of this early anthropologist's stay with a central-Indian Adivasi group.

Lucknow: Last Phase of an Oriental Culture, by Sharar 'Abdulhalim (Oxford University Press, 1989). Classic account of this highly cultured city from articles written in Urdu from around 1913.

May You Be the Mother of a Hundred Sons, by Elisabeth Bumiller (Penguin, 1990). Women's issues tackled head-on, everything from dowries to infanticide, with dozens of poignant interviews.

A Million Mutinies Now, by V.S. Naipul. The scholar seeks his roots and finds a cast of characters not easily pigeon-holed (Heineman, 1990). A more positive follow-up to his earlier **India: A Wounded Civilisation** (Penguin, 1979).

The Mind of India, by William Gerber (Arcturus, 1967). Snippets from The Vedas, Buddhism, ancient and medieval commentaries and modern mysticism all help to understand a Hindu perspective.

My Music, My Life, by Ravi Shankar (Vikas Publications, 1972). One of India's most famous musicians gives an insight into the life of a professional performer. This has now been brought up-to-date with **Raga Mala: the Autobiography of Ravi Shankar** (Welcome Rain Publications, 1999), which includes an introduction by his student George Harrison.

The Other Side of Silence: Voices from the Partition of India, by Urvashi Butalia (Penguin, 1998). Tales of families torn apart for 50 years, compellingly told by India's leading literary feminist.

The Path of the Mystic Lover, by Bhaskar Bhattacharyya (Destiny/Inner Traditions, 1993). Scoundrel/scholar delves into the lyrics of Bengali musicians, the Bauls. Obscure, but fascinating. Illustrations more 1960s than tantric.

Plain Tales from the Raj, ed Charles Allen (Rupa, 1992). First-hand accounts from ex-colonialists.

Savaging the Civilised: Verrier Elwin, his Tribals and India, by Ramachandra Guha (University of Chicago Press, 1999). Biography of the great champion of India's beleaguered Adivasis.

Fiction

Clear Light of Day, by Anita Desai (Penguin, 1982). The difficulties of post-Partition India seen through the eyes of a Hindu family living in Old Delhi.

Delhi, A Novel, by Kushwant Singh (Viking, 1989). A bawdy saga that takes us through 600 years of temptresses and traitors to unravel the Indian capital's mystique. Narrated in turns by a eunuch, an irreverent wag, potentates and poets. Superb. (It took this popular author 20 years to write.)

The English Teacher, by R.K. Narayan (various editions). Narayan depicts infuriating and endearing characters which inhabit Malgudi, a composite South Indian village. Also in various editions, are **Malgudi Days,** a series of short stories.

A Fine Balance, by Rohinton Mistry (Faber & Faber, 1996). Beautifully written but sad story of two tailors who move from their village to the city.

The Gift of a Cow, by Premchand (Allen & Unwin, 1968). The great Hindi novelist's tragic classic about the hardships endured by a North Indian peasant.

The God of Small Things, by Arundhati Roy (Random House, 1997). The Kerala backwaters are evoked in a hauntingly personal novel set in a small village pickle factory in the 1960s. Recommended.

In Custody, by Anita Desai (Heineman, 1984). The last days of an Urdu poet, made into a beautiful Merchant-Ivory film.

Kanthapura, by Raja Rao (Oxford University Press, 1947). A lyrical novel about a village in Karnataka which implements Gandhi's methods of non-violent resistance to British rule.

Kim, by Rudyard Kipling (Penguin Books, 2000, ed. by Edward Said). The wonderful adventures of a boy who wanders across North India in search of the Great Game.

Midnight's Children, by Salman Rushdie (Jonathan Cape, 1981). Rushdie burst onto the literary scene with this dazzling novel of post-Independence India. Sardonic. **The Moor's Last Sigh**, on Mumbai, also dazzles (Jonathan Cape, 1995).

A New World, by Amit Chaudhuri (Picador, 2000). Naturalistic contemporary tale of divorced Indian man, resident in America who takes his young son back to his parents in Calcutta for the holidays.

Out of India, by Ruth Prawer Jhabvala (Morrow, 1986). A collection of strong short stories that amuse and startle.

A Passage to India, by E.M. Forster (Penguin, 2000). The classic novel of the misunderstandings that arose out of the East-West encounter. After a mysterious incident in a cave Dr Aziz is accused of assaulting a naive young Englishwoman, Adela Quested. The trial exposes the racism inherent in British colonialism.

Pather Panchali, by Bibhutibhushan Banerji (Rupa, 1990). Outstanding Indian novel which outdoes the film by Satyajit Ray, depicting richness of spirit amid poverty in Bengal.

The Raj Quartet, by Paul Scott (University of Chicago Press, 1998). Four novels – **The Jewel in the Crown**, **The Day of the Scorpion**, **The Towers of Silence** and **A Division of Spoils** – set during the last days of the British Raj and charting its decline and fall.

Red Earth and Pouring Rain, by Vikram Chandra (Viking, 1996). Acclaimed debut novel, quick-paced and audacious.

A River Sutra, by Gita Mehta (Viking, 1993). Gently wrought stories which linger in the imagination.

The Romantics, by Pankaj Mishra (Random House, 2000). East meets West in Banaras.

Samskara, by U.R. Anantha Murthy (Oxford University Press, 1976). Tale of a South Indian Brahman village in Karnataka, where one Brahman is forced to question his values. Beautifully translated by A.K. Ramanujan.

The Scent of Pepper, by Kavery Nambisan (Penguin, 1996). Beautifully written family saga set in South India.

A Suitable Boy, by Vikram Seth (Phoenix Press, 1994). A huge and multi-faceted novel set during the run up to Independent India's first elections, which centres around a mother's search for a suitable husband for her daughter. Highly recommended.

Train to Pakistan, by Kushwant Singh (various editions, 1954). Gripping story of the excesses of partition, penned when scars of the divided sub-continent were still fresh.

Untouchable, by Mulk Raj Anand (Penguin, 1986). Grinding tale of poverty and discrimination.

Women Writing in India: 600BC to the Present, ed. Susie Tharu and K. Lalitha (Feminist Press, 1991). Wonderful and eclectic anthology bringing to light the neglected history of Indian women. Volume 1 includes writings from 600BC to the early 20th century, volume 2 concentrates on the 20th century alone.

Yaarana: Gay Writing from India, ed. Hoshang Merchant, and, **Facing the Mirror: Lesbian Writing from India**, ed. Ashwini Sukthankar (both Penguin, 1999). Anthologies of short stories, extracts from novels and poetry from gay and lesbian Indian writers.

Travel

Butter Chicken in Ludhiana: Travels in Small Town India, by Pankaj Mishra (Penguin, 1995). An urban Indian novelist casts a jaundiced eye over modern Indian life.

Chasing the Monsoon, by Alexander Frater (Penguin, 1991). A whimsical odyssey up the west coast, into the northeast, and onto the plains, as refreshing as the rains.

City of Djinns, by William Dalrymple (HarperCollins, 1993). Respected travel-writer's account of a year spent in Delhi, full of historical references.

Desert Places, by Robyn Davidson (Viking, 1996). A woman's story of living and travelling with the desert nomads of Rajasthan.

Exploring Indian Railways, by Bill Aitken (Oxford University Press, 1996). Highly informed and occasionally idiosyncratic tour of the Indian railway system written by a clear enthusiast.

A Goddess in the Stones, by Norman Lewis (Cape, 1991). The founder of Survival International travels among the Adivasis of Bihar and Orissa. Entertaining.

The Great Hedge of India, by Roy Moxham (Constable, 2000). One man's quest to find the hedge which marked the old British customs line. Very entertaining and packed full of historical detail. Recommended.

An Indian Attachment, by Sarah Lloyd (Eland, 1992). Insightful account of a love affair with a Punjabi Sikh which plunges the Western woman into a spiral of cultural anxieties.

Old Delhi: Ten Easy Walks, by Gayner Barton and Lorraine Malone (South Asia Books, 1997). Very useful guide to the confusing maze of streets in Old Delhi. Recommended.

Sorcerer's Apprentice, by Tahir Shah (Penguin, 1998). Travelogue of the author's attempts to learn the secrets of illusion and fraud of India's street magicians.

Three Quarters of a Footprint, by Joe Roberts (Transworld, 1994). South and Central India examined by thoughtful, unpretentious Englishman.

Food, Language & Images

Curries and Bugles, by Jennifer Brennan (Penguin, 1992). Legends and tales mixed up with the favourite recipes of Raj-era memsahibs and sahibs.

Hanklyn-Janklin, or a Stranger's Rumble Tumble Guide to some Words, Customs and Quiddities Indian and Indo-British, by Nigel B. Hankin (Banyan Books, New Delhi, 1992). Lives up to its title and is a delightful reference work.

Hobson-Jobson (Routledge and Kegan Paul, 1968), the 1886 glossary on which Hankin modelled his modern etymology. The pair complement one another.

Indian Style, by Suzanne Slesin, Stafford Cliff (Thames and Hudson, 1990). Colour prints of exterior and interior design, in exacting detail, capture the texture of India.

Mansions at Dusk: the Havelis of Old Delhi, by Pavan K. Varma (Spantech, 1992). Atmospheric photographs by Sondeep Shankar illustrate this homage to the now decaying mansions of Muslim Delhi.

Sadhus, the Holy Men of India, by Rajesh and Ramesh Bedi (New Delhi, 1991). Striking images of Indian ascetics and informed text reveal hidden life of those who renounce the world.

Taj, by Raghu Rai (Delhi, 1988). The ultimate photographic depiction of the world's monument to love. Large format, high impact.

Other Insight Guides

The **Insight Guides** series has full coverage of India:

Insight Guide: India takes you around the country state by state, from the shores of Kerala to the mountains of the Garhwal.

Insight Guide: Indian Wildlife is an indispensable guide for nature lovers, combining expert text and astonishing photography.

Insight Guide: Rajasthan features full coverage, with insightful essays and stunning photography, of the region that remains many people's first introduction to India.

Insight Guide: South India is a guide to the southern states of Andhra Pradesh, Karnataka, Tamil Nadu and Kerala.

Compact Guide: Goa is a great pocket companion to this very popular state, taking in beaches, history and the fabulous site at Hampi in Karnataka.

ART & PHOTO CREDITS

APA Photo Agency 252/253
Arun Anand/Image Vault back flap top, 64, 131
Ravindralal Anthonis 262
Aditya Arya 3, 73, 210, 233
David Beatty back flap top, back cover right, spine top, 22/23, 44/45, 46/47, 79, 123, 124, 152/153, 163, 167, 176, 177, 183R, 187, 189, 190/191, 194, 196, 206/207, 216, 217, 218, 219, 228, 232, 238, 241, 244, 246, 247, 249, 264
K. Debnicki back cover bottom
Uzra Bilgrami 234/235
A. Binavkia/Resource Foto 161
Meera Chatterjee 87, 90, 107R, 121, 127, 140, 141, 142, 143, 145, 175, 179
Asok Kumar Das 154, 155, 33
Delhi War Cemetery 115L
Gertrud & Helmut Denzau 146
Dinodia Picture Agency 75, 93, 128
Amitabh Dubey 84, 130
Marie D'Souza 214, 221
Fotomedia back cover left, 42/43, 61, 72L, 78, 86, 150/151, 178, 180, 197
Ashim Ghosh 54/55, 125, 170/171, 198
Nirmal Ghosh/Fotomedia 256, 261
Dallas & John Heaton back flap bottom, 94/95, 100/101, 212
Hans Höfer 188
Simon Hughes/APA Photo Agency 138
Images of India 74, 118
Caroline Jones 70, 76, 82, 144, 166
Ravi Kaimal 66/67, 193, 195
Rupinder Khullar 9, 69, 106R, 160, 168, 172, 225, 239L
Jean Kugler 56/57
Link Picture Library 20, 92, 98, 215
Craig Lovell/APA Photo Agency back flap bottom, 26R, 68, 99, 104R, 165, 263
Antonio Martinelli 139
Nihal Mathur/Fotomedia 173
David Messent 39, 52/53, 72R, 110, 116/117, 204/205
Shankar Narayan 254, 258, 259
Tripti Pandey 26L, 162, 169, 182R, 184
Avinash Pasricha 137, 245
Aditya Patankar 140, 164, 200
Christine Pemberton/Fotomedia 29, 34R, 260
K.T. Ravindran 134, 223, 239R, 240, 248, 262
Ajay Rohilla/Fotomedia 37R
Kamal Sahai 81, 202/203, 224
Hemen C. Sanghvi 105, 122, 242, 243
Shalini Saran 25, 27, 28, 30/31, 34L,36, 41, 103, 104L, 129, 130, 132/133, 158/159, 174, 181, 183L, 211, 220, 226, 227L, 227R, 229
Dr Geeti Sen back cover top, back cover centre,32, 38L, 38R, 89, 250, 251
Pankaj Shah/Resource Foto 109
Satish Sharma 50, 65, 77, 80, 85, 88, 91
Toby Sinclair 14/15, 16/17, 18/19, 107L, 112, 114, 115R, 120, 149
N.P. Singh/Fotomedia 185
Amar Talwar/Fotomedia 24, 37L, 192, 222
Yasmeen Tayebbhai 236 (Plan)
Topham 59, 60, 62, 63
Adina Tovy/APA Photo Agency 103, 230
Frank Udo/Resource Foto 96, 108
Joanna Van Gruisen 106L, 182L

Maps Dave Priestley

Cartographic Editor **Zoë Goodwin**
Design Consultants **Carlotta Junger**
Picture Research **Hilary Genin**

Index

a

Adilabad 139
Agra 21, 27, 28, 36, 37, 38, 40, 51, 71, 173, 187, 209, 213, 223, 228, 231, 237, 252, 253, 261
Ahmadabad 111
Ajmer 187
Akbar Road 80
Akbarnama 39
Alai Darwaza 136
Albert Hall 186, 189
Allahabad 28, 111
Alwar 199
Ambala 113, 120
Ambedkar Stadium 120
Amber 21, 27, 173–178, 181
Amber Road 188
Anguri Bagh (Garden of Grapes) 228
Anokhi 185
Appu Ghar 119
Arambagh 231
Aravali Hills 111
architects *also see* sculptors
  Ahmad, Ustad 213
  Baker 53, 71, 72, 73, 77, 78, 79
  Chakravati, Vidyadhar 162, 163, 174, 178
  Correa, Charles 82, 125
  Dick, Reid 115
  Jacob, Swinton 186, 189
  Jagger, Charles 115
  Lutyens 25, 53, 70, 71, 72, 73, 74, 75, 76, 77, 78, 79
  Medd, Henry 80
  Metcalfe, Thomas 137
  Muhammad Hanif of Baghdad 213
  Nagappa, M.S. 115
  Russell, Robert Tor 79
architecture 37
  Baroque 71
  British 40
  Gothic 137
  Hindu 36
  Imperial Anglo-Indian style 40
  Indo-Islamic style 36, 200, 240
  medieval 48
  Mughal 124, 214, 232, 243–244
  Victorian-Gothic 71, 112
Archives Office 76
Asaf Ali Road 96
Ashokan pillar 112, 120
Auliya, Kabir-ud-din 141
Aurangabad 163
Aurangzeb Road 80
Aurobindo Marg 140, 144
Avadh 65, 124

b

Baba Kharak Singh Marg 83
Baburnama 39
Bade Khan's tomb 144
Badshah Nama 215, 227
Baggi khana 165
Bagh-i-Adan 216
Bagru 194–196
Bahadur Shah Zafar Marg 120
Bakhtiyar Kaki 51, 137
Banaras 163
Bani Park 184
Bara Gumbad (Great Dome) 124
Barbar's Tomb 122
Bari Chaupar 181
Baroda 72
Barsana 263
Barton, Gayner 98
Bay of Bengal 27
Beating Retreat ceremony 92
Beg, Mirza Ghiyas 232
Bengal cotton 27
Bernier, Francois 109
Bhagvadgita 257
Bhagvat Purana 259
Bharatpur 21, 187, 209
Bhuramal Rajmal Surana 182
Bikaner 71
Birbal 247
birdlife 199–201 *also see* wildlife
Birlas 188
Blue pottery 184
Bookworm, the 83
Bopadeva 258
Brajbhumi 257, 258, 263
British Civil Lines 135
British East India Company 111, 209
British Raj 69, 71, 81, 113
Bu Halima's garden 121
Buddhism 257, 258
Buland Darwaza 239, 250

c

Central Asian antiquities 85
Central Cottage Industries Emporium 82
Central Post Office 79
Chaitanya 259
Chakravati, Vidyadhar 162
Chandigarh 25
Chandni Chowk (Moonlight Square) 79, 96, 99, 109, 115, 163
Chandra Mahal 162, 165, 166
Charbagh 248
Chatta Chowk 106
chatris 77, 178
Chauhan dynasty 49
Chaunsath Khamba 126
Chavi Niwas 166
Chini ka Rauza 232
Chippas 194
Chippa mohalla 193
Chisti, Sheikh Salim 35, 237, 250
Cholas 49
Chor Minar 144
Chote Khan-ka-Gumbad 145
churches,
  Cathedral Church of the Redemption 80
  Free Church 144
  Italianate Roman Catholic Church 80
  St James' Church 99
clubs,
  Gymkhana 80
  Panchsheel Club 140, 141
Coconut Grove 83
Connaught Place 78, 79, 82–83
Coronation Durbar Site 113–115
Cottage Industries Emporium 142
Court Baths 250
Cunningham, Sir Alexander 260

d

Daftar khana 245
dance forms,
  Bharata Natyam 65
  Kathak 65
  Kuchipudi 65
  Manipuri 65
  Odissi 65
Dariba Kalan 99
Daulatkhana-i-Khas 228
Deeg 21, 209
Delhi College of Art 115
Delhi Development Authority 135
Delhi Ridge 111, 135, 148
Delhi Town Hall 115
Delhi University 113
Delhi Zoo 147
Delhi's Golf Course 123
Digansha Yantra 167
Digantar Trust 185
Dilaram Bagh 174, 177
Din Panah 119
Din-i-Illahi 245

Diwan-i-Am (Hall of Public Audience) 105 176, 178, 243
Diwan-i-Khas 103, 165, 178, 228, 244, 246
Dominion Columns 78
Dundubi Pol 163
Dyuta Ram Sanghi 193

e–f

Eastern Court 79
Faiz Bazaar 96
Fatehpur Sikri 21, 28, 34, 35, 36, 209, 213, 223, 227, 237–250, 252
Fazl, Abul 223–225, 226
Ferozabad 51
Feroze Shah Kotla 120
Feroze Shah Kotla cricket grounds 120
festivals,
Annakut 165
Bakr Id 92
Divali 93, 165
Dussehra 93
Ekadasi 263
Holi 92, 165, 263
Id 126
Janamashtami 93, 165, 263
Muharram 92
People's Fête 81
Purnima 263
Ramadan 92, 131
Republic Day 92
Shivaratri 92
Surajkund Crafts Mela 92
Vaisakhi 92
Finch, William 225, 226, 253
First War of Indian Independence 131
Flag Staff Tower 112
forts,
Agra Fort 102, 213, 223
Amber Fort 38, 161
Badalgarh 223, 225, 226
Bala Qila 199
Bharatpur 21
Chilka-tola (Kite Castle) 178
Datia 71
Delhi Fort 28
Dhar 71
Fort Palace 96 also see Red Fort
Fortified Palaces 37
Jaigarh (Victory Fort) 178
Jankwari 199
Lohagarh Fort 201
Mahr 197
Moti Dungri fortress 200
Nahargarh (Tiger Fort) 178
Old Fort (Purana Qila) 71, 119–124, 125
Red Fort 25, 34, 37, 38, 81, 96, 102–109, 220
also see Fort Palace
Sheogarh 197
Tughlaqabad 51, 147

g

gaddi 181
Gainda-ki-Deorhi 163
Galgotia 83
galleries 84–91
Anthropological galleries 86
Arms gallery 86
Aurobindo Gallery 91
Bronze gallery 85
Buddhist gallery 85
Decorative Arts gallery 86
early medieval galleries 85
Gallerie Ganesha 91
Gupta galleries 85
History of Indian Painting gallery 86
LTG Gallery 91
National Gallery of Modern Art 90
Pre-Columbian 86
Purana Mahal 201
Village Gallery 91, 142
Wood-carvings 86
Galtaji 188
Gandhara art 260
Gandhi, Mahatma 53, 81
Gandhi Memorial 96
Ganga plain 48
Ganga-Yamuna valley 25
Garhi 91
gates
Agra 243, 252
Amar Singh Gate 226
Atish Pol (Stable Gate) 163
Badshahi Darwaza (Imperial gate) 238
Bloody Gate (Khuni Darwaza) 121
Chand Pol Gate 187
Darshani Gate 226
Delhi Gate 96, 102, 107
Ganesh Pol (Elephant Gate) 176
Hathi Pol (Elephant Gate) 226, 249
India Gate 76, 77, 81, 114, 135
Kashmiri Gate 97, 111
Lahore Gate 102, 106
Naqqara Pol (Drum Gate) 163
Salimgarh Gate 102
Sanganeri Gate 181, 186
Singh Pol (Lion Gate) 163, 175
Sireh Deorhi 163
Tripolia (Three-arched Gate) 163
Turkman Gate 141
Gautama Buddha 257, 260
George, Walter Sykes 80
Ghalib Academy 126
Ghantewala 99
Girl's school 244
gods,
Krishna 209, 257–259, 260, 261, 263
Rama 27, 173
Shiva 173
Vishnu 257
Golden Triangle 21
Gole Post Office 80
Gopal Bhawan 201
Gopal Sagar 201
Gopalji ka Rasta 181
Government Hostel 187
Graeco-Roman art 258
Grand Trunk Road 96, 119
Great Indian Desert 26
Greater Delhi 135
Growse, F.S. 260
Gujarat 163, 247
Gujarat silk 26
Gunijan khana 164
Guru Gobind Singh 122
Gwalior 227, 247

h

Hadith 250
Haji Karimuddin 131
Haldiyon ka Rasta 182
Harappa 84
Harappan pottery 48
Hardy, Faith 185
Hastinapur 48
Hauz Khas 143, 142–144
Hauz Shamsi 137
Hauz-i-Kauser 216, 218
Hawa Mahal Bazar 163
Hayat Baksh 106
Hazrat Nizamuddin 35, 51, 126–129
Himachal 40
Hindu Rao Hospital 111, 112
Hindustan Charitable Trust 188
Hiran Minar 249
hotels 279–284

i

Il-baris 49, 50, 135
Impressions of Jaipur and Amber 181

Imtiaz Mahal 104
Indian Railways 87
Indraprastha 48, 69, 119
Indus Valley 26
Interstate Bus Terminal 97, 99
Iron Pillar 136
Irving, Robert 73, 74
Ismail, Sir Mirza 187
Itimad-ud-daula 232–233
ivoryware 27

j

Jacquement, Victor 181
Jadiyon ka Rasta 182
Jag Mandir 188
Jahanpanah 51, 140–141
Jai Mandir (House of Victory) 176
Jai Niwas Bagh 162, 165
Jai Prakash Yantra 167
Jai Van 178
Jaipur 21, 25, 27, 28, 37, 38, 40, 71, 157, 163, 161–169, 173, 174, 181–184, 186–188
Jaipur Column 74
Jaipur Silawats 183
Jaleb Chowk 163
Jalebi Chowk 176
Jamali-Kamali tomb 138
Jamwa Ramgarh 187
Janpath 71, 79, 80, 82
Jantar Mantar 166, 167
Jas Mandir 188
Jasmine Tower 228
Jats, the 52, 106, 200, 209
Jawaharlal Nehru Stadium 123
Jewellery 26
Jharoka-i-Darsha 103
Johari Bazaar 166, 169, 181, 182
Juti 183

k

Kachchwaha Rajputs 27, 161, 173, 174, 196 *also see* Rajputs
Kagazi mohalla (Paper Precinct) 193
Kaki, Bakhtiyar 51, 137
Kale Khan's tomb 144
Kalikhoh 177, 178
Kalikhoh range 173
Kansa 263
Karaoli 224
Keoladeo Ghana 21
Keshav Bhawan 201
Khan, Dariya 145
Khan, Mubarak 145
Khan, Adham 137
Khan, Isa 122
Khan Market 124
Khari Baoli 99
Khas Mahal 103
Khel Gaon Marg 144
Khiljis 49, 50
Khirki 141
Khwabgah 245
Kidwai Nagar Market 145
Kinari Bazaar 99
King George's Avenue 79
King's Tower (Shah Burj) 102
Kranti Valaya Yantra 167
Kripal Kumbh 184
Kundan 181
Kuntalgarh 173
Kushan art 260
Kushans 257, 258, 260

l

Lady Willingdon Hospital 187
Lahore 51
Lake Pichola 188
Lakla Burj 201
Lal Gumbad 141
Lal Mahal 127
Lal Purdaris 104
Lalit Kala Akademi 91, 186
Left Bank, the 231–233
Lodi Delhi 144–145
Lodi Gardens 123, 144
Lodi Road 123
Lodis 51, 144, 209, 223, 226
Lok Sabha 78
Lord Curzon 135
Lord Hardinge 69, 70, 81
Lord Irwin 115
Lord Willingdon 115
Lucknow 124

m

M.I. (Mirza Ismail) Road 169, 184, 187
Machi Bhawan 228
madarsas 38
Mahabharata 26, 48, 119, 257, 259
Mahakma Khas 163
Mahal, Zafar 137
Maharaja College 187
Maharashtra 52
Mahatab Bagh 106
Mahatma Gandhi Marg (Ring Road) 96, 97, 102, 144
Makrana 72
Malone, Lorraine 99
Man Sagar Lake 188
Mandu 71, 247
Maniharon kia Rasta 184
Manihars 184
Maqdum Shah-ka-Maqbara 175
Marathas 28, 104, 106, 161, 196, 200, 209
Mathura 21, 209, 257, 260
Mathura art 258
Mathura Road 120, 121, 126
Matka Shah 119
Maurya 84
Meerut 111, 113
Mehrauli 51, 135, 137–138
Mehrauli-Gurgaon Road 136, 138
mihman khana (guest house) 217
mimar-i-kul 213
Minas 173, 178
Mint, the 249
Moatha Lake 174
Mohenjodaro 84
Mongols 51, 209
mosques
- Afsarwala's mosque 122
- Akbari Masjid 177
- Bangle Wali mosque 126
- Begumpur mosque 140
- Charbujamosque 112
- Fatehpuri Masjid 99
- Jama Masjid 70, 104, 107, 108, 120, 213, 238, 240, 242, 263
- Jamali's mosque 145
- Kali Masjid 130
- Khairu'l Manazil mosque 119
- Khirki Masjid 141
- Masjid 33
- Masjid Kalan 141
- Masjid Moth 145
- Moti Masjid (Pearl Mosque) 104, 228
- Nagina Masjid 228
- Nili Masjid (Blue Mosque) 144
- Qal'a-i-Kuhna mosque 119
- Quwwat-ul-Islam mosque 34, 136
- Sher Shah's mosque 145

Mount Abu 111
Mughal art 221, 232
Mughal delicacies 131
Mughal Gardens 75
Mughals 27, 37, 38, 39, 40, 49, 51, 52, 71, 86, 102, 103, 137, 174, 200, 209, 213, 221, 227, 231, 233, 240
Mumtaz Mahal 105
museums 84–91
- Air Force Museum 89
- Archaeological Museum 178
- Central Museum 186
- Ethnological Museum 76
- Gandhi Memorial Museum 89

Jaipur City Museum 25
Maharaja Sawai Man Singh II Museum 176
Mathura Museum 258, 260
National Handicrafts and Handlooms Museum 125
National Museum 84
National Museum of Natural History 89
Nehru Memorial Museum and Library 87
Railway Museum 87
Sanskriti Museum of Everyday Art 89
Shankar's International Doll Museum 120
Tibet House Museum 88

Musi Maharani ki Chatri 200
Muslim food 131
Mustoe, W.R. 80
Mutiny Memorial 111

n & o

Naqqar Khana gateway 105, 106
Nari Valaya Yantra 167
Nasli Heeramaneck 87
national parks *see* wildlife reserves
National Stadium 77
National Zoological Park 119, 121
naubat khanas 216, 243
Nehru, Jawaharlal 25, 59, 79, 81, 87–88
Nehru Library 79
Netaji Subhash Marg 96
Nicholson, John 111
Nicholson's cemetery 99
Nila Gumbad (Blue Dome) 122
Nizamuddin 123, 126–129, 131, 141
Nizamuddin Railway Station 123
Northern Ridge *also see* Delhi Ridge
observatories 167
Delhi 167
Jaipur 167
Mathura 167
Ujjain 167
Varanasi 167
Old Delhi 79, 96, 120, 126
Oriental Institute 76

p & q

Painted Grey Ware pottery 119
painters
Daniells, Thomas 90
Kettle, Tilly 90
Varma, Raja Ravi 90
painting
Company School paintings 86
Mughal 39
Thanjavur paintings 86
palaces
Aina Mahal 219
Alwar 21, 157
Amber 157
Baroda House 76
Bengali Mahal 224, 227
Chandra Mahal (Moon Palace) 162, 165
City Palace 199
Feroze Shah Kotla 135
Hawa Mahal (Palace of the Winds) 166, 183, 247
Hyderabad House 76
Jahanpanah 135
Jahaz Mahal (Ship Palace) 137
Jaipur 157
Jal Mahal 188
Jodhbai's palace 247
Khas Mahal 228
Man Mandir palace 227
Mariam's palace 246
Mubarak Mahal (Welcome Palace) 163, 164
Mukut Mahal 166
Panch Mahal 36, 248, 252
Pir Ghaib 112
Rambagh Palace 189
Red Palace 127
Samode 21, 157
Shish Mahal 166, 228
Tughlaqabad 135
Viceroy's Palace 53
Vijay Mandir 200
Vinay Vilas Mahal 200
Zenana Mahal 178
Palika Bazaar 83
Panchsheel Road 140
Pandavas 119
Panna Mian-ki-Kund 177
Parathas 126
Parliament House 78
Patna 51
Patte Wali Dargah 123
Peacock Throne 103
poets
Abd'ur Rahim Khar Khan-i-Khanan 123
Ghalib, Abdullah Khan 126
Jamali 138
Khusrau, Amir 51, 129
pothikhana 163
Pragati Maidan 119, 124
Pritam Niwas 165
Prithviraj Chauhan (Qila Rai Pithaura) 135
Public Works Department 81
Puranas 257
Qatb Minar complex 135–137

r

Rai Pithora 50
Railway Station 200
Raisina Hill 71, 76, 77
Rajaji Marg 79
Rajasthali 184
Rajasthan 21, 25, 27, 28, 40, 49, 72, 111, 157, 177
Rajdev 173
Rajendra Pol 163
Rajpath 71, 72, 76
Rajputs 21, 161, 173, 196, 200, 223, 224, 238
also see Kachchwaha Rajputs
Rajya Sabha 78
Ram Niwas Garden 186
Ram Prakash theatre 166
Ram Yantra 167
Ramayana 130
Ramganj Bazaar 182
Ramgarh Lake 188
Rang Mahal 104
Rangrez 182
Rashi Valaya Yantra 167
Rashtrapati Bhavan 40, 71, 73, 74, 75 *also see* **Viceroy's House**
Ravana Devra 199
Ravindra Rang Manch 186
Records Office 250
Regal Building 82
restaurants 284–286
Revolt of 1857 27, 28 *also see* Indian Mutiny
Ridhi-Sidhi Pole 165
rivers,
Ganga 26
Indus 26
Saraswati 26
Yamuna 26, 48, 102, 111, 119, 120, 135, 200, 225, 231, 257
Rivoli Cinema 83
Roberts, Sir James 189
Rohillas 106
Royal Baths 103
Royal Durbar 69, 70
rulers
Aibak, Qatb-ud-din 34 49
Akbar, Muhammad Jalaludin 28, 34, 36, 51, 119, 174, 209, 213, 223–228, 237, 238, 239, 241, 243–248, 250, 252, 253, 261
Asoka 48, 74, 84, 120

Aurangzeb 34, 99, 104, 109, 161, 215, 261
Babur, Zahiruddin 39, 49, 173, 223, 231, 238
Balban 120, 138
Chandrawati, Maharani 189
Das, Bhagwan 174
Gaekwar of Baroda 75
Ghazni, Mahmud 257
Ghuri, Muhammad 49
Humayun 36, 39, 51, 119, 121, 223, 231
Itimad-ud-daula 21, 36, 232
Jahangir 51, 209, 221, 225, 226, 227, 250, 252
Kanishka 258
Kansa 259
Khilji, Alauddin 135–137, 143
King George V 69, 76, 113–115
Kuntaldev 173
Lodi, Ibrahim 231
Lodi, Sikander 145
Mahal, Mumtaz 213, 221
Maharaja of Jaipur 27, 74
Maharaja of Mysore 88
Maharaja of Sailana 168
Nizam of Hyderabad 75, 87
Prince of Wales 81, 88, 186
Prithviraj, Raja 49, 173
Queen Mary 69
Queen Victoria 27, 115
Rai, Dulha 173
Rangila, Muhammad Shah 161
Shah, Sher 51, 119, 173
Shah, Bahadur 52, 123, 137
Shah, Feroze 112, 130
Shah, Muhammad 106, 123, 129
Shah, Nadir 52
Shahjahan 21, 25, 36, 102, 104, 105, 107, 108, 109, 209, 213, 214, 215, 220, 221, 227, 228, 252
Shikoh, Dara 99
Shuja-ud-Daula 124
Singh, Badan 200, 201
Singh, Bishan 161
Singh, Ishwari 196
Singh, Jagat 177
Singh, Mirza Raja Jai 175, 176
Singh, Sawai Jai 25, 26, 28, 157, 161, 162, 167, 176, 194
Singh, Sawai Pratap 163
Singh, Sawai Ram 163, 178, 186, 187
Singh, Suraj Mal 201
Singh, Vijay 194
Singh, Maharaja Ishwari 186
Singh I, Raja Man 164, 174, 175, 182, 189
Singh I, Sawai Madho 163, 186, 188
Singh II, Madho 163, 165, 187, 189
Singh II, Ram 163
Singh II, Sawai Man 163, 174
Singh II, Sawai Ram 184, 186, 189
Singhji, Prithviraj 196
Tilangani, Khan-i-Jahan 130
Timur 120, 143
Tughlaq, Ferozeshah 48, 120, 137, 140, 143
Tughlaq, Muhammad 140
Tughlaq, Ghias-ud-din 36, 129, 139
Zafar, Bahadur Shah 122, 129

s

Sadar Bazaar 96, 98
Safdarjang's tomb 124
Sagar 178
Sakas 258
Saket Road 141
Samode 196–197
Samrat, Pandit Jagannath 167
Samrat Yantra 167
Sanganer 193–194
Sariska 21
Sarvapriya Vihar 141
Sarvatobhadra 165
Satpula 141
Sawai Man Singh Guards Barracks 187
Sayyids 49, 51, 144
sculpture 84–85, 86
sculptors also see architects
Seismological Observatory 112
Shahjahanabad 69, 73, 96–99, 135
Shakarganj, Shaikh Farid 127
Sher Mandal 119
Sher Shah Suri Marg 119
Shir Marg 184
Shirazi, Amanat Khan 214, 218
Shish Gumbad (Glazed Dome) 124
Shish Mahal (Hall of Mirrors) 38, 104, 197
Sikandara 21, 36, 223, 252–253
Silawaton ka Rasta 183
Siliserh 21
Siliserh Lake 199
Singh, Sardar Kudrat 182
Singh, Jitendra Pal (John) 185
Siri 50, 135, 140–141, 143
Siri Fort Road 140
Sisodiya Rani-ka-Bagh 188
Sonargaon 51
Sonkh 258
State Department of Archaeology 99
State Emporia 83
Stein, Sir Aurel 86
Stream of Paradise (Nahr-i-Bihisht) 103
Subhash Chowk 183
Sufi, Inayat Khan 130
Sufis 128
Sukh Niwas (House of Pleasure) 176, 178
Sultanpur Jhil 147
Sundernagar 64
Sunga dynasty 84
Suraj Bhawan 201
Suraj Kund 112
Suryavanshis 173

t

Taj Mahal 21, 25, 28, 36, 213–220, 221, 223
Takht-e-Shahi 186
Tambi Khana 228
Tasbih Khana 103
Tehkhana 104
Telingani, Khan-e-Jahan 140
temples
- Ambikesvar Shiva 177
- Bhairon temple 119
- Charan Mandir 178
- Damdama Sahib 122
- Dwarkadhish 263
- Garh Ganesh Mandir 178
- Gopinath 261
- Govind Deva temple 162, 261
- Hanuman temple 83
- Jagat Shiromani temple 177
- Jain Tirthankara 177
- Jugal Kishore 261
- Keshav Deo temple 263
- Krishna temple 193
- Laxmi Narain temple 188
- Madan Mohan 261
- Maharani Kunti's temple 119
- Narsingh Avatar 177
- Nathdwara 26
- Nilkanth 199
- Radha Raman 261
- Ramchandraji temple 166
- Sanghiji temple 193
- Surya 177

Thar 26
Tilak Marg 185
Tilak Park 99
Tito Marg 140, 141

toshakhana 163
Town Hall 99, 166
Tughlaqabad complex 137–139
Tughlaqs 25, 50–51
Turkish Sultana's residence 246

u & v

Udaipur 181, 188
Ulugh Beg 167
Vajpayee, Atal Behari 63
Vaishnava Hinduism 257, 259
Varanasi 49, 257
Vedas 26, 257
Viceroy's House 70, 71, 73, 77, 80 *also see* Rashtrapati Bhavan
Vijay Chowk 71, 76
Vijay Mandal 140
Vikramnagar 120
Vishram Ghat 259, 263
Vrindavan 21, 257, 263

w–z

War Memorial 71
War Memorial Arch 76
Western Court 79
wildlife 147–148, 199–201
wildlife reserves 21
  Keoladeo Ghana National Park 157, 201
  Ranthambore National Park 157, 201
  Sariska National Park 157, 199
  Siliserh 157
  Tiger Reserve 199
World War I 72, 76
World War II 89
Yamuna plain 157
Yantra Raj 167
Zenana Deorhi 166
Zij Jadid Muhammad Shahi 167